THE DARK ROOM

The Dark Room

A Memoir of Triumph

Claudia Chotzen

For my husband, Hap, and our two sons,
Zach and Willy. The life and family we created is the
sweet story that I was missing as a child and one that
everyone deserves.

THE DARK ROOM

CONTENTS

Author's Note

Characters

Honolulu
1

Leschi
7

Photos

Madrona
127

Bellevue
243

Greece, Israel & Home Again
295

Washington, California, Hawaii & Oregon
331

Afterword
355

Acknowledgments
363

AUTHOR'S NOTE

In writing this memoir, I relied upon an abundance of material beyond my own memories: my personal journals, letters I wrote and received, newspaper articles, photographs, family home movies, more than twenty hours of video interviews with my parents, and interviews with my siblings and friends of our family.

All seven of my brothers and sisters graciously sat with me for extensive interviews. Where I have incorporated their reflections, it is with their permission.

This story focuses on my experiences, memories, and perceptions; for the most part it is not about what happened to others. I have changed the names of most, but not all, of the individuals in this book to respect their privacy. There are no composite characters or events.

For many years, I remained reluctant to publish; I cherish my relationships with my brothers and sisters and didn't want to intrude on their lives. Ultimately, I realized that while my story is very personal, it is also universal if it can inspire hope or be a healing force for others.

I am deeply grateful to all my friends and family who have spent years encouraging me to speak the truth and to share my story.

CHARACTERS

Parents

Walter and Carla

Children in Order of Birth

Danny & Naomi (Twins)
Leah
Claudia
Simon
Mia
Charlotte
Joey

Honolulu

1975 & 2005

T he first time my future husband met my mother she was naked. Stark naked. I was in college but had accepted a winter semester internship in Honolulu and was living at my parents' home there. Hap had flown to Hawaii to surprise me for the Valentine's Day weekend. I was surprised by his visit, but he was a lot more surprised by my mother.

My parents were aware of Hap's visit. They knew the flight arrival time and that my sister Naomi and I would bring him directly from the airport to their home. Yet my mother, Carla, answered the door without a stitch of clothing. Her body was brown from the sun, lean and strong from her daily regimen of tennis, swimming, yoga, and hiking; her breasts were small and a little saggy from nursing eight children; her hair a brilliant white. She flashed her most dazzling smile and acted coquettish, almost curtsied. She mumbled some sort of greeting and gave him a welcome hug before she walked out the door, still naked, a threadbare towel slung over her shoulder, explaining she was heading down the pathway to the beach for a quick swim before dinner.

Hap struggled to speak coherently. "Your mother. Is she usually, I mean, the lack of clothes? Did she not realize I was coming?"

"Oh, she realized," I said.

Hap was shocked not just by her naked greeting, but also by a sudden awareness that I accepted her nudity as normal, that I wasn't particularly embarrassed. I had been conditioned all my life (22 years at that moment) to admire my mother's openness, to praise her quirky behavior, to view other people who followed established social norms as "uptight." Everyone in my family celebrated my mom's free spirit.

During the prior four months of our courtship, Hap had collected bits and pieces about my family—parents who were Jewish refugees from Nazi Germany and politically active, details about my seven siblings, how everyone was expected to excel at something, how we were all compelled to enjoy skiing, hiking, tennis, and swimming. I had made my family members almost mythological beings through vivid stories. We were a proud and loyal tribe, true to each other, family first. Apparently, I had forgotten to mention that my mother didn't like to wear clothes.

* * *

Thirty years later, Hap and I and our two sons are back in Honolulu to visit my mother. I am 52, almost exactly the same age my mother was when Hap first met her. She no longer recognizes us, and as always, her behavior is wildly unpredictable. And she is still strong, athletic, and nimble. However, her advanced Alzheimer's now renders even the simplest task a formidable challenge.

We had decided to take her out for a picnic lunch, but after spending ten minutes trying to coax her into our rental car, both sides were eager to surrender.

"Where are we going?" she asks again.

I tell her for the third time that we are going to Makapu'u Beach for a picnic.

"Oh, that sounds nice," she replies appreciatively, before veering sharply into a divergent thought, "Why would I want to do that? I can eat lunch at home!"

Given how difficult it has been to cajole her into the car, and the risk in transporting her anywhere, it's a reasonable question.

The goal was to get her safely situated in the middle of the back seat, between our two sons, Zach and Willy, 18 and 14, to prevent her from jumping out of the car at a stop sign and wandering into traffic. She has already established a new pattern of fleeing from family and caregivers without warning, an escape artist, courting danger. But now that she is finally secured in the middle of the back seat, we have started the ten-minute drive.

She rubs my sons' thighs and strokes their cheeks. "Such handsome young men!" she coos. Pointing to me, in the driver's seat, she wants to know, "Is that your mom? What does she do?"

Zach answers. "Yes, Carla, that's our mom. Your daughter, Claudia. And she's writing a book."

"A book? How exciting! What's it about?"

"It's a book about her life," Zach answers cautiously.

Carla considers this thoughtfully, and then adds matter-of-factly, "I bet I'm in it. And I think I might be naked."

Leschi

1952–1963

T he story of my childhood could be told in photographs, but that would be a story through my mother's eyes. A Holocaust refugee, a college graduate at the age of 18, a translator, a bride, and a high school teacher were already part ' of her past in 1948 when she fashioned herself a new identity and career as a professional photographer.

Her new profession began—as so many other things often did in our home—with a pregnancy. My mother was 24 years old when she realized that a photography business would permit her a flexible schedule, allowing her to tend to her pregnancy, take care of her ailing father-in-law, and be available for her impending firstborn. Her first baby turned out to be twins: Naomi and Danny, my oldest siblings. My mother always loved bargains; perhaps this extra special two-for-one deal cemented her passion for pregnancy.

She put advertisements in the Seattle newspapers, purchased a used Rolleiflex camera, and rented a neighbor's coal bin for $5 a month to use as her darkroom. She visited clients' homes to snap black and white photographs of their children.

In March of 1949, shortly after the twins were born, my parents moved the family into a tiny home near the Seattle Arboretum. Otto, my paternal grandfather, moved in with them. My mother converted the living room into a photography studio and plunged into her new career with a newborn baby tucked under each arm.

A trailblazer even in 1949, she wanted her own professional identity. She decided not to use her last name, Chotzen, because it was already linked to my father's business. So she appropriated her first two names—Carla Anette—in branding her business "Carla Anette: Photographer of Little People."

As it turned out, she had a real gift for portrait photography, and it became her professional identity. Looking at her photographs, the subjects gaze back at you with a disarming honesty. "All I do is release people to be who they really are," she proclaimed proudly. "I capture essences."

Two years later, when my sister Leah was born, my mother had already established a reputation and a loyal clientele. Over the next four decades, many parents brought their children back annually to chronicle the changes in their family from year to year, and those children brought their children.

As her family-friendly business grew, my mother's own family continued to expand as well. I was born on November 7, 1952—the fourth of eight children, all of us born between 1949 and 1962.

Just after my birth, my parents moved again, this time into a larger home, at the end of a dead-end street in the Leschi neighborhood of Seattle. It was a three-story house, with six bedrooms and views of Mt. Rainer, Lake Washington, and the Lake Washington Floating Bridge.

Mom was creative about the ways in which her photography business could support her rapidly growing household. She was a savvy and thrifty bargainer, and she often traded portraits for other services—carpentry, yard work, dental care. Wherever I went in Seattle, I would find my mother's distinctive black and white portraits lining the walls of doctor's offices, neighborhood grocery stores, and local restaurants.

Even when she wasn't working with a client, she still had a camera in her hands. She was constantly taking photos of our own family, sometimes in the studio and sometimes informally, usually as a group of siblings. Individual photo shoots were among the rare occasions when Mom would focus her attention on a single one of her children.

Looking back, it seems ironic that my mother built a career taking photos of other people when she always needed to be the center of attention herself. Whenever she could, Mom would step out from behind her Rolleiflex and into the frame of someone else's camera. She was strikingly beautiful: strong, athletic, and tan, with hazel eyes and an electric smile that lit up the room. A white streak ran through her glossy black hair; it had grown there when she was just sixteen. She looked as dynamic and irresistible on camera as she was in person.

In December 1951, a year before I was born, my parents sent out their first holiday card—something that would become an annual family tradition. My mother and father collaborated on these yearly photographs—she would set up the shot, giving detailed instructions to the photographer, and my father would devise the annual pun-filled caption that accompanied the photograph.

In the third card, from 1953, my father reclines inside of a large, old-fashioned baby stroller, sporting a black fedora, the hat tipped back jauntily. He's grinning broadly and holding a cigar in his mouth. I'm bundled up in my mother's arms, and she wears a warm winter coat. Naomi and Danny (both four-years-old), and Leah (almost three) are standing behind the stroller, posed as though they are pushing it uphill. They're staring at my father with a mixture of amusement and bafflement. The caption reads, "Pushin' towards '54."

Early in 1954 my mother decided that she needed a break. She was exhausted from both of her demanding occupations— the business of photography and the business of motherhood. Though my father often travelled for work, my mother hadn't been apart from her children since the twins were born, nearly five years earlier. Unsure of how we would respond to her impending absence, Mom decided not to tell us that she and my father were leaving town together. My parents tucked us into bed one night, just as they always did, and rose early the next morning before we were awake. They climbed into their car and drove off for a ten-day ski vacation in Sun Valley, Idaho.

I was one year old, too young to remember, but this event has crystallized in my mind through letters, stories from my parents and family friends, the memories of my older siblings, and the unmistakable sense of familiarity that the story triggers. However this memory was created, I remember waking up to a house that did not contain my parents. I remember seeing Veena.

Veena was the woman my mother had hired to take care of us while she and my dad were in Sun Valley. She was a dark-skinned young woman with a green sari that draped over her body. Her black hair was pulled back into a bun, her eyes were lined in black kohl, and she had a bindi in the center of her forehead between her eyebrows. None of us had ever seen her before.

My mother had placed an ad in the University of Washington student paper, offering a home for ten days for a "student who needs a place to study." She must have mentioned the four young children that would be populating the house, but perhaps she listed us as an afterthought. Veena was hired by phone and came early on the morning that my parents left town. It's possible, I suppose, that Veena was as surprised to find us as we were to find her.

According to my brother and sisters, I took one look at Veena and began to cry uncontrollably. I wouldn't stop. I screamed for hours as my siblings—young kids themselves—unsuccessfully tried to comfort and quiet me. Veena tried, too. When Danny suggested that I might have soiled my diaper, she removed my old diaper, held me under my arms and lowered me into the toilet. She swung me back and forth, flushing the toilet repeatedly in an attempt to clean me. To my siblings, it seemed as though Veena was trying to flush me down into the sewers. Naomi remembers watching from the doorway, terrified that this unfamiliar babysitter was going to kill me.

My parents had only been gone a few hours on their 650-mile drive to Sun Valley and were unreachable during those pre-cellphone days. To complicate matters, my mother had consciously decided not to leave Veena any contact information for them in Sun Valley; she wanted a real vacation with my father, away from her kids. However, she had given Veena a list of phone numbers of neighbors and family friends in case of an emergency.

An inconsolable crying baby constituted an emergency to Veena. She called the first name on the list; as soon as this neighbor showed up at our door, Veena left. She was gone by lunchtime, never to return.

Several sets of family friends took turns helping, but reportedly I didn't stop howling. A few days later, the 3rd couple on the list, Curt and Elizabeth Nussbaum, took over. Curt was my father's employee and knew how to reach my parents in Sun Valley. His wife, Elizabeth, talked with my mom. "Claudia doesn't recognize us. She doesn't recognize anyone. And she hasn't stopped crying for four days."

My mother was unconcerned; she reassured Elizabeth, "Oh, don't worry. She'll stop eventually,"

My mom was right, because after five days I finally stopped screaming. When my parents returned from Sun Valley at the end of their ten-day ski vacation, my mother picked me up in her arms. She told me that I turned my head away from her and acted as if I didn't recognize her. I would not meet her gaze.

"That was the worst thing I ever did as a mother," she confessed to me years later.

That was the closest I ever heard my mom come to apologizing for anything. And in retrospect, I wish that had been the worst thing she ever did as a mother.

* * *

My father, Walter, was the owner of The Otto Chotzen Company. Dad had started the company with his own father, Otto, and had named it after him. The business had begun with an observation: American bobby pins were only sold in a "gross"—twelve dozen to a box. Otto and Walter wondered whether women would be more likely to buy bobby pins in smaller, more useable quantities. They pitched the idea to local five-and-dime stores, and the bobby pins idea became a hit. Soon, they expanded to other hair items and then expanded again, adding sewing supplies, ribbons, craft supplies, and baby goods.

My grandfather Otto died before I was born, but the company that carried his name grew from its humble beginnings in my grandparents' basement on Capitol Hill to a warehouse on Jackson Street, and then into a bigger warehouse on Western Avenue, near the Seattle waterfront. It took up a large section of an enormous building that covered an entire block.

Almost weekly, Dad headed off in a different direction in his De Soto station wagon, travelling to drug stores and five-and-dime stores all over Washington State to sell his merchandise. He loaded the station wagon with large leather suitcases filled with samples of his products: threads, needles, thimbles, zippers, small scissors, miniature tool kits, combs, hairbrushes, barrettes, nail scissors, clippers, emery boards, and ribbons of all widths, textures, and colors. He'd stop in a town, visit a client, display his samples, and take his customers' orders. At the end of the week, when he returned to Seattle, he and his four employees filled those orders at the warehouse, packed them into large brown cardboard boxes, and shipped them to his customers.

It was always a special treat when Dad took any of us to work with him. Even in later years, when there were eight children, he would only bring two or three of us with him to the warehouse. We wandered the aisles and, if we were lucky, we might help him fill orders for the different stores.

"Follow me," he would say. "Here is an order with a list of things Mrs. Seward in Yakima wants to buy from us. Next to the item on the list is a merchandise number. Now we need to find the aisle where this merchandise is." And then he would lead us to the correct aisle and show us how to pull the box with the corresponding product number off the shelf.

I was impressed by the exactness and organization of everything: the aisles, the floor-to-ceiling shelves stacked with white cardboard boxes, the boxes themselves so precisely labeled and numbered. I loved the smell of the large, old brick building and how the wooden floors creaked when we walked on them. What really made a lasting impression on me was the calmness and orderliness of my father's work life, which was a comforting contrast to the constant chaos at home.

If we were there on a weekend, after Dad finished his work, we would all walk over to Ye Olde Curiosity Shoppe, a few blocks from his warehouse. A crowded store with a crazy assortment of items, some just for display, others for sale, it both fascinated and gave us the creeps. Here my siblings and I could wander the aisles in wide-eyed wonder studying oddities like a model ship constructed from matchsticks, a piano that played all by itself—the piano keys going up and down without anybody's fingers touching them, a baby pig in a jar, shrunken heads with signs indicating they came from far-away places like Borneo, and two desiccated life-size mummies in a glass case, a man and a woman, named Sylvester and Sylvia. Once in a while, my father bought us an inexpensive treasure like Mexican jumping beans which we'd clutch tightly in our fists, shrieking as they wiggled and bounced and tickled our palms. Whenever it was time to leave Ye Olde Curiosity Shoppe, we begged my father to stay longer.

Back at my father's warehouse, Curt Nussbaum was Dad's only employee who never seemed to take a day off. Even on the weekends, he was always there. We would pass him in the front office, attacking the keys of the typewriter with his two index fingers. I always said hello to him; he would look up and grunt back at me in response, then quickly return to his work.

Curt's main job was to keep track of the company's finances and inventories, and to order more supplies when the warehouse began to run short. It was hard for me to imagine that such a stern man had a wife and two children of his own. It could not have been Curt's German accent that intimidated me; my father spoke English with a German accent of his own, and my parents often spoke to each other in German around the house. But my father was warm and personable, and it was obvious that his employees and customers admired and adored him. He was as charming as Curt was gruff.

My father was very loyal to Curt. "I could never run my business without him," he insisted. Though I see now that Curt's diligence must have been invaluable, as a child I attributed my father's loyalty to a shared history: Curt had escaped from Germany during the early years of the Nazi occupation, just as both of my parents had.

* * *

My father, Walter Chotzen, was born in 1911 in Ziegenhals, a small German town in the mountains near the Czech border. He was the youngest of three children, and the only son. His mother, Elisabeth, was an artist. She was fifteen years younger than her husband, my grandfather Otto. Otto owned a large factory that produced wooden plugs, or "bungs," used to seal beer barrels. The Chotzen family lived in a large villa next door to the factory and had been prominent citizens in Ziegenhals for almost a century. My grandfather served on the city council, and in 1911 (the same year my father was born), Otto and Elisabeth became the first citizens of Ziegenhals to own a car. The Chotzens were the only Jewish family in Ziegenhals; their family friends were Protestant and Catholic. My father's family celebrated Jewish holidays, but they also celebrated Christmas.

The year that Hitler ascended to Chancellor (1933) was the same year that my father finished his studies at the University of Berlin. Dad witnessed hundreds of Brown Shirts marching in the streets and wandered past bonfires burning piles of books. In Berlin, where he was working, Dad watched with trepidation as "No Jews" signs started to appear outside of shops and restaurants. He was fired within the year, at the age of 22. "I can't have a Jew working for me anymore," his employer frankly admitted.

When my father returned home to Ziegenhals, he was shocked to discover that now even his oldest friends would no longer speak to him. "Friends I had played with in my childhood would cross to the other side of the street and turn their heads so they wouldn't have to look at me," my father recounted years later.

With his father's encouragement, Walter moved to England for five months where he worked in a travel agency and improved his English.

After he moved back to Ziegenhals, his father sent him on business trips to big cities such as Dresden and Hamburg. But the political climate was shifting under his feet. When Walter walked through the door and greeted the businessmen with "Guten Tag" instead of "Heil Hitler," the business owners immediately identified him as a Jew and refused to conduct business with him. Wherever he went, my father lost more and more accounts for his father's business. It wasn't long before the Nazi government declared a nationwide boycott of Jewish-owned businesses. Otto was forced to sell the factory; the government set the price far below its actual value, but my grandfather had no choice.

Back in Ziegenhals, my father was called in by the German military to report for a physical. The medical officer ordered the men to strip, and as he marched down the rows of naked Germans he stopped in front of my father and announced to the group that he had discovered a circumcised penis. He instructed the young men—many of them my father's childhood friends and classmates—to surround my father, and he led them in chants of "Dirty Jew," as they roared with laughter and jeered.

My father realized that he had to flee Germany. As a resident of a border town, he had a permit that allowed him to take short trips in and out of Czechoslovakia. He began to smuggle money across the border, hoping that when he and his parents ultimately left Germany, they would not be penniless. He rolled paper money into medicine vials and added small chunks of lead to each vial. He immersed the medicine vials in oil cans, then placed the oil cans in his car and drove over the border. When the Nazi soldiers searched his car, they shook the oil cans, but the lead weighed the vials down, and the officers detected nothing suspicious. Once safely in Czechoslovakia, Walter poured out the oil in the woods and gave the money to a friend on the Czech side. This friend sent the money to my father's cousins who lived in Prague. Walter successfully smuggled money out of Germany in this manner six times.

One morning, when he was 26, my father was awakened by a phone call from a Gestapo officer, who demanded that Walter meet him in an hour with his car and his border crossing papers. My father said he didn't tell his parents that he was going to meet the Gestapo because they would have been terrified that they would never see him again. When he arrived at the station, two soldiers from the Gestapo got into his car and directed him to drive to a villa outside of town. They led him into an office where they accused him of smuggling money out of Germany.

Walter knew that if they could prove that he had smuggled money out of Germany, he was likely to be killed. When he denied the accusations, the officers showed him papers purporting to prove that he had crossed at a specific border station several times. When he saw the papers, my father regained hope: he had never crossed at that particular border location. The officers were bluffing. Walter produced his own documents, which proved that he had never been at that crossing. The officers, finding their claims disproved, released him.

Realizing he might not be so lucky the next time, Walter travelled to the American consulate in Berlin. The room was packed with desperate Jews, all hoping to get to the front of the line to obtain a visa. As my father stood in line, an American official rushed past him. In his best English, Walter asked, "Excuse me sir, could I talk to you?" The official turned his head. Evidently my father's English pronunciation, perfected in the five months working in a London travel agency, was good enough to catch his attention. The man nodded and motioned for my father to follow him through the throngs of people and into his office. There, he issued Walter an American visa. "That man saved my life," my father told us years later, his voice choked with emotion.

In August 1938, at the age of 27, my father boarded a train in Ziegenhals and waved goodbye to his parents, unsure whether he would ever see them again. He disembarked in Czechoslovakia, travelled to Sweden, and boarded a ship for America. His parents eventually managed to get to America, but their extended family was not so fortunate; over the next several years more than forty of my father's aunts, uncles, and cousins died in concentration camps.

Walter landed in New York City in October of 1938. The Jewish refugee committee in New York told my father they had found him a job in Spokane, Washington, but when he arrived by train in the Pacific Northwest, he learned that the company that had promised to hire him had gone bankrupt. He found employment doing various odd jobs in Spokane and then in Seattle—working in a furniture store, cleaning old stoves, and selling watches.

"I had a burning desire to get even with Hitler," Dad emphasized. However, because of his German heritage, he was labeled an "enemy alien" and not allowed to serve in the U. S. armed forces. Once the United States entered into World War II, however, policies on military service became less restrictive. My father, who had been in the U.S. less than five years, enlisted successfully in 1943 and reported for basic training in Florida. He was 32, fourteen years older than most of his fellow soldiers, who affectionately called him "Pop." A knee injury during training removed Walter from consideration for combat. He applied for a special program that trained soldiers to become interpreters. The test for the program consisted of a general I.Q. test, language tests in German and French, and a test in a fake language to assess how easily the candidate could pick up a foreign language. Walter passed with flying colors.

He was sent to Clark University in Worcester, Massachusetts, to be trained as a German interpreter. The head of the program at Clark feared my father would be bored in the German program and offered him a position as an Italian or Greek interpreter. Since Walter had taken six years of Latin, he chose Italian and passed the Italian examination in six months. Stationed in New Jersey, he worked with the "Italian Service Units"—Italian prisoners who had agreed to help the United States in non-combat roles. On the weekends, he would visit his older sister, Ilse, in New York. And it was there, in New York City, where he met Carla, and their courtship began, culminating in their marriage a mere 3 months after first meeting.

My mother, Carla, was born in Weimar, Germany in 1924. She was the second of four children born to my grandparents, Willy and Inge Glaser. Willy owned a large knitting mill in

Weimar that employed more than one thousand workers. Though Inge's father was a rabbi in Berlin, she and Willy were not religiously observant. They lived a secular lifestyle; they identified as Germans first, and rarely as Jews. In fact, when they married, Willy had insisted that his wife change her given name from "Sarah" to something less obviously Jewish. He chose "Inge" for her, a name that she would carry for the rest of her life.

Willy read *Mein Kampf* when it was published in 1925, just a year after my mother's birth, and over the next several years, he kept a wary eye on the increasingly anti-Semitic climate. In 1932, when my mother was eight, he moved the family to England. Willy felt that it was important to establish a branch of his business outside of Germany.

In England, my mother and her older sister, Ruth, were both initially placed in kindergarten because they did not speak English. They learned quickly, and before long they were conversant enough to catch up with their age-appropriate classes.

Willy had left the Weimar business in the hands of his brother, who was trying desperately to protect and preserve it. Determined to help save the knitting mill, the Glaser family returned to Germany in 1935, when my mother was eleven. Carla had never felt any personal connection to Judaism, so she was shocked to find that her heritage suddenly precluded her from participating in school sports teams, orchestras, and other extracurricular activities. Jews weren't allowed to go to public parks, playgrounds, swimming pools and theaters. Each school day now started with an assembly in the auditorium with a collective "Heil Hitler!" salute, followed by Nazi songs. When we were older my mother shared how uncomfortable and painful it was for her when every day in school, she was forced to sing lyrics translated as: "*Sharpen the knives on the pavement. Let the blood of the Jews run freely.*"

Before long, Carla and her sister Ruth were banned from attending their local school because they were Jewish. Carla was eleven, and Ruth was twelve. Worried and looking for a safer environment for his daughters, Willy took them to Switzerland and enrolled them in a boarding school. As he departed to return to Germany, Willy confided to his daughters that he didn't know if he would ever see them again. He gave the girls strict instructions to never speak German, to become fluent in French in two months, and to only speak French even when they were alone. "Throw off the shackles of Judaism," he urged them, and he warned them that, when they were older, they should marry non-Jews in order to escape future persecution.

Carla and Ruth never returned to Germany, but the family reunited in Czechoslovakia, abandoning the knitting mill, its one thousand employees, and their long family legacy as proud German citizens. They fled to America in 1937, starting over in Buffalo.

It was on a summer Sunday in 1943 at my Aunt Ilse's eleventh floor Upper Westside Manhattan apartment that my parents met. My mother, who was thirteen when she arrived in America, had rushed through the American school system. She completed high school at sixteen, received a scholarship to the University of Rochester, and graduated from college at eighteen. After working in a photo studio in Washington, D.C. and then a psychiatric hospital in Hartford, Connecticut, Carla moved to New York City to work for the American Jewish Committee translating newspaper articles from French and German into English. Her parents had known my father's sister Ilse and her husband Ernst in Germany, and when Carla learned that Ilse had a younger brother who was serving in the United States Army, she was eager to meet him. She saved her ration stamps for sugar and butter and offered them to Ilse, all to give her an excuse to visit Ilse's apartment almost every weekend. Finally, one day in the summer of 1943 when Carla was there, Walter stopped by to visit.

For my father, it was love at first sight. He was 33. Carla was twenty, a dazzling free spirit. She wore a pink, rayon, bare-shouldered dress, and her skin was tan from hours of summer tennis. When she left the room, Walter asked his niece, Steffi, to set them up on a date. When Steffi approached Carla with this request, Carla replied, "Tell him to ask me himself." He did.

A few days later, they went on their first date to play tennis on the public courts in Central Park. As the game wore on, with the weather steamy, Carla removed her blouse and was soon confronted by a policeman who told her that she could not appear in public in her bra. Carla complied and put her blouse back on. But the moment the policeman left, her blouse came off again. My father was smitten. When my mother bent down to take a drink from a water fountain, my father joked that he was envious of the lucky fountain.

New York offered few opportunities for wooing in private. To make matters more challenging, my father was often in his army uniform, which drew a good deal of attention to the courting couple. "Watch yourself, soldier, you are desecrating the American uniform," one man cautioned Walter as he and my mother were kissing at an outdoor concert. Every night, my parents stayed out late—and early every morning, my father hurried back to New Jersey to report to duty. The lack of sleep took its toll, and he was briefly hospitalized for exhaustion.

He was back to courting Carla as soon as possible. One night, as my parents canoodled in Central Park, a man dashed by, grabbed Carla's Mexican leather purse, and ran off. The joke was on the thief—the purse contained only 25 cents and the key to Carla's room in an apartment she shared, but now Carla had nowhere to sleep. My father led her to his sister Ilse's apartment. His brother-in-law Ernst answered the door and was none too pleased with Walter's request to spend the night with Carla. "You're not married," Ernst insisted. "It's not proper." "We have nowhere else to go," my father retorted, and eventually Ernst relented.

On September 24, 1944—just three months after they had met—my parents eloped to a small New York resort town. They pulled two town drunks off the street to serve as witnesses, but they were surprised to learn that the marriage was not official: New York law required a three-day waiting period between the issuing of a marriage license and the ensuing wedding.

My parents waited three days and were married a second time, this time legally. When Carla's religious grandmother expressed distress that her granddaughter had not been wed in a Jewish ceremony, they tied the knot a third time, with a small December Jewish wedding in Ilse's apartment, where they had met.

Carla's father was not present at any of the three weddings, nor had my mother given him a chance to meet Walter before they were married. He was a forceful and opinionated man, and my mother stubbornly refused to entertain his objections or displeasure. When Walter and Willy finally met, they went for a walk through the streets of Buffalo. "How do you intend to earn a living?" my grandfather demanded.

Walter, whose only goal at the time was to finish his military service and move on with his life with Carla, was annoyed by his new father-in-law's pestering questions. "I'll run a fruit stand in the Seattle Public Market," was his facetious answer.

Willy was not amused. He went home, locked himself in his bedroom, and announced that he was sick. (As far as my mother could remember, he had never been ill a day in his life.) He didn't come out of his bedroom until my father had returned to his army post in New Jersey, four days later. Upon finally emerging from his room, Willy had a few words of advice for his newlywed daughter. "Well, you can always get a divorce."

When Walter completed his military duty, my parents moved to Seattle, an area that my father had grown to like during his first few years in America. Walter and his father were busy working in their new business, The Otto Chotzen Company, and my mother grew resentful of all the time my father was spending on his fledgling business. Once, she expressed her frustration by hitting her mother-in-law over the head with a pie tin. "I was trying to send Walter a message that it was time for us to have a family," she said. "He was spending too much time with his work and his parents."

Carla wanted twelve children; my father felt that four was a more reasonable number. They compromised at eight. "I wanted to keep going," Mom would always say. But the rest of us all seemed to agree: eight was plenty.

* * *

After my birth, my parents moved into their second family home—in the Leschi neighborhood of Seattle's Central Area. Like many of their immigrant friends who had fled oppression, they identified more closely with America's minority populations than with its white majority. Residents of the Central Area of Seattle were predominantly African American, with some Asian Americans, and so my parents decided that it would be the perfect place to raise a family. From as early as I can remember, my brothers, sisters, and I were brought up with the understanding that differences of race, culture, and religion were superficial and were never reasons to be afraid of neighbors.

Though the residents of Leschi were primarily Black, a few of the neighborhood's storeowners were Jewish refugees like my parents. The local butcher, Ernie, had a heavy European accent. He greeted us warmly when we entered his shop and gave us thick, round slices of spicy bologna to munch on while Mom picked out the meat she would purchase.

After we left Ernie's butcher shop, we would often head up the street to a small bakery filled with the enticing aromas of freshly baked bread. The lady who owned the bakery was from the "old country," too, and she would give us day-old sugar cookies for free.

The Leschi neighborhood had a dry cleaner and a hardware store, too. My mother made a point of shopping within the neighborhood whenever she could. She knew everyone there, and she bargained to get good prices on everything she bought. All four of us tagged along with her on these errands—at least until the twins were old enough to start school. Mom enjoyed being followed around the neighborhood by her progeny; everyone seemed to admire our family for its size and charm. "So many children," Ernie the Butcher would grunt admiringly. "So many nice children."

When I was two, Mom became pregnant again, and just five days before my third birthday she gave birth to my baby brother, Simon. I remember waking up the morning after Mom had come home from the hospital. I wandered sleepily from the room I shared with Leah into my parents' bedroom, next door. Mom lay sprawled out on the enormous kingside bed with the tiny baby tucked lovingly under her left arm. I stared at the baby. He had big brown eyes and curly black hair and a hospital identification necklace with his name spelled out in little beads. As I watched him wriggle under Mom's arm, I felt that I had been replaced.

Danny and Naomi had moved to the top floor of our three-story home, where they each had their own bedroom. Their bedrooms had long, thick ropes coiled near the windows; Danny showed me how he could hang the rope out his window and down the side of the house and he told me, "This is how we will climb down the side of the house if there is a fire." I liked visiting him and Naomi at the top of the house. The room they had moved out of was in the basement, which was now Leah's and my room, and it was filled with dust and spiders. "You're very attached to us, Claudia. You're a very tender

girlie," my mom told me. "It's nice to be attached to me and
Daddy, but now Simon needs to sleep with us."

There was a constant stream of visitors in our home. Besides
the photography clients, our home was a magnet for friends of
the older kids, the families of those friends, neighbors, and
sometimes the mailman or milkman, when my mom invited
them for a snack or lunch.

Mom brought strangers home, too. Not infrequently she
would return from downtown Seattle with a new friend from
Seattle's homeless contingent in tow. She usually struck a
bargain with these guests, trading room and board for
housework and childcare. Though my parents' English was
good, they were both prone to occasional semantic mix-ups and
malapropisms. My parents called these people the "dredge of
humanity," although my mother said it with considerably more
affection than my father did.

No two days or evenings were ever alike. It was impossible
to anticipate how many extra bodies might join us for dinner,
or who was going to spend a few nights living with us. Through
the years, it was almost the norm to find a neighborhood child
seated for dinner next to one of my mother's friends from the
League of Women Voters, or a civil rights activist, a homeless
person, or later, one of Mom's men "friends" whom she
flagrantly flirted with in front of my father.

Fridays were always the most exciting evening because my
parents hosted their "Friday Night Group," a weekly gathering
of friends who met in our living room. Over the years, many
people drifted in and out of the Friday Night Group, but some
anchored the group right from its start in 1955 and were part of
our life during the rest of the week too, year after year.

As soon as we finished dinner on Fridays, the house would
bustle with preparation. Dad put new logs in the living room
fireplace, lit the fire, and assigned Leah to vacuum the floor.
Mom put the food away. Danny washed the kitchen floor, and
I stood next to Naomi and handed the dirty dishes to her while

she stood on a wooden stool and washed them. We all took turns holding the baby, Simon, as we hurried through the evening chores.

At 7 p.m., just as we had finished cleaning up, the guests began to arrive. John and Polly Verrall usually arrived first; my brothers and sisters and I were always excited to see them. John was a nationally recognized composer and a music professor at the University of Washington. As soon as he took off his wool sports coat, he sat down at our baby grand piano. Though I always wanted to start dancing to John's music immediately, my mother insisted that music practice come first. Danny would play his child-sized violin; Naomi would play her tiny viola. When we grew a little older, Leah played the cello and I played violin alongside Danny. My mother had assigned specific instruments to each of us, hoping to create a family string quartet.

As we squeaked out the tunes and lessons from our music books, John accompanied us by playing the same simple tunes and songs on the piano. I was always amazed by how much better he made all of us sound. He watched us carefully and often stopped playing to correct our hand positions or to have us try a note again.

If we weren't practicing with John, we gathered in the kitchen around Polly and waited eagerly as she unwrapped her wheat germ brownies, a treat that she baked specially for us every week. The brownies were still warm when she unwrapped them. We gobbled them up before the other guests arrived.

After we finished our music lessons and devoured the brownies, it was finally time to dance. John improvised on the piano while we danced around the living room. I loved dancing with my older sisters and brother—twirling and leaping as John smiled at us. His cheeks were always rosy, and he looked so happy to be playing the piano for us. I would have enjoyed being able to dance like that all night, but once the other adults arrived, John would move away from the piano to participate in their conversation.

Brian and Rita Dodd were good friends of my parents, and we often saw them during the week, as well as on Friday nights. Rita was an artist whose watercolors of Pacific Northwest scenes—boats and bridges and rivers and trees—hung on our hallway walls and in our bedrooms. Brian was a carpenter; he and his three sons performed all the repairs on our home in exchange for my mother's photography. Brian was also the editor of *People's World*, the West Coast's largest Communist newspaper. The other members of the Friday Night Group looked to him as an expert on political and labor issues. It seemed to me that when Brian came to our house during the week, he came as a carpenter, but on Friday nights, he came as a Communist.

On most Fridays, Brian and Rita often brought Zeo, a retired sea captain who lived with them. Zeo was building a trimaran in their backyard; he told us that his dream was to sail around the world one last time before he died. He arrived with pieces of driftwood and taught us how to whittle little wooden knives and forks.

Another couple, Greg and Dora Miller, were our closest family friends—probably because theirs was the only family we knew that rivaled ours in size. Eventually, there were seven Miller children—one fewer than our eight. "It's because Carla had twins," Dora would explain, as if there had been a competition. "We had the same number of pregnancies, and that's what really counts."

Dora was a natural childbirth teacher; she and Mom had met while they were pregnant with Justine and me, respectively. The Miller kids were our most frequent playmates, but on Friday nights Greg and Dora visited without children.

Greg Miller was an engineer for Boeing. Both he and Dora liked to cite studies that had demonstrated how healthy it was to be touched, and Greg spent Friday nights circling around the room, rubbing everyone's backs and necks. All of the Friday Nighters praised Greg for his great massages. Even my siblings and I would take turns receiving massages from Greg. Sometimes Mom would rub our backs, too. She was always cuddling us and "eating us up" with love and kisses. It was the greatest joy of being a mother, she said.

When Nick Farley was in town, he was a regular guest. Nick was hard to predict—sometimes he lived in Seattle, but sometimes he lived in California. Sometimes he was married, and sometimes he wasn't. I didn't know how many wives had come and gone, but I did know that one of the wives had helped him to look after us when my parents disappeared to Sun Valley. Usually Nick came alone, though occasionally he would bring a wife, or even an ex-wife, with him.

Nick was a magnetic presence, and the whole room seemed to gravitate towards him. He was a burly guy, with shaggy hair, a bushy white beard and sparkling blue eyes. He would grasp our hands and say, "Hello, I'm *so* glad to see you," as he gazed deeply into our eyes, speaking in a soft whisper. And then he drew us in for hugs that seemed to last forever. He was especially fond of my mother, and the hugs that he gave her lasted the longest of all. "Ah, Carla, such sweetness, such goodness, such beauty," he would purr as he held her tight.

Clark was an occasional guest who also appeared to take a special interest in Mom. She had met him on a train returning to Seattle after visiting her parents in Buffalo. She had all four of the children with her on the trip (Simon had not yet been born), so Clark must have noticed that her hands were quite full. According to Mom, the two of them had hit it off as soon as they realized they were both travelling all the way back to Seattle. Clark was stocky and bald, but he was also rugged—a man of the outdoors. He had been a scoutmaster and a mountaineer, as well as a tour guide at Mount Rainer National Park. He painted, too—as did Nick Farley and Rita Dodd. Clark was a widower who lived on Queen Anne Hill, all alone, and he was one of our most frequent babysitters.

The strangest member of the Friday Night Group was Waldo, the tallest man I had ever seen. Although he was in his eighties, he stood as straight as a cedar tree. He wore a green wool lumberman's jacket, had large dark hollows beneath his eyes, and lived alone in the forest somewhere near Hood Canal. The first time I saw Waldo I was convinced that he was a giant, and I immediately began to cry.

Dad told me not to be afraid. He said that Waldo went to a great deal of trouble in order to join us on Friday nights, and that we should be gracious hosts to him. Waldo took a ferryboat to get into Seattle, and his weekly visits were often his only contact with civilization. Dad explained that Waldo had lived for years with Northwest Indians. He ate vegetables from his garden. He was also an artist and often brought woodcuts and etchings of nature scenes. He smelled strongly of the forest, but once I became accustomed to the way that he smelled and looked, I grew to like him. He spoke simply and quietly, as he shared his respect for the order of the natural world and the souls that dwelt inside animals.

Once all the Friday night guests had arrived and had settled in front of the fireplace, the evening's discussion would begin. It could veer in any direction—the adults' personal lives; local, national, and international news; feelings; work; politics; fears; and dreams. Through the years, I remember listening to conversations about Edgar Cayce, reincarnation, faith healing, Ethel and Julius Rosenberg, Morton Sobell, Black Power, the Vietnam War, theosophy, and mescaline. There were no rules or boundaries about what was discussed.

Sometimes—usually only when Nick Farley was in town— the adults would paint or dance instead of talking. Mom and Nick would lock their eyes together and gyrate their bodies around the living room to John's tunes on the piano. I would sit beside Dad and watch them. On other evenings, Nick brought tempera paints and brushes and a pile of drawing paper and led impromptu art classes. As kids, this was one of the few times we were allowed to participate. Everyone squeezed around our grey Formica kitchen table, and Nick led the group in free-form painting. "Close your eyes and visualize the movement of the brush on the paper," he instructed. "Now, open your eyes and let the shapes and colors flow from your spirit." Sometimes he encouraged us to paint with our hands; we always did exactly what he suggested.

Nick loved to praise Mom's paintings in front of the Friday Night Group. No matter what she created, he would hold the paper up and insist that we all admire her work. "Isn't it exquisite?" he asked. "This stroke has such energy and grace in it." When Nick said these things, Mom's face would turn red and her voice would become higher. She would grin at Nick, and he would grin back. Nick never held up Dad's paintings for approval, but I never heard him complain or comment about Nick's obvious infatuation with my mom, or with her being so receptive to it. My mom thrived when she was the center of attention.

Usually, however, the Friday Night Group was reserved for conversation. As kids, we were allowed to stay up late and listen, but we were not invited to participate. I sat close to the fireplace, my arms wrapped around my knees, staring into the flames and trying to pay attention. Daddy poked at the fire and added more logs as the evening wore on. I didn't have a bedtime on Friday nights. Often, I would fall asleep on the floor in front of the fire, curled up next to Naomi, or Danny or Leah, drifting off to the ongoing hum of adult voices.

* * *

Our house, in the Leschi, neighborhood, was at the end of a dead-end street and surrounded by woods. The Millers lived in the Mt. Baker neighborhood, about an eight-minute drive away.

Mom and Dora Miller traded babysitting and they kept each other updated on bargains and store sales. The Chotzen and Miller kids were always back and forth between our two homes. Mom liked to say that we were shared communally. The Miller's home was a large wood-frame house painted dark brown. During the day, we played in the garage and in their overgrown yard. Grapevines covered the fence that connected the house to the garage. When the grapes were hard and green we bit into them and made sour faces. We filled buckets with them and used them as projectiles, as currency, and as marbles.

We collected real marbles, too. Naomi's collection was the envy of all the younger children from both families. Her marbles filled a giant gold, metal container with a metal lid that snapped on to keep it closed. It was one of her most treasured possessions, and she kept it hidden in her closet. She thought this secret hiding place was safe, but when she wasn't home, I loved to sneak into her room, take the lid off, and run my fingers through the hundreds of smooth, beautiful, multi-colored marbles.

In her closet, next to the container of marbles, Naomi kept a doll that had been given to her by Elizabeth Nussbaum. It was a stand-up doll in a tall plastic case, tied up in a box with wrapping paper and ribbon. Naomi told me that she didn't play with the doll. "I'm the oldest girl," she said. "I'm Mom's big helper. I don't have time for dolls." But sometimes I would peek through the crack in her door and see her untie the ribbon, remove the wrapping paper, take the doll from its case, and stare at it as she held it in her hands. Then, she always returned it to its case, replaced the wrapping paper and the ribbon, and tucked it away behind her clothes in the closet, right next to her marbles.

Naomi only took a few of her marbles to Leschi Elementary School to play marble games on the playground during recess, but she sometimes brought her whole collection to the Miller's house. When Danny wasn't building model airplanes inside with Tim, the oldest of the Miller children, he and Tim and Naomi spent hours playing marble games on a large patch of dirt in the back yard. The younger Miller kids and Leah and I watched them play and imitated the games ourselves, but we were rarely allowed into their big kid circle.

The Miller's garage was cluttered with car parts, sections of bicycles, and old bottles that Greg Miller collected. He could fix anything, and he always kept several old cars in the garage and the front yard, moving parts from one car to another as he got each one running in turn. He used the bottles to brew root beer in their basement. We loved it when Greg Miller offered us sips of the root beer while we played.

When my mother didn't drop us at the Millers, she often chose Clark from the Friday Night group to be our babysitter. Mom preferred to drop us off at Clark's apartment on Queen Anne Hill, but after our first visit there, Naomi and Danny refused to go back. Naomi threw terrible tantrums when Mom tried to take us to Clark's apartment—screaming and flailing her little body and absolutely refusing to get into the station wagon. Clark's transgressions were Naomi's dark secret.

Mom, however, was equally stubborn and saw no good reason to let a child control her relationship with a readily available babysitter, as well as a family friend. "He's a great man," she told us. "He's very respected in the community." And he was. He was a well-known Boy Scout leader and an expert mountaineer. In 1937 he had helped create a camp in West Seattle for boy scouts to learn camping skills and how to rock climb. He also designed the major attraction at the camp: a 25-foot carefully engineered artificial boulder that featured a range of rock climbing challenges that became the favorite practice site for some of the world's most accomplished mountaineers, such as Jim Whittaker, the first American to reach the top of Mount Everest.

Clark continued to babysit us at our Leschi home, but he often dropped by for Friday Night Groups, dinners, and casual visits. When he offered to paint an oil portrait of Naomi, Mom was excited. "Clark's paintings are expensive," she said. "This is a real privilege." My mother pulled Naomi's shoulder-length blonde hair into a ponytail and dressed her up for the occasion. He painted her in private in an upstairs bedroom. Selecting an outfit turned out to be an unnecessary step: Clark had Naomi strip naked and step into a pair of my mother's high heels. He painted her backside, standing in the high-heel shoes. Naomi remembers hearing the rest of us talking and racing around downstairs, wishing with every fiber in her being that she could be playing with us.

My mother loved Clark's painting of Naomi. It resonated with themes prevalent in her own photography—celebrating the human body and the precociousness of youth. She hung Clark's portrait of Naomi on the wall in a well-lit hallway; it hung there all the years we lived in that house.

Meanwhile, all throughout that year when Naomi was six, she threw violent temper tantrums. She screamed for hours and seemed to get angry with my mother for the smallest thing. Naomi's outbursts sometimes caused Mom to lose her patience and she'd spank Naomi— "whackings," she called them. Other times, Mom called my father to come home from work early. "I don't know what's going on, but I give up. I can't communicate with her," she complained to Dad over the phone. Even when Naomi wasn't screaming at my mother, she was sullen. She cried a great deal and no longer danced with the rest of us when John Verrall played the piano on Friday nights.

Naomi's eating habits changed, too. She complained that her stomach hurt, and she would sometimes lie on the floor, writhing and crying in pain, while the rest of us ate. My father tried to persuade her to eat by making her favorite food for breakfast—scrambled eggs. "Naomi Girl, I've made a whole pan for you," he told her, but she insisted that her stomachaches were too painful, refusing to take a bite.

Naomi's constant stomach aches prompted my parents to take her to the doctors at the Group Health clinic. After several visits and a battery of tests, the doctors determined that Naomi had developed a bleeding duodenal ulcer; it was the size of a baseball. Initially the doctors believed it had been caused by Naomi's diet, so they conducted an extensive analysis of everything she ate. My father just shook his head. "It's those tantrums," he insisted. "It's the tantrums." Eventually, the doctors agreed. The ulcer was caused by stress, they determined, which, in turn, was causing bile to release into Naomi's stomach.

My father begged her to stop throwing fits. "You're doing this to yourself, Naomi," he told her. "You're hurting yourself." My parents took her to three different psychiatrists and fed her a prescribed diet: nothing but soft foods for a year. Over the next year, Naomi's temper tantrums abated, and the ulcer healed. She even resumed her role as Mom's special helper: hosting photography clients as they waited for their sessions, answering the phone, cleaning up the house, and helping Mom with childcare in a manner that far transcended the abilities of any regular seven-year-old. Later that same year, in 1956, Clark died of prostate cancer. My parents brought all five of us—even me and the baby, Simon, to the funeral. There was a special tribute by the Boy Scouts, the climbing wall was named for Clark, and many people spoke about his wonderful civic contributions. "I was so glad he was dead," Naomi told me years later.

* * *

In the spring of 1956, when I was three, Brian Dodd came over to do some special construction on our house. "We're making you a bedroom of your very own," Dad told me. "Right next to ours."

"But Claudia and I share a bedroom now that is near to yours," Leah protested.

Dad shook his head. "There's a closet in the hallway between our rooms, Leah-girl. And now that closet will become a bedroom for Claudia. It was Mom's idea. Then you will each have your own room."

"It's not good for you to be so separate from us," Mom told me. "You cried like crazy when you were a baby when we left town to ski; you get scared at night. Now you'll have a bedroom of your very own, as close to ours as possible."

It was nice to be close to my parents. It comforted me to know that my parents were right on the other side of the wall, and my mother started to pay me visits during the night to make sure I wasn't lonely. I was, as my mother often commented, the "most tender of all her children."

My new room was barely big enough to accommodate my bed, so I kept my clothes in my old room, where Leah still slept. Though I missed talking to Leah as we drifted off to sleep, I felt very special that my parents had chosen to create a room just for me. My tiny room was cramped, but Brian Dodd had added a window, so it had a view outside. It only helped a little because Seattle's weather was so dreary most of the year that even as a little girl the grey skies felt like they were closing in on me.

Before I was old enough to attend school and anticipate the concept of vacations, summer already felt special. When summer rolled around, our entire family seemed re-energized.

During the summer, I put my bathing suit on under my clothes when I dressed in the morning because almost every day included a visit to Lake Washington, walking distance from our house. We swam in the lake for hours and enjoyed picnics at Denny Blaine Beach. Though Mom would sometimes accompany us for her own daily swim, she rarely supervised us when we went to the beach. We were on our own, encouraged to create our own summer adventures. It was the older kids' responsibility to look after the younger ones.

The thick, deep woods that bordered our home felt more welcoming on those long sunny days. We played in the woods, digging holes, building forts, and trying not to get stung by nettles as we chased each other through the cool forest. We swung for hours on a rope swing tied to a huge tree limb in the forest clearing just across the street from our house.

At home, we gobbled juicy cherries, apricots, peaches and plums straight out of the wooden crates that Dad brought home regularly from his business trips to eastern Washington.

Dad also seemed more playful in the summertime. When he came home from work, he changed into his bathing suit and took us to the beach to play. He picked me up by my arms and swung me around, as my feet skimmed the cold surface of the lake. He helped Danny and Naomi carry inner tubes down the cobblestone steps at Denny Blaine Beach. Once the inner tubes were launched in the water, we all climbed aboard and scrambled for position as we bobbed amidst the small waves.

Dad was great at roughhousing, too. I jumped on his back and pulled at his shoulders, while Leah attacked his legs. He scooped up Leah in one arm and swung me around to his chest with the other, dangling us both over the water as we giggled and shrieked.

Mom played too, although her favorite activity was capturing memories on her 8mm movie camera. "Keep playing," she coaxed us, as she took movies of our games. She encouraged us to take our bathing suits off while we were playing. We stripped down and continued our games, splashing and wrestling in the nude while Mom filmed. She often took her swimsuit off, too, and handed the camera to my father. "Get some film of me eating Claudia up with kisses," she told him, and she chased me into the water as my father recorded. She didn't seem to care or notice if there were other people on the beach when she was naked.

Mom used the summer sunshine as an excuse to wear as little clothing as possible, and quite often nothing at all. She loved to be naked, and she frequently wandered around the house nude, regardless of the season. Summer, however, was particularly welcoming to her nudity. When we weren't playing naked on the beach, Mom liked to sunbathe nude on the deck of our house.

She instructed us to follow her example and spend as much time as possible unclothed. It was the most natural and beautiful way to be, she explained. She laid out newspaper and paints on the deck so that we could finger paint; she encouraged us to paint with—and on—every inch of our bodies. She held the movie camera as we got naked and covered ourselves with the paint, danced in it, sat in it, and smeared it all over each other and ourselves. "Show me your orange butt," she said from behind the camera. "Now get some orange on your sisters." When we had finished playing, she took out a garden hose and rinsed all of us, and the deck, clean. "So easy," she said. "Such easy fun."

She was not self-conscious—sometimes she would go to answer the doorbell or greet her customers wearing nothing but a pair of underwear. "Carla, put some clothes on," Dad admonished her.

She was better at remaining clothed when her parents visited from Buffalo. Omi and Opi—the German words we used for grandmother and grandfather—visited at least once a year. When they came, my mother wore long summer dresses and pretty hats.

Omi was a large, fleshy woman who wore big sunhats and flowered dresses in the summer and ankle-length camel hair coats when the weather was cooler. She gave us lots of smiles and hugs and brought presents for everyone. When she wasn't around, my mother complained that she was weak. "She's not a strong woman," Mom said. "She's a hypochondriac."

Opi was shorter than his wife, and he had a stubborn and forceful personality. He dressed nicely, too—in suits and fancy dress shoes—and he taught us all how to play chess. When he greeted me, he pinched my cheeks. He and my mother argued constantly about politics, and he criticized my father. When Opi and Omi were in town, my parents usually cancelled the Friday Night Group. During their summer visits, Omi and Opi spent hours reclining on deckchairs, gazing out at Mt. Rainer from our front deck.

Mom baked fresh Northwest salmon during the summer, and for dessert she ladled hot freshly cooked rhubarb (or the blackberries we had picked that day) on top of vanilla ice cream. After dinner, we piled into the car so that Dad and Mom could play tennis at the Leschi courts near our home. If Omi and Opi were visiting, they would stroll through Leschi Park while my parents sat in their tennis whites, waiting for their turn on the courts. While we waited, my siblings and I climbed through the green ivy that grew on the overpass near the courts. The holes in the ivy were just big enough for kids' bodies, and we knew all the secret passages. We played hide-and-go-seek in the ivy, using our expert knowledge to sneak up on one another for surprise attacks.

Dad's sister, Ilse, was another regular visitor. She arrived from New York for two weeks each summer and stayed with us in our home. At first, she came with her husband, Ernst. He passed away when I was young, and after that she continued to visit on her own.

Ilse wore pearls and pretty earrings and lipstick, and her dark hair was short and elegant. Her cheeks were tan and smooth, and her eyes sparkled as much as her jewelry did. She had a big, joyful laugh, and she never seemed ruffled by the hectic nature of our household. Of all the visitors that came to our house, she always seemed the most interested in me. She never talked about "the children," the way that other people did. She called each of us by name, and she seemed to understand and appreciate the ways we were different from each other. "Claudia likes the dark chocolate best, and Leah likes the milk chocolate. I'll have to remember that" she said after we accepted her offer of wrapped candies.

She was ten years older than my father, and they loved each other's company. They played chess together, and Ilse played against us, too, and expanded upon the lessons that Opi had given us. Dad, Mom, and Ilse spoke to each other in German, telling jokes and laughing wildly at the punch lines. When we asked them to translate the jokes, they only shook their heads and laughed harder. Home felt lighter and happier when Ilse was there, and I looked forward to her visits with great excitement.

The highlight of every summer was Family Camp, a weeklong visit to a beautiful retreat in Washington State. Dad had started the camp with a few of his friends at Quaker Cove near Anacortes in the summer of 1956, when I was three. The location changed through the years—a different lake, different little cabins—but most of the same families came year after year, and new families joined in as regulars. All of the families participated in the communal chores—preparing meals and cleaning up—and in group activities like hiking, swimming, art projects, and games.

Dad was the volunteer camp director. Prior to camp, he would spend many hours planning and organizing that year's Family Camp. He selected and reserved the location, corresponded with the other families who would be attending, created a schedule of activities, and made a list of necessary food and supplies.

Every August, my family piled into our crowded station wagon and drove to Family Camp. We drove over the Cascade Mountains, shouting with excitement when we arrived at Lake Wenatchee. We unpacked the car, settled into our cabin, and then we reunited with our friends. Some of the attendees were friends we saw often in Seattle, while others we only saw during this one blissful week each year. At Family Camp, it felt like everyone was one big extended family. It grew to be a large family, too—some years, as many as one hundred people attended.

I enjoyed how everyone participated together: young kids, older kids, teenagers, and parents. Dinner was always followed by a huge group game of Capture the Flag, then a campfire with folksongs, marshmallows, and ended with my dad telling a story.

Dad was a wonderful storyteller. At home, he told us bedtime tales nightly. At Family Camp his audience expanded, and everyone gathered for his stories. Dad didn't read these stories from books; he made them up himself. I felt a sense of pride that it was my dad who enchanted everyone, and I could see that Dad loved having so many other kids and parents listen attentively as he spun his original tales.

Mom always came with us to Family Camp, but she never enjoyed it as much as the rest of us. She loved the swimming and the hiking, and the late-night conversations after the kids went to sleep, but she and Dad also fought much more often than at home. In Seattle, our world revolved around my mother; at Family Camp, the spotlight turned to Dad. He was the patriarch, the camp director, and the beloved storyteller. Dad seemed different there, more confident. Mom, on the other hand, didn't like not being the center of attention; she seemed to resent Dad for being acknowledged and appreciated. Also, at Family Camp my mother was expected to keep her clothes on. The family campers had been kicked out of the first family camp location at Quaker Cove because one time my mother's black bra and panties were left hanging over the railing of the cabin's deck, and another day my mother had been spotted sunbathing in the nude on the beach. It was a Quaker facility, and they didn't tolerate nudity.

At my mother's insistence, every year when Family Camp ended, we went on our own weeklong family vacation. My mother was much happier being in control of our world and hers.

We usually camped on the coast of Washington or took the ferry to Vancouver Island in Canada. On the Washington Coast we camped on the beaches in the Olympic National Park. Every inch of our station wagon was packed; the park rangers and other families marveled at how one car could hold two grownups, so many children, our clothes, sleeping bags, cooking equipment, food, inner tubes, and a yellow rubber raft.

Getting to the beach was equally challenging since it sometimes required a hike of over two miles from the parking lot. We carried our clothes, food, and gear in heavy backpacks and followed a trail with a groundcover of sorrel through old-growth forests of Sitka spruce, Western red cedar, and Douglas fir trees, stepping over fallen trees and crossing streams on our way down to the wild and pristine coastline.

Often, we were the only people staying overnight on these remote beaches. We set up our camp in front of the driftwood logs at the edge of the forest. My father exhaled loudly into the inflatable sleeping pads to pump them up, while the rest of us grabbed shovels and ran along the beach, digging for clams and overturning rocks in search of crabs.

In the daytime we explored the forests and played on the long sandy beaches. We had contests to see who could walk the farthest across the driftwood without falling off the logs. We chased each other across the wide expanses of sand and jumped and played in the ocean. We dove into the wild waves and swam—usually naked—in the sea that took our breath away with its chilly temperature even in the summer.

And we hiked. Wearing only our bathing suits and tennis shoes—at most—we followed the coastline, climbing over boulders, tiptoeing through tide pools, and crossing streams, side by side with the sea.

Mom and Dad cooked our dinners over a crackling beach fire as the sun dropped into the ocean and the temperature cooled. After dinner we roasted marshmallows and ate cookies.

As we watched the campfire burn down, Dad told a nightly bedtime story, just as he did at Family Camp. We all slept in a row, under the stars. My parents cuddled in their zipped together double sleeping bag; the rest of us lined up close to each other in our individual sleeping bags. We woke to the morning light on the silhouettes of the jagged sea stacks along the coastline.

A few months before my fifth birthday, Mom announced to us that we would be adding another sleeping bag to the line— she was pregnant again. "So many children," Dad would say to our friends. "We should have stopped at four, after we had Claudie-Weibly." That was his German term of endearment for me. "Now we will have six," he pretended to complain, but always with a good-natured sense of humor. My mother's charms were impossible to resist, and he was the most enchanted of us all.

* * *

On May 1st, 1958, my sister Mia was born. "Childbirth is easy," Mom explained when asked how she had managed through so many deliveries. "I'm in charge of story time and insemination," Dad joked to family friends who visited the house.

Baby Mia had tufts of blond hair, unlike the curly brown locks that Simon had sported on his return from the hospital. Danny, Naomi, Leah, Simon, and I all crowded around my mother and watched her nurse our new baby sister. When Simon began to cry, my mother handed the baby off to Naomi and picked Simon up in her arms. "You'll love your sister," she told him. It was more of a command than a reassurance. Danny held our dog Rex's collar to keep him from jumping up on

Naomi and the baby, and Mom sent me and Leah into the living room to look for Simon's pacifier, which he called his "boo."

My older siblings were eager to show off their new baby sister, so Simon and I helped Mom bring Mia to Leschi Elementary School. We visited the twins' third grade classroom and Leah's first grade classroom. The classrooms were so neat and organized, and there were so many interesting things on the wall to look at. Mrs. Kennedy, Leah's first grade teacher, let me sit at one of the desks and pretend to be a first grader. I listened attentively to her arithmetic lesson, glancing over at Leah to see how she was sitting. I tried to imitate her position exactly: hands on her lap, back straight, and feet planted on the ground—though my feet could only dangle.

That fall, I got a Leschi Elementary School classroom of my very own when I entered the world of kindergarten. I was most excited by the thought of being able to walk to school with Danny, Naomi, and Leah, but it turned out that kindergarten didn't begin until 9 a.m., an hour later than the other grades.

My teacher, Miss Christie, stressed that punctuality was one of the most important values she could instill in her young students. Not only was this a new word to me, but it was also an entirely new concept; in my family, we lived by Mom's schedule, which was the polar opposite of punctual. Often, my mother didn't leave the house until after she was due somewhere for a meeting or appointment. And frequently we would arrive home to find her photography clients waiting by the front door, squinting at their watches, wondering whether they had remembered their appointment time incorrectly. Mom was never concerned with anyone else's expectations of time, but Miss Christie wanted us to be sitting at our desks at the very minute the clock struck nine. From what Danny and Naomi told me, Miss Christie was not unusual—all of the teachers at Leschi Elementary seemed to have this rigid, objective notion of time.

My older siblings had the advantage of leaving for school together, which meant that they were able to encourage each other to get out of bed in time to eat breakfast and get ready for school. Their classes also started early enough that sometimes Dad would make sure they were awake before he left for work.

My situation in kindergarten was different. Having to be at school an hour later made my wake-up a low priority. With so much morning chaos in the house, Mom rarely remembered to rouse me as early as she needed to. And then she used a cold washcloth to make the waking-up process as effective as possible. She swiped the wet washcloth roughly over my forehead and eyes, then rubbed it down to my chin and informed me, "You're late, Claudia. Wake up! Wake up! You're late for school." The last traces of my lingering dreams fled from my mind as I snapped into consciousness. Mom grabbed my pajama top by the collar and yanked it over my head. "Get dressed!" she ordered, as she picked out clothes for me to wear.

My oatmeal was already on the long, gray Formica table, no longer hot and not even warm. Mom had set it out along with Danny's, Naomi's, and Leah's an hour earlier in order to save time. I was the last one in the Chotzen morning assembly line, turning kids out for school.

If I was lucky, Mom woke me up early enough that I could eat in the living room and watch my favorite television show, *Wunda Wunda*. On those mornings, I took my bowl and spoon and plopped down on the dark red Persian carpet, in front of the black and white TV.

Wunda had a painted face and a pointy, striped hat that looked like an upside-down ice cream cone. I liked her opening theme song, which always struck me as warm and welcoming. It felt like a personal invitation.

> *Wunda Wunda is my name.*
> *Oh, boys and girls, I'm glad you came.*
> *We'll have fun as I explain*
> *How we play our Wunda games.*

I had not yet learned how to tell time, so *Wunda Wunda* served as my *de facto* morning clock. If her show was just starting, I knew that I was able to relax and eat my oatmeal at a comfortable pace. I could finish the show before I had to grab my sack lunch and walk through the woods to school. If Wunda Wunda's show had already begun, I might need to swallow bigger mouthfuls of oatmeal. And on the days when *Wunda Wunda* was already over, I knew that I needed to run through the woods as fast as I could. I dreaded walking through the door of the classroom and hearing Miss Christie announce to all: "Claudia, you're late again. Please sit down."

In February, on one of those mornings when I had woken up too late to even catch the end of *Wunda Wunda*, I had a surprise on my way to school. As I ran through the woods, looking straight ahead and hoping that I wouldn't be late, a pair of dark, dirty jeans emerged from behind a tree and blocked my path. Looking up, I saw a tall, dark-haired man.

"Stop, little girl," he whispered. Startled by his sudden appearance, I stopped running immediately. Besides, he was in my way.

"I want to show you something," he said. Then he unbuckled his belt, unzipped the fly of his jeans, and dropped his pants and his underwear in a series of very quick gestures. "Have you seen one of these before?" he asked, putting his hand on his penis—which dangled inches away from my forehead—and wiggling it in my direction.

I had seen one before. I'd seen several, actually: Simon's, Danny's, my father's, and I had seen the penises of the Miller kids—we all played naked together. But I didn't tell all this to the man. I didn't like him, and I understood that he was doing something wrong and that I needed to get away. Should I run back home or continue running to school? I guessed that I was halfway through my morning route, which made my decision harder.

The man put his large hand on my shoulder and squeezed. I stopped thinking. I turned and ran back towards home, too afraid to look back to see whether he was following me. For a while I thought that I heard his footsteps and breathing, but then it was quiet all around me. And I was safely home.

Mom was already in a photography sitting. I knew that she didn't like to be interrupted while she was working, especially when she had customers, so I decided to make my interruption as brief as possible. I ran into her studio—the bedroom just beside the kitchen—and blurted out, "A man pulled down his pants and showed me his penis when I was on my way to school."

Mom apologized to the customer and excused herself. I followed her to the kitchen, listened as she phoned the police, heard her talking as calmly as if making an appointment with the dentist. Then she told me to wait in there until the police came, and she went through the swinging door to finish taking pictures of her customer.

When two policemen arrived at the house, Mom poked her head into the kitchen and told them I would explain the situation. "I wasn't there," she explained. "Claudia's the one who knows what happened." The policemen were very nice, and they asked me to come with them into the woods, so that I could show them exactly where I had met the man. I looked longingly towards the door, hoping that Mom would reappear and offer to come along with us, but she stayed with her customer.

I took them back to the spot where I had seen the man, but there was no trace of him. The police asked me to describe him, and I told them everything I could remember: he was tall and thin, with white skin and brown hair, jeans, and a big, wiggly penis. The policemen walked me home and promised that they would continue to search through the woods.

The next morning, Mom woke me as always with a cold washcloth and helped me to dress. She sat me at the table in front of my oatmeal. "Do I have time to watch *Wunda Wunda*?" I asked. She said that I did, so I moved to the living room. My mother disappeared into another room to work. When *Wunda Wunda* ended, I grabbed my sack lunch off the kitchen counter, knowing it was time to leave. As I came to the edge of the woods, I froze with terror. The only other way to school was up a steep hill, South Lane Street, a longer and less direct route. I knew it would upset Miss Christie if I was late, but I decided to climb the hill to be safe.

As the school year wore on, I couldn't take the long route every day and be late. I wished my mom or someone would walk with me, but I knew that would never happen. I was on my own. Most days, I mustered up my courage and ran through the woods, looking nervously behind me, flinching at every forest sound.

* * *

Because Mom ran her photography business out of our home, Naomi, Danny, Leah, and I were expected to help. She taught us to answer the phone with good manners, to speak to customers professionally, and to write down their names and phone numbers on the back of the used envelopes she kept as scrap paper on her desk, next to the heavy black telephone.

When customers arrived at the house for their appointments, we answered the door, greeted them warmly, and ushered them into the living room to wait for Mom. Sometimes she was nearby—finishing up with another client, sunbathing in the yard, or on the phone. Other times, she was gone from the house entirely—running errands or attending a meeting. Whether she was home or out, we always explained to customers that she would "be with them shortly." Because we had no control over her schedule, we learned to never estimate how long it might be before she appeared. We talked with the parents and entertained the kids with toys and books, playing host until Mom arrived.

For sittings, Mom worked out of the bedroom she had transformed into a studio. There were heavy canvas shades on the wall that she pulled down for a backdrop and snapped back up when she was done. She used dark shades for light-haired kids and lighter shades for dark-haired and Black children.

She sat the child on a card table in the center of the room. She adjusted two large floodlights and switched them on, fiddled with the position of the lights a bit more, and then, finally, lifted her black Rolleiflex camera which hung around her neck on a leather strap, and prepared to shoot. A Rolleiflex is not the kind of camera that you hold up in front of your face, but instead it has a waist level view finder and a hand crank to prepare the camera for the next shot. When my mother used this camera, she held it in front of her stomach and focused it by looking down into it; above it her gaze was free to meet the eyes of the child or adult she was photographing.

Her studio was filled with baskets of toys to help the children relax and to inspire different expressions for the photos. When I was her assistant, I stood beside her as she handed me props to use—I blew bubbles at babies, played catch with toddlers, and pulled the string on the back of a Chatty Cathy doll's neck. When I pulled the string, the doll spoke in a high, singsong voice—"I want to go to the zoo with you"—and my mom would snap a photo as the curious child turned to look at the talking doll. If a child had a tense lower lip, Mom might have them blow bubbles for a few seconds before she took a picture.

Sometimes, she gave her subject a kitten to play with. We always had at least one or two new kittens around the house. "They're perfect for cuddling and photographs," Mom said. She loved to capture the happy expressions that flooded children's faces as they played with the tiny cats. "Pick it up," she instructed. "Snuggle with the kitty. Give the kitty a kiss."

We loved the kittens and spent hours playing with them in the front yard, but Mom never allowed them to stay long enough to become fully-grown cats. My parents had enough mouths to feed already, and we also had Rex, our Border Collie/German Shepherd mix. When the kittens got older, they disappeared. "They've gone away to be teenagers," my mother claimed. What really happened was she stopped feeding them so they would wander off looking for food. It didn't bother her that she had to continually pick up new kittens from the pound. "They're only useful when they're small and cute. After that, some other family can have them."

She loved to take off children's clothes and photograph them naked, and she always praised their "beautiful skin." She didn't try to convince children to be happy. "You don't have to smile," she told her small subjects. "I like serious pictures. You can growl like a bear." Or, she might say to a recalcitrant child, "You look mad. That's okay. Go ahead and be mad." Mom rarely allowed parents in the studio when she was photographing their children unless the parents were willing to be photographed with them. I never remember anyone questioning her policy of no adults in the studio, but I wonder now why the parents didn't object.

If she noticed a mother holding her child at arm's length, my mom would encourage her to relax. "Don't worry," she'd say. "We can always cut you out of the picture." But she never did edit anyone out of her photographs—it was just a ploy to get everyone to relax. Her photos of mothers and children were especially popular—she had a knack for capturing spontaneous, tender shots.

Mom's techniques and tricks did seem to help children relax, resulting in candid photos that thrilled her clients and brought her a successful reputation, as well as word-of-mouth and repeat customers. Often, she took photos of siblings or whole families. She urged siblings to "knock their heads together" in order to bring out the playful relationship between them. She

taught me that when she photographed a group, her goal was
to get some interaction between the subjects—to encourage
them to enjoy each other.

My mother also promoted her business energetically and
creatively. She placed ads in local newspapers and on
neighborhood bulletin boards. She constantly came up with
new ideas for discounts and deals. She gave free photos to
families of local doctors and dentists; in exchange for having
her photographs exhibited in their offices we received free
medical care. She visited our classrooms, took photographs of
all of our classmates, and then sent the proofs home to their
families, letting them keep one 4x6 proof, an effort to entice
them to buy more pictures. Every Halloween, she combined her
business sense with her passion for social activism, organizing
Leschi Elementary students to trick-or-treat for UNICEF,
collecting money in tiny cardboard boxes as we went door-to-
door in our costumes. The child who collected the most charity
money won a free Carla Anette 8x10 photograph.

Mom would schedule her appointments right up until 6
p.m., when Dad came home, and we all sat down to dinner. In
the late afternoons, in between two sittings, she would toss a
whole bag of potatoes into the oven to bake and put a roast in
the pressure cooker.

We ate foods that I never encountered at anyone else's
house or in my friends' lunches, like kidneys and liver.
Occasionally, I'd arrive home from school and find a huge
cow's tongue in a pan on the kitchen counter. Even though I
was repelled by it, I often dared myself to touch it, gingerly
rubbing my fingers over its bumps and marveling at how it was
so much coarser than my own tongue. But after Mom cut the
tongue into thin slices and served them to us at dinner, I
couldn't taste the bumps at all.

At breakfast, Mom always ate a soft-boiled egg that she
placed in a special little egg cup; she whacked off the top of the
egg with a knife and scooped out the soft yolk with a tiny silver

spoon that had come from her parents' home in Germany. My parents enjoyed eating sardines, herring, salami, and liverwurst sandwiches, and they always ate their sandwiches on dark rye bread. There was no American white bread in our home.

My favorite treat was chocolate sandwiches on rye bread. Mom used a paring knife to shave slivers of rich, European dark chocolate onto a piece of rye bread, then added a thin layer of butter. In our household you had to earn the right to eat butter by passing a taste test. Until then you ate less expensive margarine. For the butter test, my parents blindfolded us, spread either butter or margarine onto a small corner of rye bread, and then asked us to determine which spread we tasted. If we passed, we were allowed to upgrade to butter, a status I proudly achieved midway through my kindergarten year.

We ate dinner around our kitchen table because the dining room table was almost always covered with Mom's black and white photos. Mom sat at one end of the table, and Dad at the other. We shared the highlights of our days, and Mom often entertained us with stories about the interesting homeless people she had met downtown.

After dinner, we all set about our chores. Naomi and Danny cleaned the kitchen. Starting when Naomi was seven years old, she did many of the household chores and became almost a substitute parent. My mother bought her a special stool so that she could reach the kitchen sink to do the dishes after dinner. Danny's chore was to wash the kitchen floor, but Naomi did everything else; she was in charge of the caretaking for us until she left for college.

When Dad was not away on business trips he helped with the bathing and hair washing, making it fun and filled with laughter. Once we were all bathed and, in our pajamas, we begged Dad to sit us on his knees and chant "Hapa Hapa Rider," a German rhyme that he recited melodically as he bounced us up and down. *"Hapa Hapa Rider, Wenn er felt dan schreit er. Felt in den graben. Fressen in die robin,"* he chanted.

Translated, it meant, "Bouncy Bouncy. When he falls he shouts. He falls into the ditch and the ravens will gulp him up." It was a strange poem, but we didn't care what it meant; what mattered was having Daddy bounce us on his lap along with the rhythm of the words. On the very last line, he opened his knees and—still holding onto us—bounced us all the way to the floor. Even though we all knew it was coming, we squealed with laughter every time.

After Hapa Hapa Rider came our favorite nightly ritual— Daddy's bedtime story. We all squeezed around him on one of our beds. "Let's see, what shall we tell tonight?" he wondered aloud before launching in. He always wove one or two of us into the story in some subtle and exciting way: he might include a detail that corresponded to something that Leah had done at school or a quality that we all attributed to Simon. He made up new names, so we had to listen carefully in order to catch the references. We hung on every word, hoping to recognize ourselves in the story and waiting to see what clever pun or moral Dad might include at the conclusion. When the story finished, it was time for bed.

Every night, as our bedtime ritual unfolded, Mom retreated to the expanded closet in the basement that she used as her darkroom, where she spent the evening developing and printing her photographs. She worked at night so that daylight wouldn't intrude upon her makeshift darkroom and because there were fewer interruptions from the children once we all began getting ready for bed. If I had a question for her, I knew to wait until I had bathed and changed into my nightgown or pajamas. Then I knocked on her darkroom door and waited until she told me to come in. "Not yet. I can't have any light in here for a few more minutes," she would call out to me sometimes. Once I had permission to enter, I slipped into the small room, shutting the door quickly behind me to minimize the light I brought with me. I was immediately struck by the dank, familiar smell of chemicals.

As my eyes adjusted to the dim red light, I could distinguish the outlines of her darkroom equipment: large, dark bottles filled with liquids, strips of negatives hanging by wooden clothespins from a clothesline above us, a large thermometer she used to test the temperature of the chemicals, boxes filled with negatives stacked high on shelves, her enlarger, and her tall darkroom chair. I watched my mother mix pungent chemicals with water and pour them into tanks and trays. She transferred the amber liquid from one tray to the next and told me that the liquids in the different trays were "hypo" and "fixer" and "stop bath." If she had just developed film, I watched her fingers twirl the spools of film in their special lightproof tanks. She cut the dried negatives into strips of five or six negatives and popped them into special, smooth gray paper sleeves. She labeled each of the sleeves in black ink with the name of her customer and the date.

Sometimes I found her rolling a large brown bottle filled with liquid back and forth on the floor with one of her bare feet. She said she was "mixing the developer," a combination of chemicals and hot water. "Want to help me?" she asked. "Rock the jar back and forth with your feet like I do." I braced my small body against her tall darkroom chair, held on to the legs of the chair, and used one foot at a time to rock the huge bottle of warm liquid back and forth, in my best imitation of my mother's style. I liked the warmth and smoothness of the glass bottle under my feet—it felt cozy and comforting on cold, wet Seattle nights.

When she printed pictures, Mom sat in her tall chair. She put a piece of special photo paper down under the enlarger. I knew the numbers of all the sizes of paper—3x5, 4x6, 5x7, 8x10, and 10x17—because I listened when she took customers' orders at our dining room table. She reached up to adjust the enlarger over the piece of paper. "You can look through it if you like," she told me gently. "I pick a spot like the hair to get the fine focus." When she had the focus, she pressed a pedal with her right foot and a bright light flashed on. She counted three seconds, out loud, and at the same time she curled her right hand above the paper to create shading where she wanted it. The dark outlines of somebody's face appeared like shadows on the blank paper; it didn't look anything like the child she had photographed, and I wondered how she even knew who the person was.

When the light went off, the paper was still blank. She carefully slipped the piece of blank paper into the first tray filled with liquid. Sometimes she used metal tongs to move the pictures from one tray to the next, but usually she picked up the photo with her fingers and moved it to the next tray to tap it under the water. Mom never wore gloves in the darkroom; her fingernails and fingertips were always stained yellow and brown from the chemicals.

The faces came to life under the liquid in the trays. This was my favorite part: it never failed to amaze me to see people and their pets appearing, as if by magic. I never wanted to leave Mom's darkroom—it was so different to see her so focused. Usually, she was running our whole household firmly, impatiently, often with a rough edge and tone in her voice. She was always in a hurry; she was always rushing, and we were always late. In her darkroom she was calm and concentrated. But if I stayed with her in the darkroom too long, I might risk missing one of Daddy's bedtime stories.

* * *

By the time I started first grade in the fall of 1959, Mom was pregnant with another baby, her seventh. Now, I could walk to school with Naomi, Danny, and Leah; I didn't have to go on my own, an hour later and worry about strangers in the woods. It also meant that I got up earlier in the morning, ate my oatmeal while it was still hot, and actually got to school on time.

My first grade teacher was Mrs. Kennedy, the same teacher whose classroom I had visited when Leah was a first grader. Mrs. Kennedy was a tall, slender grandmother-looking lady with short gray hair. She was kind, but she also had lots of rules. We needed to ask her permission to go to the bathroom, we were not allowed to interrupt her while she worked with other reading groups (the class was divided into multiple sections for group reading time), and we had to raise our hand and wait for her to call on us before we asked a question or made a comment. Some of these rules were the same ones that Miss Christie liked, but Mrs. Kennedy seemed to take them even more seriously. According to Naomi, this was just how school worked—every year you learned more and more rules, until it was almost impossible to remember all of the things that you weren't allowed to do. I wanted to remember and follow Mrs. Kennedy's rules and be a good student.

I was one of the only white students in my first grade class, and the only white girl in my Blue Bird Troop, which I joined the same year. Blue Birds was the organization for girls who were still too young to be Campfire Girls. We met at our parents' houses in a rotating fashion in order to pursue the three objectives of "Sing. Grow. Help."

When I visited the homes of my fellow Blue Birds, I was struck by how different they were—not because of race or ethnicity, but because their homes were so much calmer, quieter, and less chaotic than mine.

Our kitchen and living room always overflowed with people. Art projects were constantly spread out across the kitchen table, Mom's photographs filled every inch of the dining room table, and toys and balls were littered across the floor. Forts, caves, and tunnels constructed out of chairs and blankets often created a maze in the living room. But at my friends' houses, messes were rare, and I could usually count everyone in the house on one hand.

My friend Vicki's' home was especially calm and ordered. Vicki slept in her own bedroom, and it was tidy and decorated. She and her parents always looked as though their clothes were freshly ironed, and there were never dirty dishes in their sink. Their toilet was so clean that I wondered whether any of them even used it. When our Blue Bird Troop visited Vicki's' house, we wiped our shoes on the welcome mat and stepped cautiously onto the white, vacuumed carpet.

I liked visiting there. Vicki and I watched the "J.P. Patches Show" on KIRO-TV. J.P. was a clown who wore a patchwork coat and a tattered hat. He called himself "Mayor of the City Dump," and he resided in a messy shack where he would play tricks on his many TV guests. He would warn them as they were leaving about a hole just outside his door, always followed by the sound of crashing and banging. J.P. even did the program's commercials, telling us to eat Kellogg's Cornflakes and to drink Hi-C juice.

Vicki and I also spent a lot of time talking about the differences in our hair. Mine was naturally soft and wavy, and it was a subject of fascination and envy on the playground. At recess, my friends wanted to touch my hair, and sometimes kids from other classes—total strangers—would ask if they could feel it, too.

Vicki's hair was smooth, but nobody seemed interested in touching it at school. "Yours is naturally smooth," she told me. "That's what we want—all the Negro girls. We have to spend hours pressing it to get it to look like that. If I want to come to school with straight hair, I have to wake up so early. By the time Mrs. Kennedy lets us out for recess, I'm already tired." She confided that the chemicals, hair relaxers, and hot irons sometimes burned her scalp.

At the end of October, my mother headed to the Group Health Hospital to give birth. Dad stayed home with us, though Mom had tried to bring him along. "They won't let fathers into the delivery room," she complained. "They think the men will faint. But childbirth is the most beautiful, natural thing in the world, and I want Walter to share it with me."

"Some hospitals will let you," Dora Miller said. She was a natural childbirth teacher, and she and Mom often talked about the details of child birthing. "Greg was there for my last birth. But most hospitals are still old-fashioned about these things."

"It's ridiculous. Walter should be able to see his children being born," Mom agreed. She had argued this point with Group Health six times—before each of our births—but always to no avail. She went to the hospital alone.

The next day, Dad left to pick her up. An hour later, they returned. When we saw Dad's station wagon pull up, we flocked to the car to hug Mom and meet the new baby. Mom stepped out from the passenger's side door with a bouquet of yellow roses under one arm and our tiny sister under the other. Her name was Charlotte, and she was plumper and had darker skin than Mia or Simon as babies. "My little brown berry," Mom called her.

Charlotte was born on November 2nd, the same day as Simon—we had been celebrating his fourth birthday at the exact same time that Mom was in labor. I thought it was amazing that the nine members of our family only had seven different birthdays. Danny and Naomi shared a birthday because they were twins—that was obvious—but it seemed like an incredible coincidence that, out of all of the days in the year, two of my younger siblings would pick the same day to be born.

"It's good to share," Simon said, after he had met Charlotte. "It's good to share everything, even birthdays." Mom covered him with kisses.

Five days later, it was my seventh birthday. Even with the hubbub surrounding the arrival of Charlotte, I still got to have my own birthday party. My friends from school and Blue Birds crowded around our kitchen table as I unwrapped presents and blew out my candles. Mom held Charlotte and Dad held the movie camera. I sat between Vicki and Simon, wearing my favorite outfit: my white ballet tutu with red, green, and blue ribbons woven through the skirt.

There were lots of visitors in the house—even more than usual—during the weeks that followed my seventh birthday. Everyone was eager to meet the seventh Chotzen child. Omi and Opi came from Buffalo, and my mom's Uncle Norbert, Omi's younger brother, came to live with us for several months.

Uncle Norbert was good-humored, and he smiled patiently as we climbed on his back and clung to his arms and legs. Sometimes, he even let us take furtive puffs of his cigar. I remember him sitting in his room, smoking a cigar with a homeless woman my mother had brought home to help with cleaning and childcare. This woman was from Spain, and she kept her hair pulled back into a tight knot. She kept the curtains in her room closed, she smoked cigarettes and cigars, a stench from her cigars and Uncle Norbert's cigars permeated our home. She hated how messy our home was; she told Dad that she wanted to hammer hooks into our floor, since that was where everyone's clothes inevitably ended up.

She didn't stay long. One afternoon, when I told her mom was making steak for dinner, she looked up alarmed, misunderstanding. "Snake?" she asked.

"No," I said. "Steak."

"Snake." She repeated, and she began to tremble. "Snake. Snake. Snake." She retreated into her room and emerged ten minutes later, leaving with her single dilapidated suitcase. After that, Uncle Norbert smoked his cigars alone.

As 1959 gave way to 1960, lots of friends and neighbors continued to drop by to see Charlotte and offer their congratulations, as did many of my mother's colleagues from groups like The League of Women Voters and Women's Strike for Peace.

Along with the new baby, we also got a new dog. Rex had run away and disappeared, and so my parents filled his absence

with Shag, a white, fluffy sheep dog that looked just like the
main character in the Disney movie *The Shaggy Dog*.

First grade was more time-consuming than kindergarten,
which meant that I couldn't devote as many afternoon hours to
playing with Charlotte and Shag as I might have liked. To
compensate, I tried to wake up earlier every morning, so that I
could spend a few minutes with them both before Naomi,
Danny, Leah, and I trudged off to Leschi Elementary together.
Mom would bring Simon, Mia, and Charlotte to the front door,
and they would wave goodbye as we disappeared around the
corner and into the woods.

Most days, when school was over, Naomi, Danny, and Leah
headed directly to a variety of extracurricular activities—music
lessons, sports teams, Judo practice, Hebrew school—and it was
not unusual for me to walk home alone. I was still nervous to
walk through the woods by myself, so I often took the long way
home, through the streets of the Leschi neighborhood.

But this alternative route came with its own problems. A
pack of sixth grade girls spent their post-school afternoons on
the street between Leschi Elementary School and my house.
They were loud and tall, and to me, small for a first grader, they
looked almost like grown-ups. They sat on the steps outside one
of their homes and called out to the younger kids who walked
by, yelling things like, "Where do you think you're going?" and
"What's in your backpack? Got anything for us?" Still, I figured,
the route was preferable to taking a chance walking alone in the
woods where the man had shown me his penis.

I particularly remember a day when I decided to save the
Twinkies in my lunch to eat after school as a treat. All afternoon,
I daydreamed about the Twinkies while Mrs. Kennedy talked
about subtraction. It was rare for me to have two of them in my
lunch—perhaps Naomi had made a mistake packing our
lunches, which meant that Danny or Leah might not have a
dessert at all today. I thought about the soft, golden sponge cake,

the sweet white cream center, the moist feel of them when I held them in my fingers, and how good they would taste.

On my way home, I carried the brown paper bag in my hand, swinging it eagerly. When I saw the sixth grade girls up ahead, I ducked behind a large shrub to hide, but they had already spotted me. There were four of them, and they ambled menacingly up the block towards me. "Come out from behind that bush," they said. "We see you. You can't hide. Give us that bag."

I clutched the paper bag to my chest and ran. They chased me, and the two tallest girls outran me and stopped directly in my path, while the other two girls approached me from behind. I was surrounded. My stomach was tense, my heart was racing, and I felt my bladder suddenly release. I silently prayed—as much as I understood how to pray—that the girls wouldn't notice that I had wet myself.

They ripped the paper bag from my hand, opened it, and discovered my hidden treasures. "Twinkies!" the girl with the bag shouted out to the others with approval. "Don't ever hide your lunch from us again. We'll always find you," they warned me. And then they wandered back down the block, splitting my Twinkies between them, but none the wiser to my wet underpants.

I staggered home, uncomfortable and upset. When I saw my mother in the kitchen, I broke down in tears and told her what had happened. She sat and listened to me, expressionless the whole time, and then she pointed in the direction of my bedroom. "Go take care of it," she instructed. "Clean yourself up."

The Twinkie Incident was not my only experience wetting my underpants during first grade. One day, while working on reading groups in class, I was suddenly seized by an overwhelming urge to pee. I knew that I needed Mrs. Kennedy's permission to excuse myself to use the restroom— that was a strict rule. Mrs. Kennedy was working with a different reading group and one of her important rules decreed that no one was allowed to interrupt her while she helped classmates. I didn't know what to do. I alternated between sitting at my desk and standing next to the blackboard. Finally, when the pressure became too much to bear, I peed on the floor, just next to the blackboard. I was mortified.

Vicki was standing beside me, so she was the first to notice. "Claudia just went on the floor," she announced to all. Mrs. Kennedy broke her very own rule and tore herself away from the reading group. "Claudia, what on earth have you done?" she demanded.

Embarrassed, I explained my predicament. To my great surprise, Mrs. Kennedy's face softened. "If you ever *really* need to go to the bathroom, you can go without my permission," she told me. She gave Vicki a stack of paper towels and asked her to help me clean up the mess.

Though I had to endure a few days of ridicule and whispering from my classmates, Mrs. Kennedy never made me feel bad for my accident. Perhaps she understood that it had not really been an accident at all but rather an unfortunate result of my unwavering obedience to a contradictory set of rules.

Even though my adherence to rules caused my embarrassing accident, I actually appreciated the clear and strict guidelines at school. I knew what to expect. I always enjoyed the quiet in the classroom when we were told to work on assignments; it felt very peaceful and safe. Home never felt predictable, and often it didn't feel safe.

Despite the constant chaos in our household, it was actually the quiet times that started to make me uncomfortable. Though the activity in our house certainly made things noisy, I liked being near my brothers and sisters. At bedtime, when we donned our pajamas and retreated to our rooms, I felt a sense of eerie uneasiness.

When I was asleep, lost in my own world and dreams, Mom would often slip quietly into my closet-sized bedroom.

Suddenly, I would feel the weight of a grown-up body on top of me. I remember her smell—the strong odor of chemicals from the darkroom mixed with the heavy scent of her body and breath and skin. I couldn't move. I froze, and my body became hers.

Neither fully awake nor fully asleep, I lay as still as I could and abandoned my body on the bed. I floated away, up to a corner of the room, where the wall met the ceiling, watching my mother's grown-up body on top of my little one. She would launch into a series of movements, rubbing and writhing on top of me. She moved and sighed and made sounds and rubbed her hands all over my body—on my flat, little-girl nipples, on my thighs, on and inside my private parts. Sometimes there were words: "Your body is so beautiful, so feminine. I love you so much. You are so beautiful. So lovely."

She would start to get excited and would sometimes crawl up my body until her vagina was on my mouth and my nose and I could barely breathe. I gasped for air, her whole weight grinding on top of my mouth. Her pubic hair was thick and course, and its sour smell was overpowering. Then it would happen. She would start to make sounds I never heard at any other time: high-pitched squeals and moaning. I worried that I would die gasping for breath with her weight grinding on top of me. She was completely lost in her pleasure and had no sense of me, of Claudia.

I held my breath and continued to remind myself that as soon as the high-pitched sounds ended it would all be over. Eventually, the noises did subside, and she climbed off, silently slipping out of the room, as quietly as she arrived.

After she left, I curled up into a ball, and slowly I floated down from the ceiling to rejoin my body. I felt as though I could still see and feel and smell her body on mine.

My mother's nighttime visits began when I was three years old when they moved me into the closet room next to their bedroom. Her visits continued on a regular basis, sometimes several times a week, throughout my childhood. She told me she loved me, so the logical conclusion that I, as a young child could make was, "This is the way Mommy shows her love to me." I didn't like it, but all I could do was find a way to survive, so I developed the ability to leave my body and watch from above.

The Mommy of the Daytime was always busy, often impatient, unable to focus much attention on any one of her many children. The Mommy of the Night was different, like she was in a trance; with me, yet not really aware of me. During the day, her nighttime visits to me were never mentioned. Not by her, not by my father, nor by me. Dad must have noticed that she was absent from his bed. He must have missed her—after all, he adored her and was devoted to her. He told us often that she was the greatest woman and the best mother on earth.

In first grade, I began to have a recurring nightmare. I dreamed I was on the school playground, wearing one of the dresses that I often wore to school, when I realized that I had no underpants on beneath my dress. I was terrified that I'd be exposed—either because the wind would blow up my dress, or because other kids would see my "pee-pee" as I played on the monkey bars. As my panic intensified, I would jolt awake—usually just before the moment where my nakedness was exposed or discovered.

I wanted to tell my parents about the nightmares, but by the time I woke up, Dad was usually off to work, and Mom was already bustling frantically around the house, normally half an hour late for something. And when I arrived home in the afternoons, the dreams had drifted from my mind. Besides, Mom was so busy with her photography work, she never had much time to chat.

Looking back as an adult, even though nudity was so prevalent in our family, I must have known that something was wrong. I was having a recurring nightmare about being exposed and having my boundaries violated.

It also seems symbolic that my mother chose to violate me in my closet-sized bedroom where the shameful part of herself—her sickness—could be isolated. And by isolating me from my other siblings, she could satisfy her sexual needs and keep her secret safe.

The question that haunts me most as an adult is what Dad knew about Mom and her nighttime visits. Did he think she was working in her darkroom developing pictures when she wasn't in their bed? He must have heard her loud moaning sounds on top of me when she was in my closet room next door to their bedroom. But if he had any reservations about her molestations, he never voiced them. Did he just turn a blind eye and a deaf ear, making a conscious decision not to confront her, afraid to lose her approval and love?

On the mornings after my mother had molested me, my father would often tell me, "You have the best mommy in the world." Looking back, that seems like bizarre timing and a very weird comment. Under normal circumstances a mother is her child's fiercest protector. Instead, my mother was a predator and my greatest threat, while my father's praise of her normalized her violations.

* * *

Mom would constantly remind us that we, her children, were collectively her most prized possession. Imagine my shock when I learned that she had almost given me away at birth.

One Sunday, I rode with my mom to Herzl Synagogue to drop Danny, Naomi, and Leah off at Sunday School. I was six years old, still a year too young to begin Hebrew classes. My older sisters and brother slid out of the car, and my mother chatted with Ruth Frankel, while I moved into the front seat. Ruth was the wife of Cantor Frankel, who chanted prayers at Herzl Synagogue on holidays and presided over my siblings'

Hebrew School classes. Cantor Frankel and Ruth had one daughter, Betsy, who was a year older than Danny and Naomi.

On our way home, Mom was very quiet, lost in thought. I watched the windshield wipers rhythmically whisk the rain away. After a few minutes, Mom cleared her throat.

"Ruth Frankel is always having miscarriages." She had mentioned this to us several times, explaining to us what a miscarriage was. "Ever since Betsy, they've been trying to make another baby. Trying and trying. But no luck."

"Do you know that I almost gave you to her? It is so easy for me to have babies, and it is so hard for Ruth. After I had Leah, I thought, maybe I can just give the next one to Ruth." This would have been me!

I didn't know what to say. I was stunned. I looked to Mom for reassurance, but her eyes remained straight ahead on the road.

"Well, obviously I decided to keep you after all," she said matter-of-factly. I waited for the rest of the story—the part I wanted to know. Why had she decided to keep me? Did she fall in love with me as soon as she saw me? Was there something special about me that seemed to make me worth keeping? Had my father convinced her? (That seemed unlikely—my father rarely convinced her of anything—and seldom even tried to— but I wondered nonetheless.) But Mom had nothing more to say. She changed the subject.

When I thought about it later, I wondered what would it be like to be in a different family? What would it be like if Ruth were my mother? There was no way I could see Ruth Frankel again without thinking about this. I wondered if Ruth knew that Mom almost gave me to her. During services, when Cantor Frankel was singing the Hebrew prayers, Ruth and Betsy sat in the front row of the congregation. I watched Ruth sing and chant. When she bowed her head to pray, I wondered if she was praying for another daughter.

I studied the way that she straightened Betsy's pigtails and adjusted the pretty ribbons in Betsy's hair. I examined Betsy's crisp, clean clothes—never hand-me-downs. I observed how Cantor Frankel put his hand gently on Betsy's shoulder when he leaned down to whisper to her. When I lay in bed, I imagined what it would be like to belong to the Frankels—to be doted on the way they doted on Betsy. I fantasized about how grateful they would be to have me in their family and how beloved I would be. I would miss my brothers and sisters, of course, but sometimes I wished Mom had followed through with her idea to donate me.

* * *

In second grade, I started attending Hebrew School, too. Classes were on Sunday mornings and on Tuesdays and Thursdays after school. On Sundays, Mom or Dad drove us. During the week, we took the city bus from Leschi Elementary to Herzl. Both Leschi and Herzl were located in Seattle's Central District, but we had to transfer buses at 23rd and Cherry, right in the middle of a gritty inner-city neighborhood. The first weeks of Hebrew School, Danny, Naomi and Leah accompanied me on the bus rides.

My Hebrew School class was filled with rowdy boys who seemed to have no interest in learning the Hebrew language or Jewish traditions. They wouldn't sit in their chairs, they crumpled up their papers, and they threw spitballs and paper airplanes at the teachers. I found these boys very frustrating; I loved learning how to read ancient Hebrew, how to speak conversational Hebrew, and how to study the Torah.

On weekday afternoons, Hebrew School ended at 6 p.m. Naomi, Danny, Leah and I all watched our classmates file into their parents' cars as we waited for Mom, who was consistently the last parent to arrive. We knew better than to expect Mom to be punctual. At home, she would tell us to go wait for her in the car, and we would sometimes sit for more than an hour, wondering when we'd finally get going. My older siblings had taught me to seek out my friends' parents for rides to any truly important events. "Someday," Naomi told me once, "I'll turn sixteen and get my driver's license, and then nobody will ever have to wait for Mom."

Hebrew School sometimes conflicted with my brother and sisters' other afterschool activities, like sports practices and music lessons. On those Tuesdays and Thursdays, I would take the bus on my own. I sat on the first bus and wished it would go faster. Every time we stopped to pick somebody up, I worried that we were running late, and that I would miss the second bus and be stuck at 23rd and Cherry. I always saved my after-school snack until the second bus, because I was too nervous to eat it on the first one. Once I made the connection and was safely in my seat, I could eat my snack while I watched the busy neighborhood roll by through the smudged bus window.

After I got off the second bus, I had to walk up a steep hill to Herzl. A group of Black kids, about Naomi and Danny's age, liked to congregate at the top of the hill. Once, they shouted, "Going to Jew-Girl school!" at me as I walked by. I tucked my head and walked past them as fast as I could, without looking back. And after Hebrew School, on those days when I was the only Chotzen attending, I had to wait by myself for Mom to pick me up. It made me nervous to wait alone, especially in the winter, when it grew dark long before Mom usually arrived.

I stood on the street in front of Herzl Synagogue. If I was the only person left outside passersby from the neighborhood would sometimes try to strike up a conversation. Many of them looked homeless, and I tried to avoid making eye contact. "Hey, little girl, want to go home with me?" a derelict man asked me once. I wished they would all go away. Better yet, I wished that I could.

On those days when Mom was even later than usual, Cantor Frankel would see me waiting outside on the street as he was leaving. He would put down his briefcase and stand beside me. "I wonder when your mother will be here this time?" he would comment. I appreciated those moments—it was nice to hear him say aloud the very question I was thinking myself.

One Thursday night, I waited to be picked up for what seemed like an eternity. As usual, I was the only student left waiting outside the synagogue. Cantor Frankel stood with me in the dark for a while and finally went back into his office to finish some more work; then he came out and stood with me again. After more than two hours of waiting, he unlocked the synagogue doors and disappeared inside, returning a few moments later.

"I called your mother," he said. "I don't know how this could happen, but she told me she forgot to pick you up tonight so I'm going to drive you home."

We didn't speak in the car, except when I told him which streets to turn on. I couldn't stop thinking about how he had almost been my father. I wondered whether his wife, Ruth, was more reliable when it came to picking up Betsy. I thought that she probably was. How could she not be? Plus, she only had one child to remember. Mom had seven.

When the car stopped in front of my house, I apologized to Cantor Frankel. "I'm sorry you had to go out of your way," I said. "And I'm sorry you're getting home so late."

"It's no trouble," he said.

When I got inside, everyone was at the kitchen table, finishing up their dinner.

"Where were you?" Leah asked. "Why are you so late?"

My mother answered before I could say anything. "She stayed late at Hebrew School."

I slipped into my place at the long, grey Formica table. There wasn't much food left. Mom scraped the last bits out of the bowl and onto a plate. "This will have to do for tonight," she said.

* * *

Dinner at our house was always unpredictable; we never knew who else would join us at the table. Mom sat at one end and Dad at the other. I was in the middle, with Simon on my left and Leah on my right. Danny sat directly to Mom's right, which made him the most convenient and frequent victim of the wooden spoon that Mom kept beside her plate.

If anyone burped at the table, Mom instinctively grabbed the wooden spoon and whacked Danny on his arm or his head with it. Danny had learned long ago not to burp during dinner, but because of his position at the table adjacent to Mom he still received the punishments for the rest of our offenses. "Don't burp, or Danny will get hit," I warned my friends when they stayed over for dinner. They stared at me blankly, undoubtedly confused by the information I was offering.

Simon, on the other hand, saw Mom's wooden spoon as a tempting opportunity for mischief. He perfected a fake burp, which he frequently unleashed during dinner. When Simon burped, Danny would grit his teeth and wait for the whack of retribution.

We always ate dinner at home, except for our three annual trips to Tai Tung Chinese Restaurant. These outings were group birthday celebrations—one each in the fall, winter, and spring. Simon and Charlotte had November birthdays, just like me, so we'd share a celebration in the late autumn. At the end of January, we'd go out for Chinese food again—this time as a belated celebration for Mom and Leah's January birthdays and an early celebration for Naomi and Danny, who were born on March 1st. In the spring, we'd visit Tai Tung one more time to celebrate Dad and Mia, who were both born in May.

These three meals were the only times we went out to eat as a family and getting ready was an event in itself. My sisters and I wore our nice dresses—at age eight, I had a closet filled with orange, brown, and green dresses to choose from. Naomi and I helped Charlotte and Mia get ready, while Danny tried to persuade Simon to make his hair look nice. The boys wet their hair and combed it flat against their heads. Naomi, Leah and I braided our own long hair, and then we braided Charlotte's for her. We had boxes of colorful ribbons from Dad's business, and we tied them around the rubber bands on the ends of our braids. Mom liked to keep Mia's hair short, so she didn't get to have braids or ribbons, though we'd sometimes tie a pretty ribbon around her head and tie a little bow at the top.

We all squeezed into the Chevy station wagon and Dad drove us into Seattle's Chinatown. It was only a five-minute drive to Chinatown, but it seemed to me like a whole world away. Even before we arrived, I could imagine the tastes of the special foods I knew we would eat.

Dad steered the car down Dearborn, past the front of Tai Tung, and we all helped him look for empty parking spots on the side streets. He turned the search into a game—whoever spotted the eventual parking space was a winner, and we were all eager to be the helpful victor.

After we parked, we all wandered up the street, peering in the windows of the Chinese shops and bakeries, pointing out delicious-looking cakes and cookies, pretty porcelain figurines, teacups, and vases, and the ubiquitous upside-down hanging ducks.

The front of Tai Tung was covered in Chinese calligraphy that none of us knew how to read. I always wondered how Dad knew that we were going to the right restaurant, since he didn't speak Chinese or know the characters written on the door.

When we entered the restaurant, the same Chinese waiter greeted us. He had a very large nose with lots of pockmarks in it. He always intimidated me a little, and I would take hold of

Mia or Charlotte's hand, more for my comfort than theirs, as he escorted us downstairs to a large dining room with big round tables. I liked that he recognized our family—it made the whole affair feel truly special, as though we were important guests who could not be forgotten.

We all crowded around a single round table, and Dad ordered won ton soup, sweet and sour prawns with pieces of pineapple, fried rice, and spareribs covered in a sweet, sticky sauce. The food arrived in large white porcelain bowls with red dragons and blue designs painted on them. Dad ladled out portions of the steaming soup into smaller bowls that we passed around the table.

At home, there was never enough food for a second serving. Everyone would grab at the food as soon as it was set on the table, and it would vanish entirely from the serving plates and bowls within a few moments. The promise of Tai Tung food made me quiver with excitement, but even there I worried that there wouldn't be enough. My favorite dish was the Sweet and Sour Prawns, but they were everybody's favorite, and Dad always asked for one order. Usually, we each got one delicious prawn. If it was our birthday season, we might get two.

I knew from my friends that when their families went out to eat, they were encouraged to look at the menu and select their very own entrée. I never saw the Tai Tung menu, so I didn't know what I might have picked for myself, but I liked the regular dishes that my father ordered for the table. Eating food prepared for our family by a total stranger was a rare occasion.

We celebrated our birthdays at home, too. I always awoke on my birthday with a rush of excitement because it was a family tradition for our presents to appear on the coffee table overnight. These presents were opened on the birthday morning. Even if it was a school day, we all assembled to watch the birthday boy or girl open presents.

Some gifts were wrapped in old wrapping paper, while others weren't wrapped at all, offering absolutely no suspense about their identity. Presents were often recycled in our family; once we outgrew a toy or a game, it disappeared from our collection, only to reappear on the coffee table for a younger sibling's birthday. Often the excitement of present opening was mitigated by the discovery that our presents had broken parts or missing pieces.

We got clothes for our birthdays, too. My clothes were hand-me-downs, but not always from my older sisters. Mom scoured The Salvation Army, St. Vincent DePaul, and Goodwill for bargains, and she assembled our wardrobes from these locations. To make her shopping and laundry sorting easier, Mom chose our colors. All of our clothes had to conform to the designated colors she had selected for each of us.

My colors were orange, brown, and forest green. I envied Leah's blue clothes and wished I could wear them myself— turquoise was my favorite color—but Mom insisted that my hazel eyes were not a good match for blue clothes. Leah, on the other hand, had blue-grey eyes. "Your colors are right for your eyes, Claudia," Mom told me. I didn't understand this, since my eyes weren't orange, but I knew better than to argue about my color assignment.

We had birthday cakes and parties too. On the day of the party, the kitchen was jammed. Neighbors wandered over from up the street, Leschi classmates crowded around the table, and Dora often brought the entire Miller clan. Sometimes Uncle Norbert came, too, and by the time I was eight he brought his new wife, whose name was Bea. Before they got married, my mother declared, "Norbert is too old to get married. He should stay a bachelor." Norbert and Bea were both in their fifties.

Grownups from the Friday Night Group stopped by for Chotzen birthday festivities, too. "You Chotzens really know how to throw a party," Nick Farley gushed. He rubbed my mother's back, and she made a strange sort of purring noise and stared into his eyes for a few seconds. "A Chotzen celebration is the best kind of celebration," Rita Dodd echoed. I watched her and Brian Dodd with slight suspicion. Dad had recently gathered the older kids together to inform us that the Dodds were now our legal guardians. "If your mother and I die, they will finish raising you," he told us. "They'll be your parents." I didn't exactly understand how this would work. I liked the Dodds, and they seemed kind enough to their own children, but as I observed them, I fervently hoped that Mom and Dad would never die.

Birthdays were special occasions, so I usually wore my white tutu with the ribbons. "It's meant just for dancing," Leah said knowingly, but I insisted on wearing it for all important events (including Friday Night Groups, evening school events, and birthday celebrations). Besides, I had to be ready to seize any unplanned dancing opportunities.

Mom would emerge from the other room with the birthday cake in her hands and Mia and Charlotte jumping excitedly at her side. She tried to reuse candles for as long as possible, so by the time November 7th rolled around they were often just stubs with tiny black wicks. Still, it was a thrill to see her turn the corner with my cake and its flickering candles.

After everyone devoured the cake, we set to work on the important business of playing games. Naomi led us in several rounds of pin-the-tail-on-the-donkey, relay races, and musical chairs. My favorite birthday party game was when Naomi tied strings around cookies that had holes in their centers. She attached the strings to the ceilings so that the cookies hung in a row. My friends, siblings and I lined up on our knees, our hands behind our backs. When Naomi counted, "1, 2, 3, Go!" we stretched upwards to try to eat the cookies. The first of us to finish eating a cookie won the game, but it didn't really matter who won because we all got to eat cookies. Naomi led us in party games for hours until my exhausted friends headed home.

My birthday was the last one in our family each calendar year, so as soon as it was over, I began to anticipate Hanukkah.

For months leading up to that annual December holiday, Mom shopped in thrift stores and visited month-end sales to collect gifts for us. She stacked the toys, books, games, and clothing in a special closet that only she and Dad were allowed to open. "Don't you dare peek," she warned us, and I never did. I loved the mystery of Hanukkah presents and enjoyed the suspense about what they might be.

During Hanukkah I looked forward to falling asleep, different for me than most of the year when I dreaded nighttime, worried that I would wake up to one of Mom's invasive visits. During the eight nights of Hanukkah, Mom tiptoed into our bedrooms when we were asleep to leave gifts wrapped in recycled paper on the foot of our beds. We were not allowed to open our gifts until the next morning, and this rule heightened the excitement. Sometimes I sat up in the middle of the night to check out my gift. In the dark, I would feel the shape and size, squeeze the wrapping paper to try to guess what it might be. Then I'd drift back to sleep, waking in the morning excited to open the present on the end of my bed.

Our Hanukkah gifts, like birthday gifts, were not usually in very good condition—broken toys, incomplete games, and clothes that I didn't always like—but the poor quality of the presents didn't detract from the magical thrill of eight nights of mysterious packages.

* * *

The winter of second grade was full of excitement. In November, my baby sister, Charlotte, celebrated her first birthday, and Simon turned five on the same day. Just five days later, I turned eight, and all nine of us went out for a delicious meal at Tai Tung. Then, just a few weeks into 1961, Naomi took me to see *101 Dalmatians*, a new Disney movie.

At school, Mrs. Frost assigned a TV show for us to watch as homework. Normally in our house we weren't allowed to watch TV on school nights. So being asked to watch TV for school seemed especially exciting. I waited until Dad got home to tell everyone.

"I get to watch TV tonight!" I announced, bounding into Mom and Dad's bedroom. Dad was hanging up his coat and removing his shoes. Mom was snuggling with Charlotte on the bed. "It's for school, so I have to watch it. Maybe you can watch it with me?"

"What it's about?" Dad asked.

"It's about a man named Hitler!" I told them.

The color drained from my parents' faces. They exchanged a long look, and I wondered if I had said something wrong. Mom seemed to be deferring to Dad, which I didn't see happen very often.

After a moment, Dad spoke. "You can watch it, Claudia, but I don't think we will want to watch it with you."

Dad motioned for me to sit on the bed next to Mom.

"This man, Hitler," Dad said, "he was a monster. He killed much of our family and millions of other Jewish people. Nobody believed it was happening." He continued to talk. He told me horrible stories about how the Jews were separated from their families, forced onto trains, taken to prisons that were called concentration camps, and thrown into showers. People were told that they were going to be washed, but the showerheads sprayed poisonous gas instead of water, and the gas killed the Jews. Dad told me that these killers were called Nazis, and that the man named Hitler—the subject of the television show I would watch for homework—was the leader of these Nazis. He said that they even took the gold fillings from dead people's teeth for their own personal profit, and that they also did other things, worse things, to the dead bodies of the Jewish people. They used some of the bodies' skin to make lampshades, and other people were made into soap.

Then my mother's frozen face thawed, and she began to talk, too. She explained that this was why we had almost no extended family. Most of their uncles, aunts, and cousins had been killed.

Dad began to list the names of relatives I had never heard of before. "Tanta Ella. Onkel Sigfried. Tanta Olga. Onkel Fritz. Hedwig. Ida. All of their children who were my cousins. They all went to the concentration camps. They all died."

Dad finished his horrific outpouring simply and matter-of-factly. "Hitler killed our families because we were Jews."

"This is why I want so many children," my mom explained. "You are helping to make up for all those who died."

I wandered into Leah's room, where she was practicing the cello. I asked her if she knew about Hitler and the Nazis. "Oh yes," she said. "It's very serious. So many Jews died. Millions. We have to remember that. We shouldn't have too much fun, or else we're being disrespectful."

I felt terrible that my school assignment had made my parents so upset, and I worried that I had been disrespectful during the eight years I had already spent alive.

That evening, I sat alone in the living room and watched the TV show. It presented many of the same facts that my parents had told me, but with shocking photographs and a deep-voiced narrator who explained the black and white images that flickered on our TV screen. I had never heard the name "Hitler" or the word "Nazi" before that evening, and I couldn't stop thinking about what I had seen.

In particular, the idea of gas emerging from showers haunted me. Showers were a daily part of my life, and I had never imagined that they might produce anything other than safe water. Afterwards when I took baths or showered, I studied the showerhead and hoped that it wouldn't spray me with gas. And I examined every bar of soap, wondering whether it might have been made from my father's Aunt Ella or one of my mother's cousins. There was no way to know for sure, I decided. Not knowing made me uneasy.

After I started to learn about Hitler and the Jews, I began to realize that there was a whole community of European emigrants who had fled from the Nazis—some from Germany, and others from Poland. These were people I had seen and known all of my life. I had noted their thick accents, but I had never made the connection to Hitler before. He was the common thread between all of these people.

The tattooed numbers on some of their arms and wrists fascinated me. My parents did not have these tattoos; my father explained that it was because they had been fortunate enough to leave Europe before the Jews were sent to the concentration camps.

Ernie the Butcher had numbers on his arm, and so did the woman who ran the dry cleaners. Ida, the mother of one of my friends, also had them on the inside of her forearm. Sometimes, I'd sneak a peek at her blackish-blue numbers tattoo. Though I would sometimes whisper about the tattoos with Naomi, Danny, and Leah, we all understood that we were not supposed to stare at them or ask about them.

I knew what it felt like to be identified by a number. Because there were so many Chotzen children, my mom would often introduce us in terms of birth order. "This is number four," she would say to a new acquaintance, and gesture to me. But I only had one number assigned to me, whereas these survivors' tattoos were made up of long strings of numbers. I didn't like when Mom called me "number four," and I was glad that she hadn't decided to tattoo it onto my body.

I thought, too, about what Mom had said: that my job was to make up for lost lives. This was not a one-time comment while we were growing up. It was an often-shared sentiment in our home: our purpose on earth and our reason for being was to make up for the six million Jewish people who had died. It seemed like a huge and impossible task, a burden. I was glad to have so many brothers and sisters to help me, but even with so many of us it seemed daunting.

Danny told me that the Levines, our annual Passover hosts, had been in the concentration camps too. "They're a numbers family," I whispered to Leah. "Look at his wrist. He has a numbers tattoo, just like Ida, and like Ernie the Butcher."

Passover was the only time we saw the Levines all year, but they were very welcoming and friendly, and I always looked forward to visiting them for their annual family Seder. My mother called Paul and Ursula "The Brave Levines," because she said it took courage to host a family as big as ours.

Paul and Ursula had three children of their own, but they were all teenagers by the time I was eight. Their older children greeted us warmly at the door when we arrived. Their house was sparkling clean and neat, and I wondered whether they had cleaned up especially for Passover. I had a hunch that it always looked this tidy.

The word "Seder" means "order," and Passover at the Levines' home exuded an impressive sense of order, down to every last detail. Their table was set with a luxurious white tablecloth, fancy china plates, a bouquet of fresh spring flowers, elegant candle holders and candles, shiny matching silverware, sparkling glasses, bottles of Passover wine, and the silver cup holding symbolic wine for Elijah the Prophet. On the table were the traditional foods for the Passover service: a plate piled high with matzo, tiny bowls filled with salt water to dip the parsley into, a bowl filled with fresh charoset—the delicious apple/nut/cinnamon/wine concoction I loved so much. The large Seder Plate had the place of honor at the table; it held a roasted shank bone, bitter herbs, more charoset, karpas (fresh greens such as parsley or watercress—a sign of spring), and a roasted egg to symbolize birth and life.

Paul sat at the head of the table and led the service. Ursula took her place at the other end of the long table. All through the Seder, I glanced back and forth between Ursula and my mother, marveling that two grown women from similar backgrounds could have such different ideas about how to dress. Mom was all natural. She did not dye the streak of white that ran through her black, wavy hair, and the only makeup she ever donned was lipstick that she had received for free—sample miniature tubes given to her by the Avon women who sometimes knocked on our front door. Mom didn't shave her legs or under her arms. Her hazel eyes—the same color as mine, I thought proudly—shone against the backdrop of her tanned face.

Ursula, on the other hand, looked like she was in a fashion-magazine. She wore make-up. She dressed in ensemble outfits: silk blouses that matched her skirt, nylon stockings, and elegant shoes. Her daughters—Marion and Suzanne—were also stylishly dressed.

Paul had been raised in an Orthodox family in Europe, which meant that his version of the Passover service was very long and traditional. As an eight-year-old with a newly acquired awareness of the Jewish persecution, I noticed that the service was not only long, but also serious. We said individual blessings over every bit of food on the Seder plate, and Paul instructed us to remember how hard it was for the Jews to be slaves in Egypt. I couldn't figure out how I was supposed to remember something that had never even happened to me, but from the solemn looks on the grownups faces it seemed that they had all figured out the trick.

Still, there was much about the service that I found fun and joyous. Marion and Suzanne privately showed me how they managed to avoid eating the very bitter horseradish, which was part of the ceremony: they surreptitiously threw it under the table! There were many exuberant songs with upbeat choruses that were easy to remember and fun to sing. And even the story of the Jews' slavery in Egypt had a happy ending—God had led them to freedom through a series of signs and wonders.

Now that I was a beginning student of Hebrew, I enjoyed the added pleasure of being able to follow along with the Hebrew words in the Haggadah, the book that guides the service and tells the story of Passover. During the service, the youngest child was called upon to ask the Four Questions in both English and Hebrew. Because none of my three younger siblings were able to read Hebrew yet, I was chosen to ask the ritual questions. I had been practicing for this moment, and I was very proud to show off my Hebrew skills. It was such a thrill to participate, and I secretly hoped that Simon would take a long time to learn basic Hebrew so that I could ask the Four Questions for as many years as possible.

The Passover menu was always the same: a delicious, home-cooked meal that featured matzo ball soup, roasted chicken, and sponge cake with fresh strawberries—a special Passover dessert because it was flourless.

Toward the end of the service, between dinner and dessert, the children all left the table to search for the afikomen, the missing piece of the matzo that Paul had wrapped in a napkin and hidden somewhere in the house. It was a very important treasure hunt since the service couldn't conclude until one of the children found it. All of us sprang up from the table and scoured the house—even Naomi, who was usually too busy taking care of baby Charlotte to play, joined in the hunt.

Once one of us found the afikomen, we would negotiate our prize with Paul. Two years earlier, when I was six, Leah had asked Paul for a horse. Mia and I thought that was an especially funny request, so we had taken it upon us to pester Paul for a pony even when we weren't the winning Afikomen-hunters. "I want a pony!" Mia squealed in her high-pitched not-quite-three-years-old voice.

On this particular Passover, I found the afikomen gently pressed between two big books on a shelf in the den. When I told Paul that I wanted a pony, he countered with the offer of a live goldfish. He pulled it out from behind his back—swimming busily in a clear plastic bag full of water—and I vibrated with excitement. I rode home with the plastic bag in my lap, watching the goldfish wriggle and squirm in the water, and thinking to myself that maybe being Jewish wasn't always as serious as Leah said it was.

* * *

Sometime in the spring of 1960, Mom decided that seven children and her photography business kept her too busy to do the thorough, bargain-oriented kind of grocery shopping that she preferred. A woman named Gertie Nussbaum, another refugee from the war in Europe, volunteered to do our family's grocery shopping for us.

Gertie had a family of her own—a husband and two children—but for some reason she seemed positively cheerful about buying groceries for nine extra people. Twice a week, on Sunday and Wednesday evenings, Mom spent hours on the phone with Gertie, sifting through the newspapers' advertised food sales, and telling Gertie how much to buy of each item, from each store. Mom instructed Gertie to visit several different stores and supermarkets in order to find the best bargains.

The next evening, Gertie would pull her car up outside our house, packed with bags of groceries. "Go and help Gertie unload," Mom would command, and we would drop whatever we were doing and run out to help carry in the large brown paper bags.

In the kitchen, we would begin the project of putting all the groceries away. Our refrigerator had a large freezer on top, and down in the basement we had two more large chest freezers which we used for additional frozen sale items. Those freezers were filled with cans of orange juice, boxes of peas, rectangular blocks of Neapolitan ice cream, plastic bags of rye bread, butter, liverwurst, and salami.

We unloaded the groceries while Gertie and Mom dealt with money. Gertie handed over her pile of receipts, and Mom tallied the total cost and wrote Gertie a check. I wasn't sure why Gertie was willing to do this for our family. I knew that my mother took pictures of Gertie's children, just as she did for the dentist, the orthodontist, and our musical instructors. But I also wondered whether Gertie just loved grocery shopping. It seemed like a strange passion, but I couldn't think of any other satisfactory answer.

Mom's passions included politics and civil rights (she shared these two passions with Dad and the rest of the Friday Night Group), as well as music, photography, exercise, and nudity. She made every effort she could to instill in us an appreciation for each of these things—even the last one.

One Sunday morning, in the summer of 1960, Mom told us that we were taking an adventure.

"Hurry up and finish your breakfast," Mom announced to all of us. She had something really special planned, a surprise, and we had to get moving.

I was halfway through my oatmeal, and Leah, who was 9, had even more left than I did. I started shoveling spoonful after spoonful of oatmeal into my mouth, hardly chewing and not giving myself time to savor the taste of the brown sugar.

"Where are we going?" I asked between bites.

"A nudist colony," Mom said matter-of-factly, and then she thrust baby Charlotte into Dad's arms and glided into the next room.

"What's a nudist colony?" Simon, almost 5, asked.

"I think it's a camp for naked people," Naomi, who was eleven, explained tentatively. My father nodded. Neither of them looked very pleased.

We were used to being naked around each other, and to playing naked with the Miller kids, but we weren't accustomed to being naked in public. This idea of a whole camp of nudists seemed extreme, even to all of us.

Nevertheless, not long after her announcement we were on our way. The station wagon was loaded with food and a few backpacks of clothes. Dad drove, and Mom sat upfront with Charlotte in her lap. Naomi sat in the front too, squeezed between my parents. Leah, Mia and I sat in the backseat. Danny and Simon sat behind us in the seats that faced backwards.

After a while, Simon twisted around in his seat so that his head was facing forward and posed an interesting question. "If we're going to a naked camp, why did we have to pack all these clothes?" he wondered.

The longer we drove, the more nervous and more curious I got. Mia, who was 3, held my hand. I can't imagine she understood where we were going, but she must have sensed my anxiety. Dad was much quieter than usual during the drive, but Mom made up for it with non-stop chatting about the fun we were going to have. She was glowing with anticipation.

Finally, we arrived at Lake McMurray and followed a long road that led around the lake and into a parking lot full of cars. After Dad parked near a small building we tumbled out of the car, glancing around to see if we could spot any naked people. The door to the building opened, and a man strolled towards us and greeted us warmly. He wore nothing but beach slippers. When he leaned forward to shake Dad's hand his penis dangled right in front of my chin. I quickly took several steps back. I didn't know what to do, so I just kept staring at it as he chatted with my parents. I had seen Dad naked, of course, but the only other time I had seen a grownup penis—the one belonging to the man in the woods near our house—I had run away from it.

The man with the penis gave us directions, and then he strolled back into his office. Clustered as a family and still clothed, we walked through the grounds, passing groups of people playing tennis and shuffleboard, sitting on beach chairs, talking and reading. Everyone was naked. The tennis players were wearing only tennis hats and shoes, their interesting parts bouncing around loosely as they swung their rackets and chased the balls across the court. There were breasts of all different sizes. Some hung all the way down to the women's waists, and even some men had breasts, which surprised me. I was also astonished by all the different sizes of penises that hung from the men. There was so much to look at it took me a while to realize that everyone else was an adult, and we were the only kids at the camp. It made me feel very uncomfortable, but we always did what our mother wanted us to do.

We followed Mom along a sandy path, not daring to complain or even to express our amazement. Danny caught my eye and made a disgusted face, and I nodded at him in agreement. Simon's eyes were wide, and Leah looked frightened, but mostly we tried to pretend that this was a routine experience. We trooped through the spectacle, taking it all in.

When we got to the beach, Mom instructed us, "Okay, everybody take your clothes off!" And so we did. Altogether, wordlessly we removed our shoes, socks, shirts, pants, and underwear. Danny kept his baseball cap on, but the rest of us were all totally naked. I was embarrassed being naked, but Naomi, Danny, and Leah were entering puberty and they seemed humiliated to have strangers seeing their changing bodies. I felt very sorry for them.

I dove straight into the lake, grateful that the water was warm. Swimming naked seemed less strange to me than reading naked or playing naked in the sand around strangers. I stayed in the lake as long as possible—it gave me comfort and it also gave me some cover. I watched Mom on shore as she laughed with delight. This was my mother in her element: joyful, elated, glowing with pride, surrounded by her large, naked tribe.

When it was time for lunch, Mom called us in from the water. She spread out the beach blanket and opened the picnic basket. She poured watered-down lemonade into the cardboard cans that the frozen lemonade came in. She always packed these "cans" as our cups in the picnic basket.

She looked around at all of us and laughed joyfully. "The human body is so beautiful," she said. "This is the natural way to be."

Later that afternoon, a naked man with a camera approached Mom. He was tall and had a small beard, and the camera hung from his neck, dangling just like his penis. He called our family "beautiful" and "unusual" and asked if he could take a picture. Happy to meet another photographer who shared her passion for the human body, Mom readily agreed.

The man told us where to sit, and then he rearranged us a few times until he was satisfied with the way we were positioned. He put me in the front, next to Dad, who was holding Charlotte. Most of us tried to cover our private parts with our hands or arms. Mia started to cry and tried to run away, but Mom caught her hand and held on to keep her in the picture.

A few months later, we heard from the photographer. He sent us a print of the picture and wrote a note saying that he had sold it to a magazine. Mom swore and said that he should have asked for permission, but she also seemed proud. As far as I know, we never saw the magazine, but my mom framed the photo and displayed it on the dresser in their bedroom.

Even among the hundreds of photographs that covered every surface of our house, this one always stood out to me. My eight-year-old face, framed by my wet hair, looks bewildered. Two-year-old Mia, her little naked butt to the camera, is trying to escape. Simon, behind me, is staring directly at the camera with a sullen, frozen expression. Everyone else, including my dad, is looking at Mom, her breasts and pubic hair displayed, and her face beaming with pride.

At Family Camp later that summer, my mother bragged about our visit to the nudist colony. "Everyone was so impressed by our big, naked tribe," she told the other grownups. "Our children were the only children there. Nobody else thought to bring their kiddies."

"Maybe they thought of it and decided against it," Dora Miller suggested.

My mother's pride could not be shaken. "Anyone who understands nature understands the beauty of the naked body," she said. That afternoon, she hiked without her shirt and bra in order to prove her point.

* * *

On another hike at Family Camp that summer, I saw a different side of my mom. Dirty Face Mountain was an annual Family Camp hike. Of the hundred or so people who came for a week to Family Camp, 20 or 30 hiked this mountain together as a big group. The hikers met in the camp parking lot and piled into different cars to be driven to the trailhead. As people finished the hike, they would go back to Family Camp in different cars than they came in—when there were enough people to fill a car that driver and car would head back to camp.

Mom and I finished the hike together. There was a truck there, ready to leave for our cabins, but the front seat was already overcrowded with the driver and two others. Mom and I climbed into an enclosed camper attached to the truck bed. It was rare for me to have one-on-one time with Mom during the day, which was the only time I felt safe being with her alone. Aside from her temper, I had no reason to be afraid of her during the day. What was happening at night was buried, never talked about, and I understood never to tell anybody about it. But during the day, as one of the throng of kids, I craved her special attention, and I was glad when the truck pulled away onto the dirt road before anyone else could finish the hike and join us inside the camper compartment.

As the truck bumped slowly down the dirt road, Mom started to get very agitated. "It's so warm in here," she said. "It's too damn hot." She was sweating profusely, and she pulled off her T-shirt.

"I have to get out of here," she screamed suddenly. She wiped sweat from her face with her shirt. "Get me out of here!" she shouted.

She began to pound on the window between the camper and the cab. "Stop the truck, STOP THE TRUCK! I need to get out!" But we were in a separate compartment with a double set of windows between us and the driver's cab of the truck. No one in the driver's part of the truck could hear her over the engine noise. She became increasingly frantic. She hammered the glass window with both hands. "I'm going to smash it," she yelled, though she didn't seem to be talking to me. "Stop the truck! Stop the truck! STOP THE TRUCK!"

And then, suddenly, instead of "stop the truck," she began to shout, "STOP THE TRAIN!" She yelled it over and over again as she banged on the windows. And then she gave up. She pulled her knees to her chest and sat on the floor of the camper, sobbing. "They're taking us to the gas chambers," she wailed. "They're taking us away. We're finished. Those fucking Nazi scum!"

I watched in horrified silence, transfixed. I wanted to help her, but I had no idea what to do. I felt trapped, too. When the truck finally stopped and someone opened up the camper, we both scrambled out and sat on the ground, breathing heavily. I watched the color slowly return to Mom's terrified face, and I thought about how grateful I was to be off of that unexpected train ride and away from the Nazis my mom imagined.

* * *

I had found a different sort of escape during daytimes at school and at home—or rather, it had found me. In the spring of second grade, on a typical overcast afternoon, the Light Ladies appeared to me for the first time. I was sitting at my desk, I had just finished my math worksheet, and I was staring out the window as I often did, watching Douglas Jones' crow.

Douglas, a classmate, had domesticated a wild crow that waited outside for him all day, often sitting on the windowsill just outside our classroom. It perched on his shoulder during recess and when he walked back and forth to school.

On this particular day, however, I noticed something else besides Douglas' crow—two ladies made of brilliant, pure white light. They were standing on the ledge just outside the classroom window, almost blinding me with their brightness and their beauty. I couldn't take my eyes off of them. They were luminescent; an incredible light radiated through them and all around them.

They smiled at me and beckoned to me, and then one of them softly spoke, "You can come with us. Come, and see where we will take you."

And then, without even standing up from my desk, I was with them somewhere else, emerging into a magnificent orange grove. Sunshine gleamed on the green leaves of the trees, laden with ripe oranges. Everything felt warm, quiet, peaceful, and infused with softness and light.

The Light Ladies encouraged me to stay. "You can live here with us," they told me. I felt tempted by their offer. But then their voices mingled with Mrs. Frost's, my teacher. I could hear her at the front of the classroom talking about spelling homework. Reluctantly, I forced myself to drift away from the Light Ladies in the orange grove, back to my desk.

The Light Ladies visited me often during the last few months of second grade, and they continued to reappear for several years. Each time, they coaxed me to come and live with them in the bright sunshine of their orange grove. I did want to join them—to escape from the dreary Pacific Northwest into their radiant white light—but I couldn't leave my sisters and brothers behind. I asked whether there might be room for all seven of us, but they told me no, that this offer was only for me.

I kept the secret of the Light Ladies to myself. I didn't tell anyone about them—not my teachers, not my brothers and sisters, and not my parents. My hope was that if I did not reveal their existence, they would continue to visit.

Sometimes the Light Ladies visited me at night, too, as soon as Mom slipped through the door and came to my bed. It was a relief, a grateful escape to have them whisk me away to the orange grove while she "cuddled" on top of me.

Cuddling.

That was the word Mom used. She told us that touching was a loving thing, that the human body was a beautiful and wonderful creation, and that it was part of a mother's job to cuddle with her children. I believed her, but I also knew that I hated what she called "cuddling."

When Mommy left after she was finished with me, I would feel so dirty. I thought I should be thrown out with the garbage. And I questioned what was I doing that brought her to my bed. What made her come to me again and again? I hated my body, the one she called "feminine and beautiful." I wished I had a different body that Mommy didn't want. It seemed I was there just for her pleasure.

On the nights when Mom did not come to my room, I worried that she might be with one of my brothers or sisters, visiting their beds, using their bodies to get excited. Though I always felt relieved when I made it through the night undisturbed, I also felt terrible. It made me sick to feel that I couldn't do anything to protect my siblings and to imagine that my mother was cuddling with them as she did with me.

* * *

Sometimes, after she finished her time on top of me and had left my bed, I stayed up on the ceiling, continuing to watch myself. My body was there on the bed, but it was more like a shell; I wasn't home inside of it.

That fall, I finally told Mom that I wasn't in my body. "You can touch me, and you can talk to me, but I'm not really here," I said.

"I don't understand," Mom responded.

"I'm not in my body," I insisted.

Concerned and confused, she took me to see Dr. Luce, our family physician. "He'll examine you and tell us what is going on," Mom said.

Dr. Luce worked at Group Health, the hospital where we had all been born. Mom brought Simon, Mia, and baby Charlotte with us to the doctor. The nurse led all five of us into the room. We waited for a few minutes, and then Dr. Luce came in and poked a thin needle into my arms and legs. I saw Mia's eyes grow huge as she watched the needle disappear against my skin.

"Can you feel this?" Dr. Luce asked.

"Yes," I said. "I can feel that you're touching me with the needle, but I'm not here. I'm not inside my body."

"Are you ever inside your body?" he asked.

"Sometimes I am," I said. "But lots of other times I'm not, like when I'm at home, or at school." The truth was I was out of my body almost all the time now.

Dr. Luce was stumped. He told Mom to keep an eye on me, and then he left the room.

Later, at home, Mia tugged on my arm. "Are you back in your body now, Claudia?" she asked. "Are you back yet?"

I wasn't. I knew that Mom and Dad were worried and perplexed, but I didn't know any other way to explain it. I could walk and talk. I could feel the physical sensation of someone touching me. But I felt distant and completely disconnected from all of these physical experiences.

* * *

In spite of my insistence that I was not in my body, I loved being a third grader at Leschi Elementary. My teacher, Miss Harrison, was the favorite teacher I had ever had—and I had liked all of my teachers. Handwriting was my Achilles' Heel; Miss Harrison, like Mrs. Frost and Mrs. Kennedy before her, insisted that it was the only area in which my work was not up to her standards. In every other subject and category, she said, I was a model of scholarship and good behavior, and I found the lessons that we were learning to be easy, intuitive, and fascinating.

"You are my shiny penny, Claudie Weibly," Dad told me when I showed him my graded assignments and report cards. "You are my very shiny penny." My mother cared less about grades. "I let your daddy worry about all those marks," she told me. "So long as you did your best."

Though her photography business was still bustling, Mom was spending more and more time at activist meetings. She was a member of Women Strike for Peace, and in November 1961, nearing the height of the Cold War, she took me along on my very first peace march. About 50,000 women brought together by Women Strike for Peace marched in 60 cities in the United States to demonstrate against nuclear weapons under the slogan "End the Arms Race not the Human Race." Dad, Leah and the twins came too, and we all walked for six miles. The protest helped push the United States and the Soviet Union into signing a nuclear test-ban treaty two years later.

In addition to protesting nuclear weapons, Mom was also involved in organizing a recent protest against Central Area grocery stores that refused to hire Black employees. It's important to take action, "she told us.

Family friends often asked how my mom found the time to juggle so many activities.

"She's an amazing woman," my father said. "I don't try to figure out her methods. I just stand back and appreciate her."

On rare occasions a more peaceful side of my mother surfaced. When we lived in the Leschi area she took a class in the neighborhood to learn how to do Sumi painting—an Oriental brush painting technique that she practiced at home. She used bamboo brushes, rice paper, an ink stick with a drawing of a golden dragon, and a special stone to mix the ink. Sometimes, after the younger children were asleep, she would paint; I watched her making artistic brush strokes across the watercolor paper.

During the day, on those rare times when Mom wasn't working in her photography studio or darkroom or exercising or heading off to a meeting, she might sit down to play the piano. Classical music was important to my mother; she had studied piano when she was younger, and her whole disposition transformed when she put her fingers on the keys. Suddenly, it seemed that all of the restlessness and intensity drained out of her, and she became focused and tranquil and showed a serenity that I rarely saw in her otherwise. She only played piano when the house was quiet—usually while we were at school and the younger kids were napping. Sometimes, though, I would return home from school and hear the melodies of Chopin or Mozart emanating from the living room. On those days, I would tiptoe into the doorway and watch my mother play, trying to figure out how this peaceful woman was the same person who ruled our chaotic household with such force.

My mother was intent on the idea that her four oldest offspring would form a string quartet. I carried my violin to and from school every day, and I practiced after dinner in my tiny closet room. Next to the single bed against the wall, there was just enough room for a music stand and for me to stand up and squeak out the tunes on my violin.

Danny confessed to me that he had lost interest in playing the violin even though he was in the Junior High orchestra. "They'll be so disappointed if I quit," he confided. Danny was often the main recipient of my parents' pride. "Danny is our hope for the future," my mother said. When Danny's classmates voted him 7th Grade President and "Most Popular," my parents were thrilled.

Danny was athletic too—a quality my parents prized. The whole family trekked to local parks and sports fields to watch Danny's Pee Wee Football and Little League Baseball games. Even my father, who was dutiful about working long hours, would adjust his schedule around Danny's games. "I love it when they announce, 'Here comes Chotzen up to bat,'" he said proudly.

Like Danny, I was more excited about other activities than I was about practicing my violin. Twice a week, Leah and I went together to the Leschi Community Center to attend drama and dance classes. In Creative Dramatics, we learned different acting exercises, played fun theater games, and acted out scenes from plays. I enjoyed the world of acting and make-believe; pretending to be somebody totally different from myself made me feel as though I could lead any life I wanted to.

I decided to write a play of my own, and so I expanded the fairy tale of Cinderella into a lengthy script with parts for ten characters. I wrote it nonstop for a week: at recess, on the days I took two busses to Hebrew School, and after my younger siblings went to bed. I scrawled every line in a spiral notebook. When I finished, I cautiously showed it to my mother.

"I wrote a play," I said. "It's Cinderella, but I made it longer and wrote all the dialogue."

Mom beamed at me. "Wonderful," she said. "Are you going to put it on?"

I nodded.

"Well," Mom said, "you'll need scripts for all of your actors." She interlaced ten sheets of carbon paper and typing paper, inserted the pile of paper into her typewriter, and began to type. I stood right beside her, watching vigilantly over her shoulder to make sure she typed all of the lines correctly. As she typed, we read the play out loud together. "It's very good, Claudia," she commented. I beamed with pride.

Mom spent more than two hours typing up my play that day, and then another hour the next afternoon. When she finished, we had a separate, carbon-copy script for every character. She helped me to put all of the pages in order and slide paperclips over each individual copy.

The next day I brought the carbon copies to school and cast my friends. I was Cinderella. My friend Vicki played the Fairy Godmother. Cynthia was the prince. (I had briefly entertained the notion of casting boys in the play to make it more realistic, but I had also written a climactic kiss into the final scene. I opted to sacrifice realism rather than endure the embarrassment of kissing a boy.)

We rehearsed at recess for weeks until I finally deemed the production ready for an audience. Miss Harrison cleared time in the school day for us to perform the play for our class. She was so impressed by the show that she arranged for us to perform it three more times: once each for the two other Leschi third grade classes, and once at an assembly in front of the entire Leschi Elementary School student body.

Creative Dance was fun too. I had always loved dancing to John Verrall's piano music on Friday nights; classes at the community center weren't all that different. "Move however your body desires," the instructor told us. "Twirl! Spin! Leap! Flow!" I was good at this kind of physical free expression, since I had unknowingly been practicing since the age of three.

I begged Mom to let me sign up for other dance classes, and she obliged. I enrolled in ballet, which was very different than Creative Dance. Though ballet required more focus and precision than freeform dancing, it brought me a similar sense of enjoyment. When I was dancing my mind felt totally free.

Leah was the only member of the intended Chotzen String Quartet who found pleasure in playing an instrument. She was half the size of the cello when she first lugged it home from school, on loan from the Leschi Elementary music teacher. She wasn't good at first, and Simon and I teased her about the awful screeching sounds she made when she practiced. But she stuck with it, and before long her cello playing became too musical to merit our mockery.

"It's a good thing I'm the musician," Leah observed, "because otherwise Mom would want nothing to do with me." My mother was less kind to Leah than she was to the rest of us. She criticized her constantly and then instructed her to be happier. "Smile. Life is good," Mom told her, whenever Leah looked sullen.

"I'm not as smart or as skinny as you or Danny or Naomi," Leah complained to me. "But I do like the cello, and Mom likes that."

Mom could have never run the house without Naomi. When Naomi wasn't earning money by babysitting for other families, she was tending to our home and caring for our younger brothers and sisters. She did the dishes—no small feat in a family of nine—and cleaned the kitchen counters every night, while Danny scrubbed away at the floor. When the kitchen was clean, Naomi helped Dad to shepherd all of us in and out of our baths. She diapered Charlotte, helped Simon and Mia into their pajamas, and made sure that Leah and I had completed our homework. In my parents' eyes, Naomi was every bit the adult that they were.

One late afternoon in November, I sat in the kitchen while Mom peeled carrots over the sink and rotated the heavy lid of the pressure cooker, sealing it into place to cook a roast for dinner. I alternated between helping Charlotte to color and completing my own homework: a report on shells, complete with drawings and detailed descriptions.

It was already dark when the kitchen door flew open and 11-year-old Naomi—coming home from babysitting—entered shaking and crying. Her bare feet were covered with mud, and her long, messy hair looked nothing like the neat braids that she had left home with that morning.

"Where are your shoes?" my mother asked.

"In the woods," Naomi gulped through tears. "My schoolbooks are there, too. I saw something awful. I saw two men dragging a woman through the woods. She had red hair, and I think she was dead. When they saw me staring, one of the men stopped dragging the body and chased after me."

Charlotte climbed into my lap and began to cry. "I dropped everything," Naomi said. "I took my shoes off so that I could run faster. He chased me to the edge of the woods, but I think he stopped when I got to the street. He didn't want anyone else to see him."

"Where were you in the woods?" I asked. I remembered the man from the woods who had exposed himself a few years earlier. I wondered whether it might be the same spot, or even the same man.

"By the creek," Naomi said. "Where we always play. Where we pick watercress for Mom, right next to the place where Tim Miller first showed us the midnight berries."

Mom called the police, and within twenty minutes two officers arrived at our door. Mom suggested they join us for dinner, but they were too busy working. After Naomi described what had happened, they left to search the woods. They came back a little while later and asked Mom if she and Naomi could come down to the station. "My husband isn't home yet," Mom told them, "and I need to finish cooking dinner. Naomi will go with you. She's my grownup around here, anyway."

I watched through the window as Naomi climbed into the back of the police cruiser and drove off. More than an hour later, the officers brought her back. "I had to look through big books of bad men and criminals," Naomi told us.

"Cool," Simon said, but Naomi shook her head.

"It was scary," she informed us. "All of these men had done terrible, violent things, and I had to look at all of their faces to see if I recognized any of them."

Mom interrupted us. "Your shoes and schoolbooks are still in the woods," she reminded Naomi. "Take Claudia and go get them."

It was very dark, so we took a flashlight. Naomi led the way, and she shined the beam ahead of both of us. We didn't say much to each other as we pushed our way around bushes and under branches. I squinted into the blackness all around us and wondered if the bad men were nearby, waiting to ambush us. If they could kill a grown woman, I figured they would have no trouble with two girls. I thought of Dad, who was in Yakima on business, and wondered whether I would ever see him again.

Naomi led me to the creek, where we often played. She shined the flashlight onto her blue tennis shoes and schoolbooks, which were still on the ground, just where she had dropped them. We gathered them in our arms hastily, listening intently to every sound. Naomi's eyes were wide, and her hand that held the flashlight trembled noticeably. "Let's go," she said as soon as we had picked up everything off the ground.

With our arms full, we ran back through the woods, not bothering to weave around the muddy patches. I flinched at every dark snag and small clearing as we raced by them, terrified that we might be killed at any moment. When we emerged from the woods, we kept running. We didn't stop until we reached our front door, both of us breathless. We wiped our feet carefully before went inside. I returned to work on my shells report.

* * *

A few days after the policemen visited, Mom brought home a different kind of houseguest. Marie Dams was an old German woman who carried two brown paper shopping bags and wore the same faded, threadbare blue cotton dress every day. She was thickset and short, and her face was weathered with lines and wrinkles. Her long, stringy white hair was wound around the back of her head and held in place with two large brown combs. She spoke no English, and she reeked of urine.

"She's stinks," we complained to Mom. "She smells so bad."

"It's because she's a bum," Dad explained, wrinkling his brow.

"She's a lost soul," Mom countered. "And I found her."

She lived with us for two weeks that November. She joined us for all of our meals and slept in the bedroom that Mom used as her studio. In exchange, she mended our torn clothes and ironed everything. As a result, all of our clothing stank of stale pee.

"Get her out of here," Simon complained, pinching his nose.

"How long is she staying?" I demanded. "Even my friends at school are noticing how awful my clothes smell."

"We're helping her," Mom said. "She'll stay for as long as she needs to."

And then, without a word, she was gone. I caught a glimpse of her wandering down the front steps with a tattered brown paper bag in each hand.

"She's going back to the streets," Mom said. I didn't know whether Marie had told her this, or whether she was simply making an assumption. Since Marie only spoke German, I had no real sense of the conversations that took place between her and my parents.

The smell of pee lingered.

Shortly after Marie Dams had gone, Shag, our sheepdog, left as well. First, he bit Richard, the mailman, which instigated a lot of yelling and anxiety, especially because the mailman was an occasional lunch guest.

"We can't keep a dog who goes around biting people," my father insisted.

"He doesn't bite people. He only bit Richard," Mom argued.

"And Richard won't drop the issue," Dad said. "This isn't going to go away."

And then Shag was gone for good. Mom told us that she had found him a new home out in the country, where he could chase sheep and run in pastures all day long. "He's in a better home now," she said. I never knew if my mother had really found him a new home or if she had abandoned him somewhere like she did with our kittens.

Though I couldn't have articulated it at the time, the safe places in my young life were at school with my teachers. That December, I decided to thank Miss Harrison for her exemplary third grade teaching and her buoyant support of my burgeoning creativity. Though it was customary for each of us to give our teacher a small gift at Christmastime—some item from Dad's business, wrapped in festive paper—I determined that this year no ordinary gift would do. Miss Harrison was an overwhelmingly good teacher, and so it was imperative that I gave her an overwhelmingly good gift.

Since the gifts available to me were limited to the contents of my father's warehouse, it would be nearly impossible to give Miss Harrison something lavish. The solution, I decided, would be to impress her with the quantity of gifts. With my parents' permission, I picked out all my favorite items from Dad's business: a sewing kit, a tool kit, a collection of ribbons, a set of combs and brushes—at least twelve items in all. I wrapped them each individually and presented them to her on our last school day before Christmas break.

When I returned to school that January, Miss Harrison handed me a lovely card. I ran my hand over the elegant, imprinted design on the front, and then I opened the card to read her hand-written message, scrawled in perfect teacher cursive. I felt a surge of sadness that my own handwriting left so much to be desired.

In her note, she thanked me for each item, one-by-one, and the list took up the entire inside of the card. She ran out of room inside the card and had to sign her name on the back. As I read her litany of the gifts I had given her, I began to feel embarrassed. When she listed all of the little items in this way, the sheer quantity of gifts I had wrapped seemed silly and excessive.

I showed the thank-you note to my mother, who affirmed my feelings of humiliation. "Usually, Claudia, people appreciate one thoughtful gift more than lots and lots of gifts," she told me. I wished she had told me this back in December, when I was wrapping all of the presents.

Naomi and Danny were especially busy during that winter of 1961 and 1962. In addition to the rigors of seventh grade, babysitting jobs, sports teams, and household responsibilities, the twins were also studying for their Bat Mitzvah and Bar Mitzvah, respectively.

These traditional ceremonies, held when Jewish children turn thirteen to mark their transition into adulthood, turned out to involve a lot of preparation. Danny and Naomi already functioned as adults in our family, but the qualifications for traditional Jewish adulthood were very different from childcare and housekeeping: they had to learn to chant portions of the Torah, and to recite other Hebrew prayers and blessings.

Because they were twins, it made sense to hold a single ceremony for both. I learned in Hebrew School that this was called a "B'Nai Mitzvot." Bat Mitzvahs were for girls, Bar Mitzvahs were for boys, and B'Nai Mitzvot were for girl and boy twins, like my brother and sister. There had never been a B'Nai Mitzvot at Herzl before, and my mother's request to have Danny and Naomi's ceremonies combined broke a tradition for our synagogue. But my mom said she had no intention of having two separate rituals, and Herzl finally acquiesced. The event was planned for March of 1962, just after the twins would turn thirteen.

"Chotzens can't sing." That's what Mom always told us. "It's not our fault," she said. "We just don't know how to carry

a tune. Don't try to sing in public because it won't be pretty."
But Danny and Naomi were required to sing some of the
prayers for their special ceremony. They attended weekly study
sessions with Cantor Frankel to practice the singing and
chanting.

Naomi and Danny's preparation for their B'Nai Mitzvot
made me think about how closely Judaism was tied to my
family's identity. I knew that my heritage was Jewish, in the
way that other people's heritage might be Mexican, Irish, or
Japanese. But those kinds of heritages were all tied to a country,
and my parents didn't take that kind of pride in their country
of origin. Sometimes they identified themselves as German,
especially when they told stories about their childhoods. But
when they talked about another German couple in our
neighborhood, they called them "The Germans," as though
they were foreign or different. "Damn it, the Germans are on
the tennis court," my father would complain when he and my
mother showed up at the neighborhood court to play and found
it already occupied.

I didn't understand whether or not I should identify as
German. When I told grownups my last name, they repeated it
thoughtfully and said, "Chotzen. Chotzen. Are you German?"
I never knew how to answer the question.

"We're German Jews," Dad told me. "When I was a boy,
that distinction didn't matter. Everyone was German. But ever
since Hitler and the war, it means something different." I didn't
know anyone else who announced their religion when they
were asked what country their family had emigrated from.

I refined my answer to questions about my heritage. "I am
American. My parents were born in Germany. I'm also Jewish."
I practiced it on Dad, and he seemed pleased with the
thoroughness and accuracy of my answer.

According to Mom and Dad, some of the values in our
family were closely tied to the terrible things that had happened
to Jews in Germany. My parents constantly expressed gratitude

for the smallest or most mundane things—things that other people took for granted—and they encouraged us to do the same. They appreciated everyday things like fresh air, having food to eat for dinner, or colorful maple trees in the yard, because so many of their relatives had died in concentration camps. Since we were so lucky to be alive, making up for millions who weren't, it was our job to be useful, productive, and to appreciate the little things that those who had perished could not. It was also our job to be especially loyal to our family. "This is our precious unit," Mom told us. "Our first duty is to one another. We are the Chotzens, and we are not like the rest of the world. And no one will ever love you as much as I do."

Boys' Bar Mitzvahs were traditionally held on Saturday mornings, but girls were not permitted to lead the Saturday service. For this reason, Danny and Naomi's B'Nai Mitzvot was scheduled for a Friday night. Danny complained that he was being deprived of the traditional opportunity, all because he had to share the event with Naomi, but my mother fixed him with a powerful warning glare. We all understood what the look meant: family loyalty was foremost among Chotzen values, and Danny ought to be grateful to be sharing his Bar Mitzvah with Naomi. He got the message, and he seemed resolved to be excited about the joint venture from that moment on.

We spent all week helping Mom prepare for the reception: cleaning and rearranging furniture and picking out the tablecloths that didn't have too many stains.

On Friday afternoon, the day of the ceremony, Mom dropped all of her daughters off at a Black hair salon in the Leschi neighborhood. "We're having a big family event," she told the lady who greeted us. "They need to look nice."

Charlotte was only two years old, and Mia—with her little boy's haircut—was not quite four. I was nine, Leah was eleven, and Naomi had just turned thirteen a few days earlier. None of us had ever been to a hair salon before. We sat, side-by-side-by-side-by-side-by-side in the waiting chairs. Our hairdresser took Leah first and set her up in the tall chair. She ran her fingers through Leah's hair, and then beckoned to the three other hairdressers in the salon. They left their customers and came over. All four of them whispered and laughed as they ran their hands through Leah's locks. "It's so soft," one of them said. "I don't know how to style white hair," our hairdresser complained.

Finally, they agreed that it would be best to use the flat irons to straighten our wavy hair and then the curling irons to curl the ends. One of the other hairdressers finished with her customer—an elderly Black lady who didn't have much hair at all anymore—and took me next. I sat next to Leah as the hot irons singed my scalp.

Once all five of us (even Mia) had been styled, Naomi paid with the money that Mom had given her and we walked home, our pressed hair falling in soft ringlets around our necks. We donned our five matching grey wool dresses, which had been made especially for the occasion. (Mom had taken photographs of a local seamstress' family in exchange for the five dresses.) Mom had also laid out clean white socks for us to wear, along with new black patent leather shoes.

It was so special and exciting to wear new clothes—let alone ones that had been sewn just for us—and I felt proud to match my four beautiful sisters.

The nine of us drove to synagogue together. Naomi and Danny hopped out of the car to go meet the Rabbi while Dad parked, then the rest of us filed inside. We sat in the front row, where we had never sat before. Omi and Opi and Aunt Ilse joined us—they had come all the way from Buffalo and New York City for the occasion—and Norbert and his wife Bea slipped in beside them. I waved at Justine and Phoebe Miller, who sat with the rest of their family a few rows back. They had never been in a synagogue before, and Phoebe looked especially fascinated.

I stared up at Naomi and Danny, standing tall on the *bimah*. Up above them, high on the wall, hung the everlasting light, which never turned off, even when the synagogue was closed. The light shone out of a carving of two hands, with the thumbs touching and the other fingers splayed out forming two V-shaped symbols (exactly like the Star Trek greeting but I didn't see that until years later). Sometimes, when I was bored during synagogue, I stared at the everlasting light and imitated the V-shapes with my own hands. Today, however, I did not need to find ways to distract myself during the ceremony; I was utterly riveted to see Danny and Naomi standing in front of the congregation.

They were great. They took turns chanting their Torah portion, which they read from the actual Torah. Then, they each gave a short speech, in English, about the significance of their Torah portion. Then, they helped to lead the regular Friday night service! They led the entire congregation in prayers, and even though Mom told us that Chotzens couldn't sing, I thought that their voices sounded strong and beautiful.

At the end of the service, Naomi hugged the Rabbi and the Cantor, and Danny shook each of their hands in a very grown-up manner. Then, still standing on the *bimah*, they hugged each other. I was so proud of them for their performance in front of the whole congregation, and also for all the hard work and preparation that I knew they had done together. It made me envious that I didn't have a twin; if I had a Bat Mitzvah, I thought, I would have to study and sing all by myself.

Everyone came back to our home for the reception. It was quite an event: there were flowers, fruit punch, deviled eggs, and a cake in the shape of a Torah. Mom wore silver jewelry and scurried gracefully around the room, laughing with our guests and flashing her beautiful white smile. She was glowing.

About a week after the B'Nai Mitzvot, when my two oldest siblings had become official Jewish adults, Mom sat the whole family down to share some news: she was pregnant again, for the eighth time. For two years I had been the middle child, number four of seven. Now I would have four younger siblings. I was excited to be one of the older kids. I was enjoying the end of third grade and felt confident that I had lots of important knowledge to impart upon Simon, Mia, Charlotte, and the unborn baby.

A few nights later, my father made his own announcement at dinner. "I'm having a vasectomy," he said. "I will be voluntarily neutered," he added, in answer to the puzzled looks on our faces. "Enough. Eight is enough." Mom didn't look pleased, but Dad was resolute. "We simply can't afford any more children."

Pregnancy didn't slow Mom down at all. In the mornings she did calisthenics in our living room while watching "The Jack LaLanne Show," a television fitness program. She ordered a taut, black rubber cord from the toll-free number they advertised on the show, and she pulled it while she did the exercises. Jack, clad in a jumpsuit, instructed and encouraged her from within our black and white television, shouting cheery aphorisms such as, "Train for life like it's an athletic event!"

Every day, regardless of the weather, Mom went for a swim in Lake Washington. In the winter, she bundled Mia and Charlotte up in snow boots, mittens, hats, and heavy jackets, then brought them along to sit on the freezing beach. She stripped down to her one-piece bathing suit and dove into the lake. "I started in the summer," she explained to friends at the Friday Night Group, "but it was so easy that I just kept going."

Skiing was a mandatory family activity, and my parents brought us along to the slopes before we were even old enough to walk. They had each of us on skis by the time we were age three. As a baby, Mom wrapped me in blankets, put me in a basket, and left me next to the rope tow or chairlift while she, Dad, and my older siblings skied. When I grew old enough to ski myself, I watched my mother repeat the process, bundling the most recent infant and setting them beside the chairlift. "I never let the kids get in the way of my needs," she said with pride. I remember her stopping between ski runs to breastfeed Charlotte, before returning her to the basket and heading back up the slope for another run.

During the winter, we skied almost every weekend. We piled into the station wagon and drove the hour from Seattle to Snoqualmie Pass, which was sprinkled with commercial ski areas with chairlifts, rope tows, T-bars, and poma lifts. On other weekends, we skied at The Mountaineers Club, a member-based organization to which my parents belonged. This was a cheaper alternative; it only offered rope tows, and though it also had a day lodge where we sat and ate our picnic lunches, they did not sell any food or hot chocolate. Once a year, over winter vacation, we stayed for a week in a Mountaineers lodge at Mt. Baker.

Skiing made me nervous, especially during snowstorms. The blustery snow covered my goggles and made it hard to see; it hurt to fall on the icy slopes. I was skinny, and the cold always numbed my fingers and toes. It scared me when I removed my gloves at the end of a run and saw that my fingers had turned white; I worried that the tips of my fingers might break off. I felt a knot in my stomach as I rode the chairlift to the top of the mountain and skied warily towards the edge of the slope. But as soon as I pushed off, I gave into the exhilaration of flying down the hill, carving my skis around the moguls as the wind whipped against my face and hair. I enjoyed my time on the slopes when the snow was soft and the weather was clear, especially when we skied in the spring, and it was warm enough to wear shorts and a T-shirt.

My parents insisted that we ski in all types of weather. Even on stormy days there were strict rules about when we could break for lunch or quit for the day. It was expected that all of us get in a full day of skiing to get our money's worth. It was equally important that we demonstrate our skiing ability—my parents created a high degree of competition to be the best at everything we did. During the ride back to Seattle my parents would share their observations and evaluations of our daily performances. They only offered praise, but criticism was implicitly obvious—if Mom and Dad didn't mention your skiing, you had clearly not performed well that day. It wasn't important to ski well as much as it was important to ski better than others. I was a good skier, but there was never any assurance that I would impress Mom and Dad.

Every autumn, Dad prepared for ski season by measuring the previous year's skis against our growing bodies. We reached an arm straight out in front of us, and Dad placed one ski on the floor under our arm. If it reached our wrist, it was the right length. If we'd outgrown it, we graduated to the next pair of skis, previously used by the sister or brother just above us. Only Danny and Naomi had the luxury of new skis: because they were the oldest, they were able to grow to heights that were still unprecedented among the Chotzen siblings.

My father shared my mother's appreciation for athletic pursuits, especially when they also allowed him to revel in the beauty of nature. He was an avid skier, hiker, and tennis player—a sport that he and Mom often played together in the summer, and which we were taught as soon as our hands were big enough to hold a child-sized racquet. Athleticism was mandatory: we participated in family tennis competitions, swam daily in the summer (only Mom was brave enough to swim in Lake Washington in the winter), and hiked often. We held races, played croquet, and spent hours playing "Pole"—a game that my father played as a child in Germany, and which resembles tag.

My mother wasn't just physically fit—she was tough, too. She had insisted on natural childbirth for all seven of her children, and her eighth baby would be no exception. Physical pain and discomfort seemed to have no effect on Mom. She had no patience for sickness, which she associated with weakness. I never saw her show any sign of a cold or flu, and she taught us that such ailments were unacceptable for us, too. "If you are sick, you are not my child," she told me once, when I complained of a fever.

When I did get sick, I felt that I was a disappointment. Mom quarantined me in my bedroom, put a cup of canned orange juice on the nightstand, and instructed me to stay put until I felt better. If I was nauseous, or if I was already vomiting, she handed me a bucket. Then she would leave the house to do errands or go to meetings.

* * *

Mom was eight months pregnant with my seventh sibling when she took us to the World's Fair, in September of 1962. They called the Seattle World's Fair the "Century 21 Exposition." It included a tour of the future and a couple of monumental urban developments: a huge pointy building that stretched up 600 feet into the sky, "The Space Needle," and a very fast train that ran on an elevated track over a mile of the city, "The Monorail."

I had been begging to go to the Exposition since April, when it had opened. Finally, while Dad was in Wenatchee on business one weekend, Mom took us. The eight of us plus several of the Miller kids piled into our old station wagon. (Dad always got the new station wagons for his business, gave his older car to Mom, and traded in the oldest car.)

We spent the afternoon enjoying rides and cotton candy. Phoebe Miller and I took an elevator to the observation deck of the Space Needle and looked out over downtown Seattle. "It's like being the tallest people in the world," Phoebe said. I was the shortest kid in my class, and I liked Phoebe's idea. I imagined that Phoebe and I were benevolent giants, towering over the city of Seattle, enjoying the hubbub of the World's Fair.

When we piled back into the car, at the end of the afternoon, it felt a little roomier than it had before.

"Let's go," Mom said.

I began to count my siblings and the Miller kids. "We can't," I told her. "Hold on."

"We're going. No talking," she insisted, turning the key in the ignition.

"We're missing Mia," I said. I had figured it out.

"Shit," Mom said. "Come on."

She bolted out of the car and back into the crowds of fairgoers, and we all took off after her. After questioning two security guards and a soda vendor, Mom led us to the Lost and Found center.

"I'm missing my daughter," she said.

"Sorry ma'am," the attendant told her. "We found a little boy, but no girls."

"I'm not a boy," someone piped up in a very small voice. Mia had wandered up behind the attendant, her hands on her hips. "I am Mia," she added.

I felt an enormous wave of relief wash over me. I heard Naomi exhale, too, as though she was releasing a lot of anxiety and fear.

"That's her," Mom confirmed. "That's my daughter."

"Sorry," the attendant mumbled, glancing at Mia's bowl haircut. "She sure looks like a little boy." He gestured to Mom's very pregnant belly and joked, "Anyways, it looks like you've already lined up a replacement." I didn't think the joke was funny.

Mom whisked Mia away, and Danny thanked the attendant for his help. Back in the car, I switched seats with Phoebe Miller so that I could sit beside Mia. I held her hand on the drive home. "I am not a boy," she whispered in my ear.

* * *

For Mom's seventh and final delivery, Group Health Hospital finally consented to allow my father into the room.

"Finally," Mom said. But when they left for the hospital, my father inexplicably returned home a few hours later. "I got to the room, and they shut the door in my face," he told us. "They wouldn't let me in." He was frustrated, and my mother was furious.

Mom gave birth to my new baby brother on October 23rd, 1962, just a few weeks before my tenth birthday. Dad brought us all to the hospital to pick Mom and the baby up. My father filmed with the movie camera while my mother, baby in her arms, posed for the camera. Naomi carried Mom's suitcase to the car.

My parents named the baby Joseph, but we all began calling him "Joey" right away. Joey seemed to me to be the smallest baby of the four younger siblings I had encountered, but Dad suggested that this might have just been my perception. "After all," he said, "You're the biggest sister that you've ever been."

I observed Naomi carefully and tried to be as good a caretaker to Joey as she was to Mia and Charlotte. Mom told me that the family needed me now more than ever, and I was eager to rise to the challenge. The baby kept Mom awake during the night, which meant that she needed to take a nap in the afternoon. Often, she would wait until I was home from school to retreat into her bedroom. "Claudia, don't let anyone disturb me," she instructed.

After dinner, while Mom worked in her darkroom, I helped Dad and Naomi get the younger kids ready for bed. After Dad's goodnight story, I would tuck Joey in his crib.

Just a few days after my tenth birthday, I came down with the measles. Simon, 7, and Mia, 4, got them, too. All three of us had to stay home from school for several uncomfortable days, which presented Mom with an opportunity: instead of dragging Charlotte and Joey along to her errands, meetings, and appointments, as she usually did, she could leave them at home with us.

She put me in charge, and for the next two days she didn't come home until dinnertime, after even Dad had returned from work. "Claudia is taking care of the babies and the measles gang," she cheerfully announced in a letter she wrote to my grandparents in Buffalo.

I missed Mom that week. A fever and an awful itchy rash made me feel like a young ten-year-old, not a grownup responsible one. I understood that the family needed me, but it wasn't easy to take on so many caretaking responsibilities when I felt miserable myself.

* * *

Our evening routine changed dramatically when Dad was away on his business trips. He would usually be gone for three days. Everyone seemed anxious for his return. Mom didn't even like to spend an evening in the house if Dad wasn't home. Instead of cooking dinner, she'd set out cold food or leftovers on the table and instruct Naomi to "feed the children," and then she would rush off to a meeting. After dinner, I tried my best to help Naomi replicate Dad's nighttime rituals, but nobody seemed to be very interested in hearing me tell a story or bouncing on my knee while I chanted "*Hapa Hapa Rider.*" It took all of my energy just to help Naomi get everybody bathed, into their pajamas, and into bed.

I missed Dad desperately when he was away. On an unconscious level, I believe I worried about Mom's nighttime visits—although this was still something I never talked about with anyone. I fretted that Dad might decide not to come home to us; and I couldn't tear my mind away from tragic images of him crashing his car on a dark, slippery road. What would happen if he died? I didn't think I could live without him.

Dad must have known how much I worried during his absences, because he always came to my room first when he arrived home from a business trip. He opened my door quietly and peeked into my room. I would sit up in bed and throw my arms around him and cry with relief; he would give me a kiss on the top of my head and tell me to sleep soundly.

My world revolved around Daddy, and his world revolved around my mom. He was totally smitten by my mother. "My life was nothing until your mother came into it," he liked to tell us, as he gazed adoringly at my mother while she bustled about the house.

"Men like me don't often get to love women like her," he said. His back was hunched from a childhood bout of scoliosis, and he lived gratefully in the shadow of my mother's striking beauty. When Mom was angry, Dad seemed to shrink in size and hunch even more. He nodded meekly when she yelled, and he always did exactly what she demanded. But when she laughed and smiled and wrapped her arms around him, Dad seemed to grow taller, and happier. My mother was so beautiful and perfect in his eyes. He worshipped her.

My father was a gentle man, but he sometimes flashed a temper that took us by surprise. Little accidents propelled him into a sudden rage. If he spilled flour while making waffles for our weekend breakfast, or if he chipped a plate while washing the dishes, his relaxed demeanor vanished in an instant, and he launched into a torrent of German swear words.

My father's anger was mostly directed at himself and his own trivial mistakes. Sometimes, though, he would go after one of us—usually one of the boys. My father was tough on Danny, for whom he had very high expectations, but he was even tougher towards Simon who teased Mia, Leah, and me relentlessly and often neglected the chores that my mother assigned him. This behavior ignited my father's temper. "Simon!" he would bellow, chasing my younger brother around the house in a blind fury. "When Carla tells you to take out the garbage, you must do it!"

* * *

The rest of the fourth grade school year passed uneventfully. I did my homework, attended Hebrew School, Creative Dance and Drama, and continued to practice the violin. Joey learned how to crawl, Mom was busier and more beautiful than she had ever been before, and Dad seemed to be away on business almost every week.

One of my good friends was Justine Miller, who was my age. Justine and I talked about books we liked and things we had studied in our different schools, but when our siblings bolted out the door to play outside, Justine often held back. "I think I'll read," she said.

That was how I ended up spending more time with her older sister, Phoebe, who was twelve—the same age as Leah. Phoebe and I had similar interests, and we enjoyed telling each other funny stories about our younger siblings. As the spring of 1963 turned into summer, we spent hours together jumping rope, walking on the beach, picking blackberries, and chatting. Amidst the mayhem of two oversized families, it was a great to have a confidante and a playmate who didn't require supervision like my younger brothers and sisters.

On August 1st, 1963, our world changed. Mom picked us Chotzen kids and some of the Miller children up at Mt. Baker Beach after a long morning of swimming and playing in the sun. After lunch at our house, she dropped Phoebe and her little brother, Tommy, who was four, back at the Miller house because they wanted to pick blackberries. They headed down the street from their house to a nearby vacant lot where wild blackberry bushes were abundant.

When Phoebe and Tommy reached the lot, there was a stranger there. He knocked Phoebe to the ground and then he pulled out a small knife and brutally stabbed her over and over in her chest. He stabbed her twelve times in all, leaving wounds two-to-three inches deep all around her heart. Tommy ran away, terrified.

The attacker pulled Phoebe's blue shorts down around her ankles and stabbed her twice more in the abdomen. He left her unconscious behind the bushes and brambles, her green plaid summer blouse soaked with blood.

I don't know how much time passed before she was found. Another group of neighborhood kids arrived at the lot to pick blackberries and heard a whimpering sound from the bushes. They investigated the noise and discovered Phoebe lying in a small clearing, hidden by tall grass. The kids fled to a nearby apartment complex and found the manager, who came running with one of her tenants. The manager and the tenant attempted to stem the flow of blood oozing from Phoebe's body. The manager yelled for neighbors to call police and an ambulance.

Tommy was discovered several blocks away, lost and crying. A neighbor who knew the family walked him home. "Phoebe was hurt by a mailman," Tommy cried to his mother. Phoebe was already in an ambulance by the time Dora placed her own call to the police.

Dora called Mom who told us the news. She phoned Dad at his Seattle warehouse, and he came home from work immediately. Mom left for the hospital. Naomi and Danny stayed at home with our younger siblings. Simon and I rode with Dad to the Millers' house to collect the rest of their kids and bring them back to our house. On the car radio we heard the news: "Mt. Baker girl stabbed and beaten, left for dead."

We were not the first car to arrive at the Millers' house: police and reporters already lined their front yard. Dora was at the hospital, and Greg was on his way there from Boeing, where he worked. The Miller kids piled into our station wagon. I squeezed Justine's hand as Dad turned the car around and steered it back to Madrona. Nobody spoke.

We sat in our living room together: Dad, surrounded by fourteen Chotzen and Miller children—everyone but Phoebe. Many of the Friday Nighters arrived too. We didn't talk; no one knew what to say.

I had never seen my father so distraught. He sat with his head in his hands, hiding his face, and he only looked up whenever the phone rang. He and Brian Dodd took turns answering the calls. The sun had nearly set when my mother finally called from the hospital.

My father blinked back tears as he reported the news to us. "Phoebe is on the edge of death. They've given her seven pints of blood, and she has eight doctors working to save her life," he told us, his voice faltering.

Brian Dodd answered another call from Greg Miller. Brian's voice trembled, too, when he told us, "The police found Phoebe's flip-flops in the bushes. They are searching the Mt. Baker neighborhood for the person who did this."

Watching these two grown men overcome with despair, I felt that I ought to be similarly tearful. "Phoebe was stabbed. She might die," I kept repeating to myself, thinking that if the reality really sunk in, I would feel the appropriate emotion. Instead, I just felt numb. It didn't make sense. I had picked blackberries in that vacant lot dozens of times. Why would a man do that to a stranger, especially to a young girl?

Our house was packed with friends that night. Gradually, the younger kids drifted off to sleep. The older siblings tucked them into beds and stayed up with the adults, waiting.

At 10 p.m. the phone rang. Dad answered it in the next room. We all strained to listen, but his voice was soft and solemn. When he returned, he looked so frightened and weary that I was sure Phoebe had died.

His voice came out as a low whisper. "Phoebe is alive, but still in grave danger. She needs all our help and all the love we can give her."

The next call came around midnight, though it felt like we had been waiting for weeks, not hours. Dad reported back to us, "Phoebe is still in great danger, but the doctors think she's going to live." We all sat and watched as he stood alone in the middle of our living room and wept, his body quaking with each sob. I had never seen my father cry before.

The next morning was a Friday. Our kitchen was filled with people and newspapers. "Mt. Baker Girl Stabbed, Police Hunt Assailant," shouted one headline. "Stabbed Girl's Condition Is Still Critical," blared another. One of my mother's photographs accompanied the articles: a close-up black and white picture of Phoebe, her long hair flowing behind her.

I read every word of the newspaper articles. *"Thirty-five police officers scoured the area of the vacant lot and went on a house-to-house search of the neighborhood hoping to find a clue." "Physicians said Phoebe's condition was still critical and she has a fifty-fifty chance of surviving."* The bleeding had been stopped and her wounds had been stitched, but the articles said she might still die from infection and shock.

The Seattle Times was our afternoon newspaper. "Wounded Child Winning Fight: Hope Buoyed," it announced, above a large photograph of Greg Miller sitting with his three youngest children on his lap. *"Greg Miller with three of his children after father's return from the all-night vigil with wounded daughter,"* read the caption.

The doctors allowed Phoebe to be taken off the respirator long enough to give a description of her attacker. It matched the one that 4-year-old Tommy had given. The next day, the police visited Phoebe again. They told her that they were going to bring three men into the room, one of which might be her attacker. They promised her that the man would not be allowed to hurt her again, and they instructed her not to say anything while the men were present in the room.

Then, they marched a line-up of three postal workers in their uniforms into Phoebe's hospital room. They held them there for a moment, while Phoebe looked at each of them from her hospital bed. As soon as the men were led out, Phoebe identified her assailant without hesitation. He was a twenty-two-year-old substitute postal worker just out of the army. He had grown up in a prominent family that lived in the neighborhood and had attended nearby Garfield High School. His brother was a minister.

The six Miller children stayed at our house all week, while Phoebe continued to recover in the hospital. According to her parents, she was growing livelier by the day—chatting with visitors and reading books. I wanted to go see her and sit beside her and help to lift her spirits, but Mom had other ideas. "We're sending you away," she said. "You need a distraction."

The distraction Mom had in mind was two weeks at Camp Solomon Schechter on Whidbey Island. Danny, Naomi, and Leah had all been to this camp before—and they had gone again, that very July. Sessions were divided by age, so there was no way for any of my siblings to accompany me.

Danny, Naomi, and Leah came home from camp and shared stories about all the games and sports they got to play, how much fun they had from morning to night. In spite of the rave reviews from my three older siblings, I had no interest in going to camp. I pleaded with Mom to let me stay home, at least while Phoebe was still recuperating. But Mom, as always, was resolute. "The older kids love camp, and you'll love it too. Keep sending Phoebe your good thoughts, and maybe she'll be able to join us at Family Camp at the end of August."

Naomi reassured me that camp was fun. "Everyone liked me and Danny a lot," she said. "We've both been Camper of the Day every year we've gone, and so has Leah. Danny and I won Best Boy and Girl Camper for the whole session, too. They really like Chotzens at that camp." I knew this already—my parents had made a big deal out of the honor when the twins had returned from camp.

A few days later, Mom dropped me off at the Herzl Synagogue parking lot, where all the campers were gathering. We loaded our suitcases and sleeping bags onto a big bus, then climbed on board ourselves. I watched out the window as Charlotte, Mia, and Simon waved goodbye to me. Simon even shook Joey's arm so that he, too, was waving. Tears streamed down my face as the bus pulled out of the parking lot. When I looked back, my brothers and sisters got smaller and smaller as we drove away.

The bus took us onto a ferryboat that crossed part of Puget Sound and then it drove us on to Fort Casey on Whidbey Island, a former army base. We disembarked and carried our bags into what had once been the barracks. The girls' barracks were a large building with a dining hall downstairs and bunk beds upstairs. The boys slept in barracks on the other side of a large soccer field.

I wrote to my family within an hour of arriving.

"Dear Family,
We just got here and unpacked. On the bus I just sat there. I didn't say much to anyone. My counselor is Karen. She seems really nice. Is she the one you guys said was shy? It seems all the girls here are pretty different than me. Guess what? At least fifty people recognized me as a Chotzen. They all say I look like Leah. I'm not exaggerating the number either.
Love, Claudia."

I worried constantly about Phoebe, and I missed my brothers and sisters and parents. I was so overcome by homesickness that I had trouble participating in activities or making friends—things that usually came easily to me. I couldn't bring myself to talk to the other girls. A few of the kids tried to invite me to engage with them. "Want to join our group, Claudia?" or "Do you want to sit with us?" they asked. I declined—amazed at how unrecognizable I was to myself. I simply had too much on my mind to make small talk or participate in trivial activities. After a while, the other kids stopped asking and inviting. They walked past me without a word.

Evenings were the worst. At sunset, everyone gathered outside the dining hall: the campers, the counselors, the staff, and Rabbi Stampfer. We formed a circle around the flagpole, a counselor played Taps on her bugle, and we all sang, "*Day is done. Gone the sun, From the lake, From the hills, From the sky. All is well. Safely rest. God is nigh.*" The song seemed sad and grim to me—it signaled the onset of another lonely night with solemn foreboding.

The flag was lowered, and then one of the counselors announced and honored the Camper of the Day. Every afternoon, I wondered when it would be my turn. Even if I didn't have fun, at least I could uphold the family tradition and redeem my experience at Camp Solomon Schechter by being named Camper of the Day. Each evening, my stomach tensed as the bugle played and the flag was lowered. I held my breath and waited, repeating the words, "Please pick me. Please say my name," over and over in my head. I had to be picked. But I wasn't.

Ruth Frankel, the cantor's wife, one of the female staff members, noticed how unhappy I was. She made a point of visiting me in the girls' barracks each night, sitting on the edge of my bed, talking to me, and listening while I cried. Each night I told Ruth how much I wanted to go home, how much my friend Phoebe needed me to be there, and how much I missed my family. She listened to me with her full attention and nodded as if she understood. She had a gentleness and patience that I wasn't used to at all.

I remembered that Mom had thought about giving me away to Ruth when I was a baby. I liked Ruth; she was kind and caring, but now I felt so attached to my own family that, despite the chaos at home and the traumatic night visits from my mom (which I still never told anyone about), I could not imagine being separated from my parents and all my brothers and sisters.

"*Dear Mommy, Daddy, and Family,*" I wrote.

"I didn't feel very good last night (about to throw up), and they gave me an aspirin. It's in the night when I get the most homesick. As I said before, <u>everyone</u> except the campers knows that I'm a Chotzen. They all judge me on who I look like. I'll write you another letter this afternoon. Love the whole family <u>always, forever</u>.

Love, Claudia.

I covered the margins of the paper with the word *"<u>Love</u>,"* underlined over and over again.

My family got the message, and soon I received a pile of letters. *"Claudie, my lovely Lady,"* Dad wrote. *"I want to tell you that I miss you and love you very much. Nevertheless I think it would be good for you to stick it out there if for no other reason than as an exercise. Make the best of all the good things you enjoy there and figure that the days will go by very fast. Much love, kiss between the eyes. Cheer up, old girl!"*

"You're having more fun now, aren't ya?" Naomi wanted to know. *"Have you been picked as Camper of the Day? Have you a lead in the camp play? Take the very best of camp. I loved almost every minute of it. We miss you."*

Danny convinced an older friend of his to drive him to camp so he could visit me for a day. When the counselors and staff members saw him, they practically cheered. "I love this place," Danny said, trying to encourage me, but it just made me feel more like a failure. He stayed through the evening flag lowering—long enough to see someone else chosen as Camper of the Day—and then he headed home. When he left, I cried so hard that Ruth Frankel promised to call my mother.

"Dear Claudie-lady," Mom wrote. *"I'm glad you're a brave girl and staying at camp. Ruth Frankel called Sunday to let us know that you are lonesome at bedtime. That is understandable. Phoebe Miller had an operation. It will take a little while longer to get her well. The younger Miller kids have been with us for several days. Lots o' love, Mom."*

Those two weeks of camp seemed like an eternity. When the last morning of camp arrived, we packed our clothes and rolled up our sleeping bags, cleaned our rooms, scrubbed the bathrooms, and swept the hallways. I attacked these final chores with more enthusiasm than any previous camp activity.

The bus retraced its route from two weeks earlier and finally drove up to Herzl Synagogue where we had started. I claimed my duffle bag and sleeping bag and watched from the curb as the other campers bid each another tearful farewells. As usual, Mom was the last parent to arrive. She pulled up in the station wagon, packed with all the little kids. I hugged Mom first, then Mia, Simon, Charlotte, and Joey. I was so happy to see each of them. When Dad came home from work, I wrapped my arms around him and wouldn't let go.

And I got to visit Phoebe. When she was finally released from Harborview County Hospital, Leah and I spent many afternoons sitting by her side until she was strong enough to play outside.

Adults in the Millers' neighborhood responded to Phoebe's stabbing by launching a campaign to clear the brush out of the vacant lot. When both the City of Seattle and the landowner failed to respond to their efforts, these neighborhood mothers and fathers wielded machetes, rakes, and scythes and cleared the lot themselves.

"The bushes aren't the problem," Dora Miller said. She spoke to the local papers about the issue. "New York City doesn't have blackberry patches, and that hasn't lessened their problem," she told reporters. She praised the neighbors' zeal in cleaning up the site of her daughter's attack and said that she hoped they wouldn't find her comments offensive. She explained that the problem wasn't caused by the existence of blackberry bushes but by violence perpetrated by mentally ill people who needed help.

Dora and Greg Miller remained concerned, not just for their daughter, but also for the perpetrator. At the Friday night group, they told us they had learned that Phoebe's attacker knew he was having a serious mental health problem for several days but was unable to find the help he needed. They felt the incident might have been prevented if her assailant had received counseling assistance when he needed it. They decided to start an emergency service to be a resource for people afraid of hurting others or themselves. A few months after Phoebe's brutal attack, Dora and Greg helped to establish the first Crisis Clinic in Seattle. It was one of the earliest crisis centers in the country; it's still going strong, now almost 60 years later.

The way the Millers transformed a devastating family tragedy into emergency support for desperate individuals made a big impression on me.

* * *

That August, as our family continued to support the Miller family, Mom came to the realization that our home was now too crowded.

"Joey barely takes up any space," Naomi argued. "And nothing else has changed." Dad, however, seemed to agree with Mom; we needed a bigger house for eight kids.

A realtor drove my parents around Seattle to look at houses for sale. My younger siblings and I rode along on the house-hunting trips, and I was excited to participate in scouting our potential family homes.

Mia, Charlotte, and I were with Mom and the realtor when they saw Mom's favorite house—an enormous three-story home with a huge yard, just a few blocks from where the Millers lived in the Mt. Baker area. The previous family had already moved out, so the house was empty. It had dark wood floors and high ceilings, a large front yard, and a huge back yard that was big enough for our family games. It even had a staircase that led from the kitchen into the maid's quarters—where my mom could house her frequent homeless guests.

The dining room had floor-to-ceiling windows that looked out onto the backyard. The room was so big that you had to shout from one end of it to the other to be heard. When Mom and the realtor walked on to see other rooms, Mia, Charlotte and I stayed in the dining room. We twirled in circles, and I practiced some ballet moves. "This would be a perfect room for dance concerts," I shouted up the stairs to Mom.

When my father saw the house, he was less enthusiastic. "It's too big and it's $35,000; that's too expensive for us," he insisted. "We can't afford a mansion."

My mother argued. "This is the only house I want. It's the only house I'll live in. It's perfect. I won't look at another house."

"Well, Carla, you'll have to look at other houses," Dad replied.

"I won't. I'll never live in any house besides that one."

Dad held his ground. "Under no condition will we ever buy that house." I had never seen him stand up to Mom with such stubbornness and conviction before.

Mom yelled. Dad stood firm.

Mom cried for days, but eventually she relented. Within two weeks, they found a house in the Madrona neighborhood. It was smaller and less expensive than the Mt. Baker mansion, and even Mom seemed surprisingly cheerful about it. My father was thrilled. "It's $20,000," he announced at dinner. "We can afford it."

The Madrona house was not as large as the mansion, but it still offered more space than our Leschi home. It sat on a hillside at the bottom of a curved street, overlooking Madrona Park and Lake Washington. Like our Leschi house, this new one opened onto woods, but it didn't feel as isolated. There were more houses all around us.

As August crept into September and the start of fifth grade loomed, we packed our belongings, loaded all of our furniture into a moving truck, and left the Leschi house for good. Brian and Rita Dodd had bought our old house from us, and their family moved right in. As they settled into Leschi, we unpacked in the Madrona house. We got a new dog, too: an Irish Setter named Tasha with beautiful, deep red fur and a very friendly disposition. It was fun to play with our new dog, unpack boxes of belongings, and explore a new neighborhood with my brothers and sisters.

"We'll have a good life here," Dad said. "This neighborhood is peaceful."

This photo is of my parents on a hiking trip in the Pacific Northwest before they had children.

Here's my mother in 1945, at age 21 or 22, a year after her marriage to my dad.

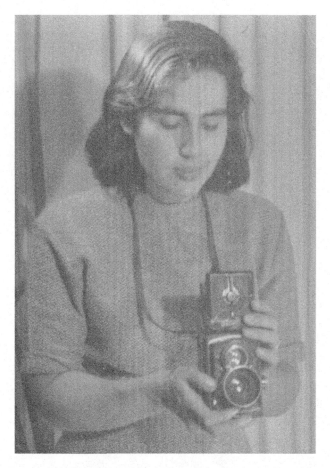

A photo of my mother, with her Rolleiflex camera, in 1951, early in her photography career which she started in 1949.

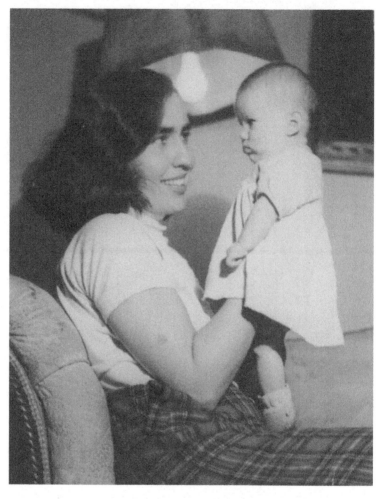

A photo of my mother admiring me when I was a month old in December 1952.

This is our family's holiday card photo from 1953.
I am the youngest of the four children.

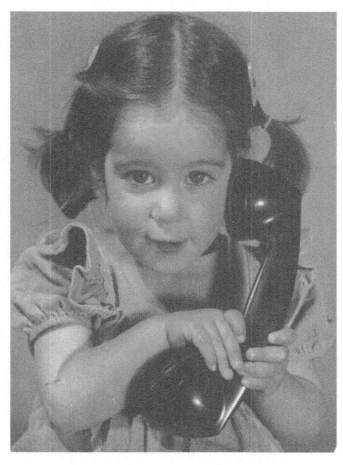

This is a photo of me, taken by my mom, when I was two; it is typical of the kind of photos she often took of other children.

Here I am at four years old, wearing my Davy Crockett hat, on
the steps of our home in Leschi.

This portrait was taken of me by my mother when I was seven years old.

This was my Blue Bird Troop; photo taken by my mom in her studio circa 1959.

This was the photo taken by a photographer we met when we
visited the nudist colony in 1960. I am in front and center
sitting next to my father. My mother loved this photo and had
it framed and displayed in our home.

This photo of my mother and me was taken on the deck of our
Leschi home, circa 1961, when I was nine years old.

This photo of me at ten years old is typical of how my mother often posed me. Many of her pictures of me are more provocative and some might say border on pornographic.

My mother took this photo of Danny and me at Swarthmore College, the day before the three of us attended the March on the Pentagon, in October 1967.

These are five photos my mother took when Danny, my mother, and I marched on the Pentagon on October 21st, 1967. I was fourteen years old. The second photo on this page is almost identical to photographer Marc Riboud's famous photo which became a defining image of the Vietnam antiwar era.

We often took family camping trips. This photo is from La Push Beach on the Washington coast in 1969 when I was sixteen. My mother is holding her Super8 home movie camera.

Here I am on the island of Paros, Greece at age 18.

On the island of Paros, I visited with this charming couple, Kula and Demetrius, who brought me to their home via a donkey. They had lived and farmed on Paros for their entire lives.

After I returned from Greece and Israel, I worked as a
substitute mail carrier for the Bellevue Post Office for two and
a half years.

This photo is of me dancing at an outdoor performance in Seattle at age 21.

We took this photo of the ten of us in front of our Bellevue
home in the early 1970's; my parents and my four youngest
siblings moved to Honolulu in 1974.

I moved to Olympia, Washington to attend The Evergreen
State College in 1974, when I was 21.

A photo Hap took of me at Hood Canal on one of our first
dates, in the fall of 1974.

These two photos with Hap were taken in 1975.

My mother took this photo of Hap and me in her studio in
Honolulu in the early years of our romance.

Wishing You Armfuls of Aloha
for 1985

Hap and I started sending out our own holiday cards in 1983
when we lived in Hawaii. This card is from 1984.

This photo of my parents was taken shortly after they celebrated their 50th wedding anniversary.

My mother always used a Rolleiflex camera, from the time she began her profession in 1949 in Seattle to this photo in Hawaii in the mid 1980's, when she still had her successful career.

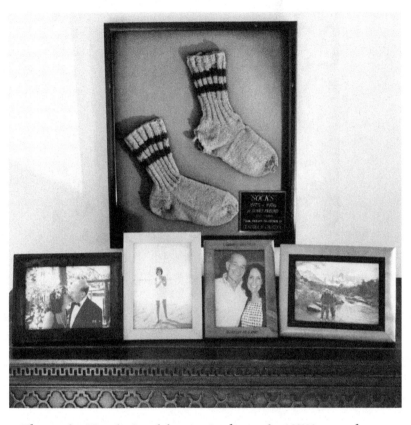

The socks Hap knitted for me in the early 1970's now hang
above a dresser in our bedroom.

This is a photo of us hiking with our dog Felix in the Eastern Sierra mountains on our 42nd wedding anniversary in June of 2021.

Madrona

1963–1969

A new home in a new neighborhood meant a new school. Usually, I approached the start of each school year with a sense of excitement, but that wasn't true for fifth grade; it was trepidation. I wanted to go back to Leschi, where I had friends, familiar teachers, and five years of experience.

I begged Mom to let me return to Leschi—politely at first, and then with desperation.

I cried and pleaded, "Don't make me go to Madrona."

Mom would not be swayed. "Go to your room and don't come out until you are happy about attending Madrona," she ordered.

I lay on my bed, curled up in a ball, crying. Charlotte watched me from the corner of the bedroom I shared with her and Mia.

"I won't go!" I shouted down the hallway. "You can't make me!"

"You can't make her," Charlotte echoed.

Mom burst through the door, whopped me on the butt, and barked, "Enough! Enough complaining! Madrona is your new school!" And that was how that discussion ended.

Things took a turn for the better by the end of the first week of school. My teacher, Mr. James, was very solicitous about making me feel welcome in my new classroom and school, and the adjustment turned out to be less painful than I had expected. On the third day of class, he selected me to lead my peers in the

Pledge of Allegiance. I was honored to stand before the class and recite the Pledge, and I could hear my voice growing stronger and more confident as I proceeded. When I walked back to my seat, some of my classmates smiled at me. For the first time, I thought it might not be so hard to make friends at Madrona after all.

The next afternoon, Mr. James held class elections. When he asked for nominations for Class President, a girl whose name I didn't even know submitted me for consideration. Mr. James instructed us to close our eyes, put our heads down on our desks, and raise our hands to vote. When we raised our heads and opened our eyes, he announced that I was the new fifth grade Class President.

"How was school, Claudia?" My mom asked me that night at the dinner table.

I was reluctant to admit that Madrona Elementary really wasn't so bad. I scowled and said, "I still hate it. I still want to go back to Leschi." Then, as an afterthought, I added, "But today I was elected president of my fifth grade class."

My older siblings were all together at the same new school—Meany Junior High. Naomi and Danny were in ninth grade, Leah in seventh. I was in fifth grade at Madrona Elementary School, where Simon and Mia also now attended.

In addition to adjusting to a new school, I also had new household duties. I was responsible for setting the table before dinner, which was easy, and for washing the kitchen woodwork weekly, which was neither easy nor fun. Mom showed me how to mix "Spic and Span" cleaning powder with hot water in a bucket to scrub dried food from the kitchen cabinets and walls.

Making school lunches was my third new chore. With such a large family, we usually all took lunches with us every day, even my dad.

For years I had watched my mother wrap our rye bread sandwiches in re-used plastic bags still coated with breadcrumbs or bits of old broccoli. When making lunches became my responsibility, I had a wish list ready. I immediately asked Mom for real sandwich bags and white bread—two changes that I thought would make a big difference in lunch quality. Surprisingly, Mom granted my first request, and I was supplied with boxes of small wax sandwich bags.

My other request, for Wonder Bread, which advertised that it helped "build strong bodies in twelve different ways," was firmly rejected. White bread was out of the question. Rye bread was what she and my father had eaten since they were children in Europe, and it remained the only bread that she would allow.

After dinner, while Naomi washed the dishes, I laid out my materials: a tin cookie sheet, a knife, and a loaf-and-a-half of pre-sliced rye bread from Gai's Bakery. I spread the slices out across the pan, with extra ones lapping over onto the Formica table, and, when a sandwich required mayonnaise, spread the mayonnaise onto each slice. There were seven of us who needed to have lunches to take on a daily basis—everyone except Mom, Charlotte, and Joey. Each person had special requests or needs that I needed to cater to. Danny got two sandwiches, except on days when he played football; on those days, he got two-and-a-half. Simon usually needed one-and-a-half sandwiches, but on days when he stayed late for tutoring, he received two full ones. Dad took one-and-a-half every day. Each of the girls always got one sandwich, regardless of our afterschool activities. So, there were nine sandwiches on regular days, nine-and-a-half on days when only Danny or Simon stayed late, and ten sandwiches if Simon stayed after school on the same day that Danny played football.

Calculating the number of bread slices was simple compared to the next challenge-making sure that everyone received the correct ingredients. Dad always wanted at least part of his lunch to be a cheese sandwich. Often, he would want one cheese sandwich and one half-sandwich of something else, but sometimes all one-and-a-half sandwiches in his lunch were cheese. Leah and Simon wouldn't eat cheese sandwiches, so it was my job to find alternatives for them on the days when I made cheese for everyone else. On those days, Simon would get peanut butter and jelly, and Leah—who didn't like that, either—might get tuna fish. Danny couldn't stand tuna fish, so he had peanut butter and jelly on days when the rest of us ate tuna. No one besides Danny and Simon liked peanut butter very much, so on some days I would scour the fridge for leftovers and create a combination of roast beef, chicken, or jelly sandwiches for the rest of the family.

Of course, all of these efforts were ruined if I didn't put the correct sandwich in the right bag. After cutting each sandwich in half, I allocated the halves. If someone was supposed to receive a half sandwich of something, I had to determine who should take the other half of that sandwich. Each night, I spread out six new brown paper bags, along with the wrinkled one that my father brought back home daily. I wrote each person's name on a bag with a bright marking pen, and I always added a little note in Dad's bag, just to remind him that I loved him.

If I messed up and distributed the sandwiches incorrectly, I was sure to hear about it that night. Everyone knew what they were supposed to get, and they would complain if they received the wrong quantity or the wrong ingredients.

When I finished making and wrapping and distributing the sandwiches, I added the milk money. A nickel, wrapped in a napkin, was dropped into each bag except for Dad's. Then came a piece of fruit: apples and bananas were easy, but oranges had to be "scored." (Mom showed me how to do this—slicing just enough into the skin so they could be easily peeled later.)

Though Mom was very health-conscious, she always let me put a Hostess dessert in each bag. Twinkies and Snowballs came in packets of two, so I had to remove them from their packaging in order to ration appropriately. I separated them into individual wax paper bags and added them to our brown bags. Once the sandwiches, milk money, fruit, and desserts were in their proper sacks and the bags were correctly labeled, I had to find room in the refrigerator to house them overnight.

My lunch-making duties included one other important responsibility: inventory. I had to keep track of what I needed for future lunches and tell Mom if we were facing a shortage of brown bags, sandwich bags, peanut butter, cheese, tuna, fruit, jelly, mayonnaise, or Hostess desserts. Failure to maintain an adequate inventory would set off a disastrous domino effect that would make it impossible to correctly complete my task.

Invariably, someone would forget a lunch amidst our daily morning chaos. If Mom had the time, she would drop it off at school. But sometimes she was too busy with her photography clients, getting Charlotte to and from preschool, taking care of Joey, attending political meetings, and exercising to Jack LaLanne on TV. Actually, it was good news for me if Mom didn't have time to drop off a forgotten lunch. That sibling would find a way to eat some of a friend's food; the forgotten lunch could be used again the next day, which meant that I had one fewer lunch to prepare after dinner that night.

There were only two school days each year when I didn't have to make lunches. On the last day of school just before the Thanksgiving and Christmas breaks, Mom would let us buy our lunches in the cafeteria. Madrona served delicacies like creamed chunks of turkey over white rice, sweet, canned peas, and ice cream bars. These days were doubly joyous for me—not only did I get to enjoy a special school lunch, but I was also liberated from my sandwich-making responsibilities. My only job the night before was to make six piles of lunch money— thirty cents apiece—on the counter. Dad bought his lunch on those days, too, but he had his own spending money that he could use.

I also had a new responsibility at school—the student patrol, which meant I had to arrive half-an-hour before school started and don a fluorescent orange vest. I stood on the street corners near school—glinting even in the dreariest weather—

and held my pole with the bright red flag on the end of it, stopping traffic to help other students cross the street safely. At lunchtime, I volunteered in the school lunchroom, where I sat at the milk table and sold individual cartons, five cents each.

After school, Mia and Charlotte and I played in the new green park across the street from our Madrona house. "Go outside," Mom told us, every day after school. "Go be wild. Go get exercise."

We bounded out the door, down the cement stairs, across the street, and onto the grassy park alongside the lake. And we were wild—wild horses, to be exact. Though it was a great dream of all of ours—Mia especially—to own a horse, we preferred to imagine that we were actual horses rather than horse owners. My name was Scarlet Red, Mia was Blackie, and Charlotte was Star. We bucked, neighed, and galloped through the park, racing with abandon and delight until dinner.

When we were inside, Mia and I often played house. I was the husband; she was the wife. As the husband, I arrived home from work and shouted, "Hello, dear, I'm home." Then, in celebration of my return home, I would instruct her to lie down on the floor and I would climb on top of her. I would writhe on top of her—just like my mother did on top of me at night—until I determined that the game was over. Years later, as an adult, I felt terrible that I had played in this way with my younger sister. In therapy, I began to understand that I had been acting out the sexual acts my mother was perpetrating on me, a common way that children deal with childhood sexual abuse.

At night, my two little sisters and I slept in our new bedroom. After years of my isolated closet/bedroom, it was a comfort to share a room with Charlotte and Mia. Our new room was spacious, with eight large windows; it had an expansive view of Madrona Park and Lake Washington. Mia, who was five, slept in a single bed near the windows. My bed was on the other side of the room, against the wall, and Charlotte, who was three, slept beside me on a trundle bed that we stored underneath my bed during the day. Each night when we lifted Charlotte's bed and tightened the lever that held it up, my bed became a cocoon between her bed and the wall. It was one of the few times in my childhood I remember feeling comforted by being "closed in" instead of feeling claustrophobic. As we drifted off to sleep, Charlotte grabbed my hand and held it in her smaller one.

I hoped that sharing a bedroom with my sisters might offer me protection from Mom's intrusive "visits." At first, this seemed to be the case. My mother was so busy settling us into our new home that she was truly exhausted by the day's end— too exhausted for her secretive "cuddling." I felt much safer sleeping in a room with Mia and Charlotte.

But by the fall, her visits had resumed and sometimes I awoke to the weight of her body on top of mine. She was undeterred by the presence of her two youngest daughters.

I was allowed to stay up later than Mia and Charlotte, but I didn't want to. I hurried to finish my homework and chores before they fell asleep, so that I could hear their voices and hold Charlotte's three-year-old hand. "Charlotte, are you awake? Can I hold your hand?" I whispered. There would be a long, silent pause. I held my breath, and then her little hand would reach up and grab mine. "Here I am," she would murmur in her sleepy voice.

Though I pretended that our nightly handholding ritual was for my little sister's benefit, Charlotte seemed to sense the immense comfort she gave me. As I floated into my dreams with my arm stretched towards my littlest sister's trundle bed, her hand wrapped in mine, I felt calm and protected and hopeful that tonight—whatever night it was—we would all be safe.

* * *

As refugees from Nazi Germany, my parents cherished the values that their new country represented—particularly freedom of speech and the freedom to dissent. They took full advantage by joining peace groups, being involved in civil rights activities, attending protests, and writing numerous letters to the editors of both Seattle newspapers.

Our family gathered in our Madrona living room and watched the major events of 1963 unfold on our television. I saw the tragic aftermaths of Medgar Evers' assassination and the Birmingham church bombing by the Ku Klux Klan. I embraced my parents' outrage when the newscasters informed us that Governor George Wallace had defied court orders and refused to integrate the University of Alabama. Though Mississippi and Alabama were far away, the consequences of these events felt personal—these struggles were happening in Seattle, too. According to the news, the fight for civil rights was truly nationwide.

My mother kept books about the civil rights movement on our living room coffee table. The book that intrigued me most was called, <u>The Movement: Documentary of a Struggle for Equality</u>. It was a large book of black and white photographs, and though that was also my mother's profession, these pictures were dramatically different from the portraits she took. I spent many late afternoons plopped on the couch, with this oversized paperback book sprawled across my lap. The pages included text by Lorraine Hansberry—which I read—but I was most fascinated by the images. I pored over pictures of James Baldwin, Martin Luther King, Jr., Dick Gregory, Fannie Lou Hamer, and Malcolm X. These were our household heroes.

But other photographs—ones of people who weren't famous—shocked me the most. The book's cover depicted a white police officer choking a young Black man. And inside, between the pages of great leaders and protests, were terrifying images that have never left me. Two Black men hanging, with ropes around their necks, from the limb of a tree while a crowd of white men and women stood beneath them, some of them pointing and even smiling. And another photo, of a Black man lying dead and burned on top of planks of burning wood, as a different group of white men gawked and—again—smiled.

In October of 1963, shortly after the start of fifth grade, I found a book that Naomi had read for her ninth grade English class. It was called "Black Like Me," a true story by a man named John Howard Griffin. I could hardly breathe as I devoured this incredible account. Mr. Griffin, a white journalist, had darkened his skin so that he could experience the life of a Black man in the American South. As I read about the injustices he suffered and the atrocities he encountered, I felt personally hurt. I could not believe that this country, which had been my parents' refuge from the Nazis, could allow such rampant and violent discrimination.

I decided to make a stand. When I found black and white tennis shoes on sale at Chubby and Tubby's, our neighborhood discount clothing store, I asked Mom to buy me both pairs. Every day, I showed up to Madrona Elementary School sporting one black shoe and one white shoe. "I'm for integration," I explained to my teachers and classmates when they questioned my unorthodox fashion statement.

That same October, Brenda Lewis, our eight-year-old neighbor, called early one morning. The Lewis' daughters, Brenda and Dana, were close in age to Simon and Mia. The four of them had all become good friends and they played together often.

"Is Simon there?" Brenda asked my mother when she answered the phone.

When Simon got on the line, Brenda simply told him, "Come over. Quickly. Before school. I want you to meet our houseguest."

Simon and I usually walked to Madrona Elementary School together, so I joined him to go over to the Lewis'. We met

Brenda and Dana on their front porch; Brenda ushered us inside, while Dana jumped up and down, excitedly.

In their living room a tall, handsome, young Black man, dressed in a nice suit, rose from the couch and bent down to shake our hands.

"This is our friend, Cassius Clay," Brenda beamed. "He's famous."

We all moved outside to sit on the Lewis' front steps. Cassius Clay sat and chatted politely with us. I liked him immediately—he was soft-spoken, gentle, and very friendly. He asked us which subjects we liked in school, and which sports we liked to play. And he told us that he had been an Olympic champion and was now a professional boxer. Brenda nodded proudly.

Finally, Brenda and Dana's mother joined us. "Brenda," she said, "You and Simon and Claudia are going to be late for school. And let's give Mr. Clay some peace and quiet now, shall we?" We shook his hand again. "It was very nice to meet you both," he told us. Then we walked to school, peppering Brenda with questions about Mr. Clay and how long her family had known him. "He's an athlete, but he cares a lot about politics and civil rights," Brenda said.

From that day on, I read the sports pages of the Seattle newspapers in hopes of finding news about Mr. Cassius Clay. I was not disappointed. It was hard for me to believe that the friendly man who had inquired about my favorite school subjects was actually famous for knocking people out in the boxing ring, for taunting his opponents, and for calling himself "The Greatest." According to the newspapers he was a boastful and formidable presence, but I knew that he was also a very polite houseguest.

"He's an American hero," I told Simon, quoting one of the articles I had read. "We got to meet an American hero in the Lewis' living room." A few years later, I realized what a hero he was when he changed his name to Muhammed Ali, took a principled stand against the Vietnam war, refusing to go, serving prison time during the prime years of his athleticism which led to his being stripped of his boxing titles.

At school, Mr. James taught us about other American heroes, ones who were no longer living except in spirit and memory. Inspired by a lesson on Betsy Ross, I wrote a play about the creation of the American flag. I cast four new Madrona friends as Betsy Ross, her helper, her father, and President George Washington; I was the narrator. We painted several flags to illustrate how the flag had evolved through history—from a thirteen-star handwork piece to the modern version. With Mr. James' help, we performed the play twice on November 8th, the day after my eleventh birthday, in honor of Veterans' Day. A reporter from the Seattle Post Intelligencer even attended the performance, and the next day's newspaper featured a photograph of the five of us in costume. The caption explained that we had performed the play "before an amazingly well-behaved, packed auditorium of 400 first, second and third graders and then again for students in grades four through six."

Mom praised me for my performance as the narrator. "You projected your voice beautifully," she said. "Everyone in that big auditorium could hear you. You taught them all something about American history."

On November 22, 1963, I encountered American history of a different sort. President Kennedy was killed. I cried uncontrollably, emerging from my room only to sit with my family and watch the news, which only made me cry harder. Back in our room, Mia and Charlotte watched me, both of them too young to understand the significance of the day's sad events. Charlotte stretched out her little hand to me. "Time to sleep?" she asked.

Amidst my grief over the President's assassination, I went out of my way to save newspaper articles about the event. I kept the Seattle Daily Times' afternoon edition from November 22nd, which blared the headline, "Assassin Killed Kennedy. Johnson Sworn in as President. Governor of Texas Wounded." I kept the next morning's Seattle Post-Intelligencer, which featured a full-page picture of Kennedy above the word "Martyr." I kept articles from the Seattle Shopping News, National Geographic, Life Magazine, and Look Magazine. I even held onto the program from the Memorial Service that our family attended together at Herzl Religious School.

"This is history," I told Mia. She watched me curiously as I piled these articles and clippings in the corner of our bedroom. "It's the worst, saddest kind of history, but it's still important to remember it."

I stowed the newspapers and magazines that I had collected about President Kennedy's assassination in the huge cedar closet in the bedroom Mia, Charlotte and I shared. This closet was so big that it was almost a secret room unto itself: our thrift store dresses hung on wooden rods, and built-in bookshelves and drawers held an array of other clothes, toys, games, and books. The sweet aroma of cedar emanated from the planked walls. It had an overhead light bulb with a chain and a little window that let in natural light. It was a cozy place, and I often went there to hide out, read, or just to have quiet.

Despite my initial resistance to attending Madrona Elementary School, I grew to love it. Mr. James was a very supportive teacher, and I had a new best friend too. Her name was Phyllis, and she was a beautiful Black girl who had a very nice family. When I played at Phyllis' house, her mother greeted us with milk and home-baked cookies. Phyllis only had one sibling—an older brother, who was away serving in the military. She kept a picture of him, wearing his uniform, on her desk, and she had a special collection of dolls and stuffed animals that were always arranged tidily on her bed.

Sometimes, her big brother came home to visit, and I could see why she adored him so much. He was so handsome and mature, and he was very polite at the dinner table.

Phyllis wasn't boring, even though she came from a tidy home and a well-mannered family. We had a great time together in Mr. James' class. We passed notes back and forth all the time, and we even developed a secret code so that the content of our messages would be secure, even if the notes were intercepted or fell into enemy hands.

When we returned to school from Christmas Break, in January of 1964, Phyllis told me that her brother had taken her to a carnival. "I think it's still running," she said.

Naomi had heard about it, too, and we convinced my father to take us to the carnival on Sunday morning. As it turned out, the carnival wasn't nearly as big or eventful as the Seattle World's Fair; mostly it was full of vendors selling items.

"It's all junk," Dad said, shaking his head. I knew that it would be no use to ask him for money, since he wasn't terribly fond of the items being advertised and shouted about.

"I want a sweet," Naomi whispered to me, pointing towards a stand that sold cookies, cakes, and cotton candy. We each had a handful of our own coins. I followed her over to the stand. She bought herself a cotton candy, and I bought two cookies to give to my parents.

When Dad saw us walking back to the bench where he sat with Joey and Charlotte, clutching sweets in our hands, his face turned red and taut, and his eyes bulged.

"What are you doing?" he demanded. "What the hell did you just buy?"

"Mine are for you and Mommy," I explained, holding out the powdered sugar cookies to him.

He glared. "This is a waste," he shouted. "You've wasting money on garbage! We're going home."

He was furious all the way back to the Madrona house, and he avoided Naomi and me for the rest of the day. I cried that afternoon, not because Dad was angry, but because I had apparently handled my money in a childish, irresponsible manner. I was inconsolable—I couldn't even stop when Mia and Simon teased me, or when Naomi told me to grow up.

That night, Dad didn't come into my room to kiss me goodnight, like he usually did. And when I woke up the next morning, he had left for a three-day business trip to Kennewick.

I wrote him a letter.

"Dear Daddy,

I didn't get anything at the carnival except I spent fifty cents of my own money on those white cookies for you and Mommy. Since you think it was wasted, I'm going to save 50 cents out of my milk money to make up for what happened. I wanted to tell you last night (Sunday night), but you didn't even kiss me goodnight. Now I don't even think I should send this letter because it sounds stupid now that I read it over. I just can't express myself in letters I guess. I cry every night you're gone because I'm a baby. That's what everyone says, so I suppose I shouldn't mind being called one by my brothers and sisters.

Love a zillion times (or the highest number there is),

Claudia.

P.S. Love is just a word and NO word can express my feelings for you. No word. Again and more, your crybaby (which is my name to everyone) daughter, Claudia."

I asked Mom for Dad's hotel address in Kennewick, found a stamp in her desk, and mailed the letter.

When Dad returned home that Thursday, he scooped me up in his arms and held me tightly. "I wrote a letter back to you, my little lovely lady," he said. "But I think I probably beat it home. The cookie you bought me was delicious. I ate it on the road, and it was a thoughtful and nice treat."

"It was a waste," I said.

"No," he corrected me. "I was wrong to get so angry. It's not healthy to get angry like that. It just builds and builds, and then I don't behave as I should."

His letter, which arrived the next day, said the same thing. *"Getting mad is just like hating. It feeds on itself,"* he wrote. *"Once I started I got madder and madder and I said things I should not have said. Words which upset you. I don't want you to save your milk money."*

A few weeks later, however, I made another mistake. A horrible one.

One afternoon when I was reading in the cedar closet, I discovered a book of short poems on a shelf. When I read through them, I was particularly taken with a clever four-line rhyme, written by Anonymous.

I often pause and wonder
At fate's peculiar ways
For nearly all our famous men
Were born on holidays

I read it several times, delighting in the whimsy of the rhyme and the hilarity of its subtle joke. I was sure that my teacher, Mr. James, would also find it entertaining so I carefully copied the rhyme onto a piece of scratch paper, making sure that I got it exactly right. The next day, I brought it with me to school.

When I showed the poem to Mr. James, he laughed. "Claudia, this is wonderful! Did you write this?"

Suddenly I was overwhelmed by a burning desire to be the little poem's author. I told him the answer that we both wished were true. "Yes," I confirmed.

Mr. James smiled. "Terrific," he said.

Just before lunch, the principal, Mr. Caldwell, entered the classroom and pulled me aside. "Mr. James showed me your poem," he said. "I think it's very good. One of the cleverest things I've read in a long time. And just in time for Washington's Birthday, too. We're going to print it in the school newsletter that we send out to all the parents and families. We want everyone to see that one of our fifth graders wrote this little gem."

A sick, hot feeling rose inside me. My intention had been just to please my teacher, to satisfy a fleeting desire for his praise and admiration. It had never occurred to me that my lie might linger for more than a moment. I wanted to correct the mistake, but now both my teacher and the principal were beaming at me with such pride. I was terrified to disappoint them.

I spent the rest of the school day worrying about the poem and the newsletter. My mind continually drifted to the little poetry book in the cedar closet—the evidence of my lie. What if someone else found it and read it? As soon as I got home, I bolted upstairs, found the book, and frantically ripped it to shreds. I hid the scraps in a drawer under a pile of books and toys.

Wracked by guilt and worry, I decided to confess to my father. He was wise, and he adored me, and he knew how to handle difficult situations. I sat on my bed, nervously waiting for him to come home from work. When I heard his car on the street in front of our home, I steeled myself and headed downstairs to greet him. I followed him into my parents' bedroom, where he planned to take his customary pre-dinner nap.

"Daddy," I said. "I need to talk to you." He was still wearing his white, long-sleeved shirt from work. I took one big breath, and my story came tumbling out: how I had found the poem, liked it, copied, it, and taken it to school. I explained how badly I had wanted to impress Mr. James, how I had answered his question with a lie, how he thought I had created the poem, and how the principal now planned to print it in the school newsletter under my name.

Within seconds, my father's face twisted into seething rage. His words and hands hit me at the same time. "You plagiarized," he bellowed. I cowered on the bed as he pounded me with his fists, shouting, "You plagiarized! You cheated! You are no daughter of mine! You are not a part of this family! No child of mine cheats and plagiarizes!" Dad's fists collided with my back, my arms, my ribs, then my back again. And then he stopped.

"Are you listening, Claudia?" I nodded between panicked, muffled sobs. "You may stay in the house tonight," he said. "But you will not come home from school tomorrow until you take care of this problem. If you do not fix it, you are not welcome here." This was devastating to me. The father who had been my only safe harbor had now turned on me with his full rage and fury.

I spent the evening in my room, repeating *"plagiarism"* over and over in my head. I had never heard the word before, but now I was sure that I would be labeled with it for the rest of my life. I did not join the family for dinner—I wasn't hungry, and besides, my father had told me that I was no longer a part of the family. I hoped that someone—one of my siblings, maybe, or my mother—would pay me a sympathy visit, but nobody did. I didn't even know if they knew about the serious crime I had committed.

When I rose the next morning, my father was waiting for me. "Hurry up," he grunted. "I'll drive you to school on my way to work."

I sat next to my father in the front seat, clutching my books and my violin. It was the most interminable car ride of my life. I avoided his eyes, but continually glanced over at him to see whether he was preparing to hit me again. I had never been afraid of him before.

Dad stopped the station wagon across the street from Madrona Elementary. Without looking at me, he simply said, "Get out. Don't come home until this is taken care of."

The playground was empty, the principal's office was locked, and even the student crossing guards had not arrived. I sat on a chair in the secretary's office, right outside Mr. Caldwell's door. Miss Beverly, one of the sixth grade teachers, stopped by to pick up her mail. "Claudia, you're trembling. What's wrong, dear?" she asked. "Did you forget to do your homework?"

I shook my head and tried to hold back my tears. If only it was that trivial.

"What's wrong?" she asked again.

"I have to see Mr. Caldwell," I said. I was too ashamed to elaborate.

"I'll sit with you until he arrives," she said. She pulled up another chair and sat beside me, patting my arm. When Mr. Caldwell arrived, she gave me a little squeeze. "Claudia has been waiting to talk with you," she told him.

I followed Mr. Caldwell into his office. The second he shut the door, I blurted out my secret. "I didn't make up that poem that you're going to print in the newsletter. I didn't make it up. I copied it from a book. I didn't mean to plagiarize."

Mr. Caldwell was very calm. He sat down behind his big desk and listened, and his face did not contort into fury. "Well then," he said finally, "we'll get it out of the school newsletter. We've already printed it, but it hasn't been mailed yet. We'll have to take it out and print a new batch."

I kept waiting for my punishment, but it didn't come. He opened his office door and indicated that I could go. "To class?" I asked, unsure of whether I would still be permitted to attend the fifth grade. Mr. Caldwell nodded.

The rest of the school day passed without any further mention of the poem. If Mr. James had been informed of my plagiarism, he kept it to himself.

When I returned home, Mom made no mention of the issue, either. But when Dad arrived from work, the poem was clearly on his mind. He would hardly look at me, even as he ushered me back into his bedroom and asked, "Was it taken care of?"

I told him that it was. And that was it. He had no further questions. The conversation was over. When I came down to dinner that night, nobody mentioned the plagiarism of the cedar closet poem. But I could tell that the whole family knew I had done something unspeakable. It was one of those things we never talked about.

* * *

Earlier that same the school year, our family had experienced another incident involving a lack of truthfulness. Charlotte had started at Madrona Elementary School in September. According to school policy her birthday made her too young to begin kindergarten until the following fall. Mom insisted that Charlotte was ready, and that it would be ridiculous to wait an entire year. "Why should we waste a whole year of her life?" Mom demanded.

"The rules seem really clear," I reminded her, being careful not to argue or contradict her. "Rules are never a valid obstacle, Claudia," Mom informed me. "You should know that." She said she had done the same thing to get Simon into school a year earlier than the school district allowed. So, she adjusted Charlotte's birthday on the registration forms making it seem that Charlotte made the cutoff age for kindergarten.

"Is my birthday still the same as Simon's?" Charlotte wanted to know. (Simon and Charlotte were both born on November 2, but Simon was four years older than Charlotte.) It made Charlotte nervous to think that her birthday might suddenly be changed.

"It's still the same," Dad reassured her. "Just not on the registration forms."

Charlotte's early induction into elementary school meant that the four of us—Simon, Charlotte, Mia, and I—were able to walk to school together in the mornings.

We left Charlotte at the door to her kindergarten classroom, where she looked positively overwhelmed. "There are so many kids in there," she whispered, peering through the door at her thirty little classmates.

Charlotte's school days ended early; she was usually back home by the time my classes ended. When I asked Charlotte how she had enjoyed kindergarten, she said that it was fine. And yet, each morning for the first couple weeks of the school year, she lingered outside the door to her classroom, looking terrified.

We were all very confused when someone from school called to ask my parents why Charlotte hadn't been attending classes. "Is she sick?" the administrator wanted to know.

My parents called Simon and me into their bedroom, looking for an explanation. Stunned, we insisted that we had done our job: we had left her at the door to her classroom each morning.

Only Charlotte knew the answer. After attending a few days of kindergarten, she had decided that she didn't like it. Too many students and too much commotion. She didn't want to go. She had taken matters into her own four-year-old hands. After we left her at the classroom door and hurried off to our own classes, she turned around and marched right off the school grounds.

"Where have you been spending your mornings?" Mom wanted to know. And Charlotte told us that she had gone to the Fire Department station house and kept the firemen company. She had visited the IGA grocery store, where one of the cashiers liked to buy her an ice cream. She had dropped in at the dry cleaners and the bakery and all the other nearby shops. She had even visited neighborhood homes to play with her friends who weren't yet enrolled in school. "Sometimes people would ask me where my mom was, but I would just say she was shopping," she explained, clearly proud of her own ingenuity. Charlotte said she waited until she saw the other kindergarten kids in her class leaving the school, and then she walked home, timing her arrival for when my mother expected her to arrive at home.

My parents were not amused. Dad called her a liar and spanked her hard, and Mom made arrangements for her to attend Epiphany—a nearby private Catholic school. "You can go back to Madrona next year, for first grade," Mom informed her.

From Charlotte's experience, and then mine with the poem, it was clear that lying would not be tolerated in our home. Telling the truth wasn't always easy, but it was important. And we all had a lot to learn from Mom and Dad about how to be honest. But I did wonder why Charlotte and I were both punished for lying but Mom and Dad didn't see anything wrong when they decided not to tell the truth about Simon and Charlotte's birthdates.

* * *

As winter thawed, so did my sense of shame, and my terrible act of plagiarism seemed to fade into a painful memory. Mr. James was as warm and encouraging at the end of the school year as he had been during that first week, and even my father once again seemed to dote on me.

In March, Mom took off for the east coast and left Dad in charge of us—a rare reversal of parental roles. She took Joey, who was two years old, with her to visit Omi and Opi in Buffalo.

Mom continued to run the family from Buffalo, through an ongoing exchange of letters. She scheduled family visits for us with the Millers, and she wrote to my father to instruct him on what time to arrive, what food to bring, and what everyone should wear to dinner at Uncle Norbert and Aunt Bea's apartment on Capitol Hill. (At the very least, she said, Charlotte and Mia should match. If it was possible for all five sisters to match, that would be preferable.) She urged us to go skiing for the weekend and reminded Simon to lend Mia a pair of his warm socks. She also planned ahead for our final ski trip of the season, at Mt. Baker Lodge during our late March vacation, and told my father which days he should plan on taking off work. (*"Remember, you want me to force you into taking more vacations,"* she wrote.) She suggested which Miller children might want to join us on the slopes (Tim and Phoebe, who had made a full recovery), and asked my father to arrange to leave Joey and Charlotte with Greg and Dora for the weekend. She told Danny to help Simon get a haircut and encouraged them to play basketball together, and she thanked Naomi for being in charge of tucking everyone in at night.

"I'm happy in tears thinking about all my lovely people at home. What wonderful people, perched on the hilltop over the big water," she wrote. She called my father "Daddy Boy" and Danny "Danny Boy," and she urged us all to *"Give Leah a kiss on the neckline, if she'll permit it."*

She also sent me my own, private letter.

"Dear Claudie-girl,

I feel I'm letting you down. When you come to cuddle in bed or in the bath, you're looking for a warm flesh to flesh like I give Joey. And I just don't come through. You have a beautiful body, almost a bit sacred to love up like a little girl. I'm unsure of myself in this new relation. You'll need to help me work it out.

I love you.
Mom-Carla."

I saved this letter from March 1964 and found it a few years ago, stored with so many other childhood items I had kept. Re-reading it as an adult, I felt sick to my stomach. And, for a few moments, I also felt confused. Had I initiated or encouraged my mother's aberrant behavior? Had I asked her to routinely molest me? With the help of my therapist, I realized how her letter was another of her ways of manipulating her deviant behavior so she could continue to sexually assault me and justify it in her mind by pretending I had asked for it. She was absolving herself of responsibility for her own actions, blaming me. It was always my mother who came to "cuddle" me when I was in my bed—not the other way around. Children don't ask or want to be abused.

My mother's nighttime molestations continued on a regular basis the entire time we lived in the Madrona house. I felt suffocated by her. I left my body. I stopped moving, stopped existing while she writhed on top of me. I waited for her movements and her sounds to finish, when I knew she would climb off me and leave the room. This was my role, to be the body, the shell, that she demanded of me, to lie on the bed and serve her needs. This was my life. I learned to cope with it by being numb and by compartmentalizing the experience. I had no other options, and eventually I was living outside of my body all the time.

During the day, I worked hard to win my mom's approval, to be a good girl. I was quiet, obedient, and desperate to please her, afraid of her harshness and unpredictable angry outbursts. I craved her love. But when she nuzzled my hair, or caressed my arm, when her fingers stroked the side of my face, or she pretended to "gobble me up," part of me recoiled.

It was during fifth grade that Mom announced that she was going to buy me a new dress. As far as I could remember, those words had never been spoken before in our home. All of our clothes came from second-hand stores or were hand-me-downs from family friends or older siblings.

Mom left Joey and Charlotte at home with Naomi and just the two of us drove into downtown Seattle where we parked in front of "The Merry Go Round on Fifth Avenue," an upscale children's clothing store.

Mom picked out several different dresses for me to try on, while the sales ladies buzzed around us, giving suggestions and bringing more choices to my dressing room. I had never tried on clothes in a dressing room before and never been helped by eager sales ladies. I felt like a princess.

Mom did not let on that Chotzens were unaccustomed to this kind of shopping experience. As a girl, in Germany, she had grown up with stylish clothes, elegant stores, servants, and money. It was hard to tell whether she was drawing from that long-ago experience, but somehow she knew just how to behave. "She'll try that one on next time we come," she said to the sales ladies, dismissing their suggestions and giving the impression that trips to stylish clothing stores were part of our routine.

"You are so beautiful, Claudie Girl," Mom told me, as I modeled each dress for her and the sales ladies. "Your body is so slender and feminine." Was this why I had been chosen to receive a new dress, as a reward for my lithe figure?

Finally, Mom settled on a soft, blue, cotton sleeveless dress with little ruffles, and a matching sleeveless white coat that went with it. Reluctantly, I took it off and changed back into my hand-me-down clothes, so that the saleswomen could fold my new dress and wrap it in tissue paper.

Back at home, Naomi and Leah were livid with jealousy. "How come Claudia gets to go to a fancy store like The Merry Go Round? Naomi demanded, glaring at me. "Why is she the only one who gets a new dress?"

"I thought blue was my color," Leah complained.

"I don't need to explain myself," Mom responded, and swept out of the room.

I looked at my sisters apologetically, and they stared back at me with looks of envy and confusion.

"She loves you best," Naomi said. "It's not fair. I do everything, and I don't get anything. It's rotten." It was true. Mom demanded a lot of adult responsibilities from Naomi—so much of the clean-up, chores, and childcare.

I kept the blue cotton dress in the closet but was afraid to wear it. Sometimes I tried it on when everybody else was busy or outside, but I didn't feel like a princess anymore. I felt guilty, as though I had betrayed my sisters. I had never meant to hurt their feelings. I hadn't asked for the dress in the first place.

Years later, as an adult, I wondered: *Was buying me this fancy new dress somehow connected to her nighttime visits—treating me differently, specially, because she chose me to lie underneath her and serve her insatiable sexual needs?*

My shopping trip to The Merry Go Round and the new dress she bought me was one of the rare occasions when I was with Mom one-to-one outside the home. Often, I had individual time with her in her studio. My siblings and I were our mother's favorite subjects; she photographed us in every possible arrangement: in pairs, trios, large groups, all together, and individually.

Though some of our sittings were clothed, nude portraits were an integral component of Mom's art. Bare chests and bare backs—of babies, children, teenagers, and adults alike—were her hallmark. "The most beautiful pictures show the human body in its natural form," she preached.

On many evenings she beckoned me into her studio. She turned on the hot floodlights and instructed me to remove my clothes. She brushed my hair, gently shaping it around my neck with her fingers, and told me how to pose. "Stand here with your backside facing me. Now, tilt your head and gaze at me over your shoulder."

She juxtaposed my naked body with props and objects, so that the starkness of my nudity would spring to life. She draped a shawl over my shoulders, its fringe tickling my skin as she captured a shot of my back and legs. Or, she placed a tall vase

of flowers and branches she had picked in our yard on the floor
of her studio and had me sit on the floor beside it. "Sit like this,
facing away from the flowers, and wrap your legs back like this,"
she showed me. "Now, turn your head and peek at me over
your shoulder."

On some nights, when the floodlights warmed her studio,
she would urge me to dance for the camera. These sittings when
I got to dance were my favorite because dancing was my special
talent. I knew that my siblings could sit, stand, and pose, and
they were all perfectly capable of wearing shawls, but Mom
promised me that I was the only one who danced for her
photographs.

At her urging, I moved my naked body around the studio—
sometimes to the choreography from my dance classes, and
sometimes in a manner that was completely improvised and
original. She didn't play music, and I didn't need it. Mom
watched looking down into the viewfinder of her Rolleiflex and
up again at me and murmured her approval. "You dance so
beautifully, Claudia," she cooed. "Dance like that some more."

I ignored her camera and focused on my dancing, leaping
myself around the studio as my mother clicked her Rolleiflex
and muttered, "Beautiful," under her breath. She handed me
props to incorporate into my choreography: hats to wear, silky
scarves to wave, feathers to wiggle, and a long strip of bells to
hang in front of my private parts. "Try using this," she'd say.
"But don't stop dancing. You are so lovely." And she snapped
picture after picture after picture.

When I left the studio and returned to the rest of our
Madrona house, I felt as though my skin glowed with the light
of my mother's affection and attention. So many things made
her anxious and frustrated—war, injustice, money—that it
made me happy to feel that I made her happy. Though I knew
that she photographed all of her children, our sessions in the
studio still felt like a secret we had shared: I had danced for an
audience of one, and the crowd had gone wild.

A few months later, as the trees grew bare and frost clung to the needles of the evergreen trees, Mom announced that I needed a new coat. I had outgrown my old one and Naomi and Leah's didn't fit me.

Instead of another mother-daughter shopping trip, Mom handed me her charge cards to three major Seattle department stores: J.C. Penney's, the Bon Marche, and Frederick and Nelson. She handed me a piece of paper, too. It read: *My daughter Claudia is allowed to use this card,"* with her signature at the bottom.

This amount of trust was unprecedented, and the pressure I felt to do it "right" was immense. What if I picked the wrong coat, or spent too much money, or simply couldn't make a decision? I stuffed the plastic charge cards and permission slip deep into the pocket of my old coat.

We set off at the same time. Mom was off to Gai's Bakery to pick up a day-old cake for Joey's second birthday. She took the car, while I crossed the street and walked to the bus stop on Lake Washington Boulevard. The bus picked me up and made its looping, end-of-the-line turn by the lake, before it started back up the hill, through the Central Area, then on to downtown.

The three department stores were located close together. I navigated my way through each of them, comparing prices and jackets. At the Bon Marche, I picked a light brown quilted parka, one of my assigned colors, which was also cheaper than the other options. When I arrived home with my purchase, Mom approved of my choice—and the bargain price ($11)—and I basked in her approval.

Naomi, however, had been surly to me ever since Mom had taken me dress shopping. And now she was rude and snippy. "All of my younger siblings are a big responsibility," she said. "But you are the worst."

On my birthday a few weeks later, Naomi pulled me aside. "This is for you," she said. She gave me a little purse and a doll and long note. "Happy Birthday, Claudie Girl," her note said. It was the same thing that my mother called me.

In the letter, she told me that the doll was supposed to represent my past, and the ways in which I was still a little girl. The purse was for my future, and the "big lady" shoes that I was stepping into. The letter was full of sentiments that felt angry and loving at the same time. *"Over twelve long years you've managed to stand up to anyone for anything. My goodness, but you're simply the most aggressive child I know! I admire and respect you as a person—all 59 pounds of you! You've always been my little birdie. Tiny-winey petitey in stature, yet big on the inside,"* she wrote. Mom called me "her little birdie," so I knew where Naomi had picked it up.

She ended the note with this: *"Wherever you go in the years to come, please remember that your biggestest, tyrantest, swearingest, bossiest, bitchiest, witchiest sister loves every petite little inch of your darling self."* She didn't exactly apologize for being surly, but she let me know that she felt bad. I felt bad, too, that I made her so angry and upset. She seemed to think that Mom gave me more attention than anyone else, but I still felt like I had to compete with Naomi and Danny and Leah and Simon and everyone just to be seen or heard.

* * *

That December, as the ten of us tackled the enormous challenge of packing for our annual ski trip, I put my new parka at the top of my bag. I wondered whether it might give me a whole new outlook on skiing.

In our house, preparing for a ski trip involved even more than the usual quantity of bustle. Mom packed a week's worth of food, while the rest of us helped Dad to load the station wagon with nine pairs of skis (Joey was still too little, but it was time for Charlotte to hit the slopes), ski poles, ski boots, after-ski boots, sleeping bags, parkas, gloves, hats, ski goggles, and our suitcases filled with sweaters, long johns, socks, and flannel pajamas. In later years my father bought a rooftop cargo carrier for the top of the car, but in the early years all of our ski equipment was crammed into the back of the station wagon. As we looked at the car—filled to the brim with our food, gear, and winter clothes, it was hard to imagine how it could fit any passengers, let alone ten of us.

Dad always drove, and Mom always sat in the passenger's seat. Everything else was up for grabs, and so we all rushed to claim our places in the crowded car. The most coveted spot was in the front seat, between my parents. Because I sometimes became carsick, I had an especially persuasive case for sitting up front, but I could only use the carsick excuse so many times. And now that I was bigger, Mom often suggested that she and my father could squeeze both Charlotte and Joey between them. When they sat up front, I squished into the back with the rest of my siblings. The station wagon didn't have seatbelts, but we were packed together so tightly that it was impossible to be dislodged—or to move at all. The worst spot was the far back because no one would feel comfortable wedged against all the skis, ski boots, and ski poles. In later years, when Joey and Charlotte grew too big for both of them to squeeze between my parents, we sat with three people in the front (my parents, plus one of us), three in the middle, and three facing backwards in the third row. Joey, the tenth, lay sideways in the narrow luggage compartment between the middle and third rows. He couldn't see where we were going, but he would pop his head up to ask us about our progress. "Tell me if you see anything good," he'd chirp. Dad would exclaim, "Joey! Choo Choo train!" but by the time Joey pushed himself up to look out, we had passed the train that Dad was pointing out.

That winter my parents rented a cabin at Mt. Hood, in Oregon, instead of our usual trip to Mountaineer's Lodge at Mt. Baker. After driving four hours on a very cold and dark winter evening, we arrived. "We made it!" Simon cheered from the far-back row. Even the long drive couldn't dampen his enthusiasm for a family ski trip. It took the better part of an hour to unload everything from the car, and it was after midnight by the time we all settled into bed. Knowing that my parents would try— as always—to get an early jump on our ski day, I drifted off knowing it would be a short night.

My parents' desire was to be at the slopes shortly after they opened, to allow for the longest ski day possible. That was the goal; in reality, getting ten people dressed to ski, plus their gear and our lunches packed and in the car, meant that we never arrived at the slopes as early as we intended. Still, my parents were determined that one day, we would hustle through the exhaustive morning tasks and be skiing by 9 a.m.

That morning at our Mt. Hood cabin my father awoke to his travel alarm clock and roused the rest of us when it was still pitch-black outside. "Seven o' clock" he announced cheerfully. We launched into our usual ski-morning routine: rising sleepily from bed, bundling up in our numerous layers of ski clothes, eating bowls of oatmeal, packing the cooler with our lunches, claiming our equipment, and piling into the car.

There were blizzard conditions, and so my father put chains on the car while the rest of us finished our morning preparations. We drove for twenty minutes up the snowy, winding road to the Timberline Lodge ski area. Though I was still half-asleep, I noticed that there were no other cars on the road. The parking lot was empty, too. The only people around were employees, clearing away huge snowdrifts with their heavy machinery. And as we approached the lodge, we saw that the ski area wasn't even open.

"What's going on here?" my father demanded. He checked his watch. "It's after nine in the morning. What the hell is this?"

"Maybe your watch is off," my mother suggested.

My father shook his head. "My alarm clock went off, too."

He pulled up next to a man operating a snow blower on the main road and yelled to him over the noise. "Where is everybody?" he asked. The man gave my father an incredulous look. "It's barely 6 a.m., sir. The lift doesn't open for three more hours." "This doesn't make sense," my father grumbled. Beside him, my mother shook her head in confusion. "It's not that hard to figure out," Simon volunteered. "I fooled you. I fooled all of you. I set the clocks forward three hours last night after everybody fell asleep." He laughed and clapped his hands victoriously.

Suddenly, the sleepy car was abuzz with conversation. We all had questions for Simon about his terrific prank.

"So it's not 9 a.m.?" Leah wondered.

"Did you change Dad's wristwatch, too?" Danny asked.

Simon nodded. "I changed the alarm clock and Dad's watch. Naomi helped me plan it."

Simon and Naomi: an unconventional but effective team. Even at nine years old, Simon was our family's resident mischief-maker, while Naomi—sixteen years old and Miss Responsible—was an ideal consultant. They had turned the clocks forward three hours: we woke up at 4 a.m. thinking it was 7 a.m.

"You should thank us," Simon suggested. "We finally figured out how to be on the slopes by 9 a.m."

We laughed, but my father didn't think it was funny. An explosive rage spread over his face as he launched into a storm of German expletives. He turned around in the drivers' seat, reached back, and lunged for Simon.

Acting on impulse, Simon swung open the back car door and took off running at full speed. My father opened his car door, jumped out and chased after him. Simon was swift, and for a moment he seemed to think this was all a game. He grinned as he lingered behind a boulder, waiting to see which side my father would come around. Then, as Dad approached,

Simon dodged him and sprinted around the hood of the car, with my father on his heels.

Simon ran past the car and towards a snowbank and tried to leap over it like a hurdle. It was too tall. He shoved his shoulder against it, but it was too solid to budge. He turned back in the direction of the car, looking for a new escape route, but it was too late. My father caught him a few feet from the snowbank, and the mischievous smile vanished from Simon's face with the impact of my father's right fist. There was nothing playful about the way my father hit him.

We all watched in silence. Simon seemed to crumble under the fury of my father's beating: he sank lower and lower to the snowy ground and curled himself into a ball. My father sank with him, pummeling him with both fists all the while. I was terrified that dad might kill him. I felt powerless to help my little brother.

After several minutes, Dad slowed down, and then he stopped altogether. He stood, stepped away from Simon's trembling frame, and trudged through the snow and back to the car. Simon stood, too, and stumbled slowly after my father, leaving a good fifteen feet between them. He tucked his chin into his chest so that no one could see his face. At the car, my father turned back to my brother. "Get in," he growled. Simon did.

No one spoke as Dad drove the car to the parking area. We filed out, unloaded our equipment, and sat in silence as we waited for the ski lifts to open. We bought our tickets and stapled them to our parkas. Mom bundled two-year-old Joey in an extra coat and left him by the chair lift, with instructions to guard the cooler that held our picnic lunches. The rest of us climbed aboard the lift and spent the day skiing.

I watched Simon carefully, and a few times I caught his eye and gave him a quick smile. I hoped that these glances communicated everything I wanted to say: "That was an excellent prank," and "I'm so sorry Dad beat you," but mostly,

"Are you okay?" I wanted to tell him all these things to his face, but I was terrified that my father might hear me.

Simon skied all day without complaint, but I did see him wince a few times as he transferred his weight or lifted his arm. He was a little less agile and daring than he usually was on his skis, but my parents didn't seem to notice. On the ride home, they praised Mia and Danny as the skiers of the day. We all stole glances at Simon, seated in the far back next to Mia, but nobody asked how he was feeling. The events of that morning became another one of those things we never talked about.

* * *

Our lives revolved around my mother's increasing activism. Mom was still involved with some of her old groups, like the League of Women Voters, the Urban League, Women Strike for Peace, and the National Association for the Advancement of Colored People. But now she spent most of her time devoted to the Seattle branch of a newer organization named The Congress for Racial Equality, or CORE. Her meetings frequently overlapped with dinner, which then fell to Naomi to prepare. If Mom was in a rush when she picked me up from Hebrew School or dance lessons, she might take me with her to a meeting at the YMCA or a local church, and I would skip dinner altogether and wait for her in the lobby or entryway.

Though we waited outside the room when we accompanied Mom to meetings, she proudly included us in rallies, picketing, sit-ins, and demonstrations. For Vietnam War protests, she painted five reader boards with the letters "P," "E," "A," "C," and "E," and instructed five of us to wear them over our clothes, marching in the correct order. At civil rights events, we chanted along with the throngs of other families, and continued to chant as Mom drove us back to Madrona. "What do we want?" I shouted. "Integration!" Simon and Mia responded. "When do we want it?" I yelled. "Now!" They answered. It was electric.

The Congress for Racial Equality had experienced success with their protests against businesses with discriminatory hiring policies, and now they turned their attention to the problem of school segregation. Though the Supreme Court had officially integrated public schools in a 1954 decision, ten years later our schools were still segregated. My brothers, sisters, and I were the rare exception: white kids who attended otherwise mostly all-Black schools. In other parts of town, most students had never even known a Black classmate. My mother showed us the statistics that her fellow CORE members had obtained: 90% of Seattle's Black elementary school children were enrolled in the same ten schools—out of eighty-six schools in the city!

In the spring of 1964, CORE established an Education Committee, and in January of 1965 my mother was named the committee's co-chair, along with Beatrice Hudson, an impassioned Black woman whose family also lived in the Central Area. Together, Mom and Beatrice worked to raise money for "Operation Transfer," a program that would provide bus fare for Black students interested in transferring to predominantly white schools in distant Seattle neighborhoods. Their initial goal was to raise $347: enough money to provide twelve students with a school year's worth of transportation.

"It's a small difference," my mother explained to the Friday Night Group in January, "but it ought to be the start of something."

* * *

Early that summer in 1964, Naomi came to me with a job offer.

"I want to put on puppet shows," she said. This sounded appealing to me: I loved puppet shows, although I was surprised that my fifteen-year-old sister still wanted to play with puppets. But there was more. "You can be my assistant. We can make money."

Naomi had been earning paychecks for years as a babysitter and a lifeguard, but her newest idea would take more creativity and initiative. Her scheme was to perform for a fee at birthday parties.

"Are Danny and Leah going to do this too?" I asked. "Will Simon and Mia also be your assistants?"

"I think it will work best if it's just the two of us," Naomi said.

I was sold.

Our first step was to create the puppets. We sat together on the sun-drenched cement patio outside our kitchen with a bucket of thick, wet Plaster of Paris between us. Carefully, we crafted the lumpy plaster into puppet heads, smoothed it, added bits of plaster to make noses and mouths, and created dents where the puppets' eyes would eventually go.

Next, Naomi opened her special bin that I had admired and envied for years—the two-foot-high, round, gold metal container filled to the brim with her marbles. We selected the perfect marbles to serve as the puppets' eyeballs and inserted them into the eyeholes in the plaster heads. We spread out newspapers across our outdoor picnic table, placed the wet puppet heads on the newspapers, and left them to dry overnight.

We returned the next day, armed with tempera paint. We gave each puppet its own distinct features and colors, specific to the characters in the stories we planned to tell. "We could give the king wrinkles on his forehead, to show that he's older," I suggested. Naomi liked the idea.

We used strips of cloth and yarn to make the hair, and we formed the puppets' bodies out of old socks or colorful old shirts that we cut up and re-sewed. Naomi knew exactly what she wanted, and she was insistent about the look of each puppet, but I didn't mind; I was happy to be her assistant on this ambitious project.

Naomi found a huge, discarded cardboard box, which we transformed into our puppet theater. We folded the two sides of the box so that it could be freestanding, and we cut a half-circle out of the box to make our puppet stage. We painted the cardboard theater with a bright, cheerful design. The box folded up neatly, and we kept our puppets in a large green suitcase; our equipment was completely portable.

I painted a stack of fliers (under Naomi's close supervision), which we taped to the dusty windows of neighborhood grocery stores and dry cleaners and tacked to the bulletin board outside Madrona Elementary School.

We rehearsed together, in preparation for our shows. Naomi was even more explicit about the content of our puppet shows than she was about their aesthetic elements, and she often snapped at me when I said the wrong line or didn't express a character's voice exactly to her liking.

We had several different stories we could perform, depending on the occasion. My favorite was the story of a princess who couldn't stop laughing; she thought that everything was hilarious. Her father, the king, worried that it wasn't healthy for his daughter to laugh constantly; he wished that the princess also had the capacity to shed tears. The frustrated king consulted his wise old advisor, who suggested that he spread the word throughout the kingdom to find a suitor for his daughter who could teach her to cry. The man who succeeded would receive the princess' hand in marriage as a prize. Several suitors appeared at the castle and tried to make the princess cry: they told her sad stories, they tried to hurt her feelings, and one even bit her finger, but the princess just laughed and laughed. As the king despaired, a clever suitor arrived. He removed an onion from his bag, sliced it in front of the princess, held it near her eyes, and—lo and behold—she began to weep. The king was thrilled, and the princess was relieved and delighted, too. She married this final suitor, and everyone lived happily ever after.

When we performed this show, I played the princess and the advisor while Naomi tackled the parts of the king and the many suitors. I got a real kick out of playing the princess—I got to laugh hysterically for most of the story, and then transform my peals of laughter into dramatic sobs at the end.

Most of our initial clients were families that Naomi had previously babysat for. But word spread, and soon parents we had never met wanted us to come and perform puppet shows. Seeing an opportunity for expansion, Naomi decided that we should coordinate entire birthday party events: planning and facilitating party games and party prizes, in addition to our signature puppet show event. Mom drove us to our gigs in the station wagon. We unloaded our cardboard theater, green suitcase of puppets, and boxes filled with balloons, party hats, and party supplies. We entertained the children for two or three hours, then we stepped back and graciously accepted all the mothers' compliments. Naomi saved most of the money and gave me a small fee for my help; mostly, I was thrilled to be a part of her thriving business venture.

* * *

Our puppet enterprise was interrupted in August, when my parents sent me back to Camp Solomon Schechter for a second two weeks of misery.

My older siblings peppered me with wisdom about how to enjoy my session in Coupeville. Danny was concerned with making sure I upheld a vital Camp tradition: midnight raids on the boys' barracks. The boys would, inevitably, retaliate, but if I didn't rally the other girls to make the first attack, we ran the risk of no barracks wars at all. And that was inconceivable. He used his insider knowledge of the boys' sleeping quarters to give me all the advice he could. His loyalty to his sister outranked his loyalty to his gender, he explained.

My mother wasn't so pleased with the letters that Danny wrote to me.

"As far as raiding the boys' barracks, don't take your brother Danny's advice too seriously," she suggested. *"He just thinks it fun to plan such a raid. But the rabbi has to cope with the uproar afterwards. Perhaps Danny will change his mind when he becomes a counselor and has to tame a bunch of unruly campers."*

Naomi sent me a letter describing how Joey had cried for me when she tried to put him to bed. *"It was only then that I realized what a lovely little person you really are,"* she said. *"Sometimes, most of the time it seems, we aren't getting along, but inside I respect and admire you as a person, a sister, and a very special little girl."* It made me miss her and Joey and everybody even harder.

Though my parents and siblings had plenty of opinions about how I should enjoy camp, I was every bit as lonely and homesick as I had been the first time around. I felt like a failure and a disappointment. Chotzens were known at Camp Solomon Schechter for being happy, talented, enthusiastic leaders. For the second summer in a row, I had proved myself an exception to the family tradition.

In retrospect, it may seem surprising that I resisted going away when camp was an obvious temporary escape from my mother's nighttime visits. I didn't have the understanding or the words to question what my mother was doing, nor the language to call it what it was—sexual abuse. My mother wrapped her molestations with the phrase every child craves, the whispered words, "I love you so much." And my father reinforced that message by telling us that we had the best mother in the world. These two adults created my reality, ruled my world. How could a child know anything different?

On the bus back to Seattle, I flipped through the Camp Solomon Schechter memory book, which featured photographs and highlights from our two-week session. There were hardly any mentions of my name. I stuffed it into the bottom of my bag.

Mom and my youngest siblings picked me up at the Herzl parking lot, just as they had the previous year. I rode home in the front seat, with Joey on my lap. "I don't need to sit here," he said in his know-it-all toddler voice.

"Yes, you do," I told him, as I wrapped my arms tightly around him. I was immensely relieved and happy to be with my adorable little brother and home again.

When we got home, I ran straight to my bedroom, where I was greeted by a nasty surprise. The walls next to my bed were dirty and disgusting looking. On closer inspection I saw they were covered in dried snot and smeared boogers; my sheets and pillowcase were similarly coated. My stomach turned, and I felt an urge to puke.

Mia had followed me into the room, and she watched from the doorway as I surveyed my bed and battled nausea.

"Gross, huh?" she asked.

"Repulsive," I answered. "Who did this? Whose snot is that?"

"When you were at camp, Mom met a stranger from Yakima," Mia explained. "She had her two granddaughters with her, too. They needed somewhere to stay, so Mom put the girls in your bed and Charlotte's bed. Charlotte slept in Naomi's room. I guess that's probably their snot. There was always more of it in the mornings after I woke up."

I raced outside and found my mother, who was chatting with a group of neighbors. "Mom, you've got to see this," I insisted, grabbing her hand and leading her into the house, upstairs, and through my doorway.

She gave the snot-covered walls and my bed a cursory glance. "Claudia," she said impatiently. "It's your room. It's your bed. You take care of it. What do you expect me to do?"

I got an old rag and some warm water and a dinner table knife and began to scrape, pick, and wipe the sticky, dried snot off my walls. I peeled it off, piece-by-piece, top to bottom. Then I gingerly removed my sheets and pillowcase, put them in the wash, and found clean linens for my bed.

That night, I lay awake in the bedroom that I had been so anxious to return to. Despite hours of cleaning, I still felt enveloped by the dried boogers of strangers, as though they had seeped into the walls and mattress and pillow and were therefore indelible. My skin crawled as I squinted through the dark and wondered whether my scrubbing and scraping had had any real effect—would I awake in the morning and find the wall caked in snot again? A heavy weight of hopelessness descended over me; a grayness inside of me that matched the overcast skies I lived under. The sense that I would be trapped forever and that my mother's visits would never be over.

From the other side of the room, Mia's sleepy voice called out to me. "Claudia?" she whispered.

"Yeah?" I murmured back.

"Are you asleep?" Mia wanted to know.

"If I was asleep how could we be talking?" I asked.

There was a long pause, while Mia contemplated. "I guess you're awake," she said finally.

"I'm glad you came back," Mia whispered into the stillness. "Our family should stay together forever."

I told her that I felt the very same way.

* * *

Soon after Camp Solomon Schechter, we went east of the mountains to Family Camp; it was such a relief to experience the version of camp that I knew and loved, back on familiar turf and surrounded by family and old friends. I was grateful for the familiar games like Capture the Flag, the familiar songs, and for my favorite Dad campfire stories. Family Camp felt like an oasis.

Mom had learned to enjoy Family Camp, too, in her own way. She took advantage of the abundance of family friends and used the week as an opportunity to rest from the usual strains of parenting eight children. At Family Camp, childcare duties were blithely distributed amongst anyone willing to lend a hand.

I remember a soldier, wearing his military uniform, who appeared at Family Camp one afternoon that summer. Nobody knew him—he said he was just passing through—but he sat at the picnic tables and ate lunch with us. He seemed to take a special shine to Mia, whom he nicknamed "Smiley." After lunch, the family dispersed: Simon ran off to play with Danny and the older boys, Naomi put Charlotte down for a nap, and Leah wandered away with a few of the girls her age. Mia wanted to go play on the beach, and so Mom asked the soldier to take her. I watched them wander off together.

"Where is Mia?" my father asked, about an hour later.

"I sent her off with the military man," Mom explained.

When Mia returned with him in the late afternoon, her eyes were red and puffy. The military man coaxed her, "Smile for me one last time, Smiley," but Mia wouldn't look at him. He hopped in his car and drove off, never to be seen again. We were accustomed to these impromptu, one-time "babysitters."

Years later, when we were adults with children of our own, Mia described to me in horrific detail how the soldier had molested her. I still weep as I write these words today: My beautiful, innocent five-year old sister, another victim of my parents' neglect and abuse, and their almost total abdication of their responsibility to keep their children safe. I would do anything on earth to be able to go back in time and protect my precious little sister; to be able to rescue, defend, and safeguard all my beloved brothers and sisters.

* * *

My sixth grade teacher was Miss Beverley, the same woman who had comforted me outside of Mr. Caldwell's office the previous spring. I was glad to have her as my teacher, although I was concerned that she might suspect me of plagiarism from the outset of the school year.

After a year of experience as a Madrona Elementary Milk Box Distributor, I was promoted to Cafeteria Helper. I was excused from class early every day before lunch. I reported to the cafeteria, put my hair up in a net (just like the paid lunch ladies did), and stood with them behind the serving counter. As students filed by, I helped to ladle lunch onto their plates. The ladies were friendly and appreciative of my help. I enjoyed hearing about their lives: they all had husbands and children who were, from the sound of it, very aggravating. Best of all, I got to eat a free cafeteria lunch every day: hot, delicious school food ladled onto divided plates. It was heaven. There was meat loaf, fried chicken, creamed turkey, mashed potatoes, and carrots, sweet peas, and corn that came from the huge cans that were kept in the kitchen. On Fridays, we served fried fish.

At home, my chores remained the same: setting the table, washing the woodwork, and making lunches. But now, when I made lunches, I only prepared seven paper bags; I skipped myself. While my siblings endured rye bread, I ate delicious, canned meats and vegetables heated on the enormous cafeteria stove.

On the weekends, I sought out one-on-one time with my father by helping him with his own household tasks. My favorite chore was polishing shoes with him. First, he collected all the leather shoes from everyone's bedroom. He hauled a large wicker laundry basket, overflowing with shoes, down to the basement. I helped him to line up the shoes—fifteen or twenty pairs, ranging from Joey's tiny loafers to Danny's and Dad's bigger shoes—in a long row on the basement's wooden countertop. Once the shoes were in formation, Dad set out his supplies: shoeshine cloths, brushes, and several tins of Kiwi shoe polish in black, brown, and neutral shades. We always began by polishing the black leather shoes Dad wore to work, then we moved on to the other shoes.

I twisted open the small metal brackets to pop the lid off the tin of black paste. I breathed in deeply, savoring the intoxicating aroma of the rich, dark paste. Dad rubbed the thick paste into the grains of leather for several minutes, then he whipped a rag and a brush back and forth across the tops of the and sides of his large shoes. I worked beside him on my siblings' smaller shoes, applying polish and trying to imitate his motions with the rag and brush.

"Do you see the sheen?" He asked me, pointing to the shoe he was polishing. I would nod and try to emulate the shiny gloss he achieved so expertly. Dad was quiet and purposeful while he polished; though we didn't chat much, I knew that he enjoyed my company.

I also liked to help Dad wash the windows. He added ammonia into a bucket of water. Then he dipped crumpled newspaper into the pungent liquid and wiped the glass with the paper, moving from window to window throughout our big Madrona house. While Dad worked on the outsides of the windows, I cleaned the insides. As he peered in at me from outside, he pointed his long fingers and directed me to smudges I had missed on my side of the glass. I cleaned those spots again, until he gave me a smile and the thumbs-up sign. Then, I was able to move on to the next window.

"Very good, Claudie Weibly," he said. "Very nice cleaning." But once, after we had finished, I saw him re-scrubbing the insides of the windows. From then on, I tried to elevate my own window cleaning to an even higher standard.

* * *

On March 3rd, Miss Beverly's class took a field trip to the state capitol in Olympia. "If you see any congressmen, tell them Seattle CORE needs to set up a meeting," Mom instructed.

"Tell them I want a pony," Mia added.

There were several other schools visiting the Washington State capitol that day, and we were one of the last groups to arrive. We filed into the State Reception Room and lined up in the back, behind more than a hundred other students and teachers. I peeked between the torsos of two tall boys in front of me, but all I could see were more bodies.

But then, one of the guides announced, "Please move back and let the littler ones through," she yelled out. "Smaller students to the front, so that everyone gets to see."

"Make room for Claudia," Phyllis called out, nudging me forward. The crowd in front of me parted and I squeezed through. Suddenly, I had a front-row view of the entire room: the massive walnut table, the impressive chandeliers, and the vast marble walls.

The guide led us out of the State Reception Room, and down a corridor. We passed the committee rooms in the Senate Gallery, lined with legislative photographs that dated all the way back to 1889. I stayed at the front of the group the whole time, which meant that I was among the first students to see everything. When we passed anything particularly exciting, I looked a few rows behind and gestured to Phyllis so that she wouldn't miss it.

Sam Smith, Seattle's Central Area State Representative in the Washington Legislature, stopped by to explain how bills were passed. "How many of you are from the Central Area?" he asked. My classmates and I proudly raised our hands.

Our whole class got our picture taken with Senator Fred Dore, who also represented the Central Area. I got to be in the front row of that photograph, too.

"You are the voters of tomorrow," Senator Dore told us encouragingly.

"We already vote for class president and secretary," Phyllis explained to him.

Back at home that evening, I sat down to write my required report on the day's exciting field trip. I thought back on the all the first-rate views that I had been privy too, thanks to the guide's insistence that smaller students should move to the front. I titled my report, "It's Good To Be Small (Sometimes)."

A few days later, on March 7th, 1965, Alabama state troopers responded to silent marchers with horrific violence. The newspapers called the event "Bloody Sunday," and five days later we gathered with two thousand other Seattle residents at the federal courthouse downtown, where we held a silent vigil. I was used to yelling and chanting at big civil rights events, but this time our mission was to be silent and respectful.

"What do we want?" Simon whispered. Though he was nine and I was twelve, he was already an inch taller than me, and he had to stoop slightly to be sure that no one else would hear him.

"Integration," I whispered back.

"When do we want it?" He breathed.

Charlotte tugged at each of our pant legs with one hand. "We want it later," she whispered. "Right now, we want to be quiet like everybody else."

* * *

When we weren't helping Mom save the nation, we were helping her save money. Despite the size of our family, I knew that my parents' financial situation couldn't be totally dire: Dad made a good living, and Mom contributed with her successful photography business. Besides, few of my friends' families could afford ski trips, summer camp, and private violin lessons. Still, money seemed to be constantly on my parents' minds.

Often, when I asked Dad how he was doing, he would respond, "I'm worried about money."

"We don't have enough, Carla," he'd sometimes say to my mother over dinner. "We don't have enough." This caused me to worry; I didn't want to create financial stress or be a burden to my father. Consequently, I was conscious and careful to not eat too much, and I never requested money for activities like movies or shopping.

Mom didn't make overt pessimistic statements about our family's financial situation, but her resourceful frugality spoke volumes. Under her watchful eye, we learned to re-use almost every bit of household trash. We drew pictures on the blank side of used order forms; we copied down phone messages and her customers' photo orders on the backs of used envelopes. When we ate outside, we drank from repurposed empty cardboard orange juice containers as cups.

Being wasteful was a cardinal sin to Mom. If she found a discarded chair on the street in front of a neighbor's house, waiting to be collected by the garbage truck, she'd snatch it up and add it to our living room. Once she caught me dropping an old toothbrush into the wastebasket. "Don't you dare throw that away," she chastised me. "We can use it to scrub the woodwork."

The first question from my mother about any purchase was always, "How much did it cost?" I never knew the reasons why my mother was concerned about money—was it from having so many children? Was it from going through World War II and having her parents' livelihood and security snatched away from them overnight? Her family had lived in an elegant house in Weimar, Germany when my mother was growing up. They had a cook, a driver, and household servants. They escaped with their lives, but with little on the material level.

Convinced that our local grocery stores had a habit of discarding perfectly good food on a daily basis, Mom set out to change their policy. She introduced herself to the managers of the grocery stores in the Central Area and informed them that she considered the waste their stores produced to be "criminal."

I stood next to her and watched, uncomfortable, as she reprimanded these managers passionately. She appealed to them to save their bruised and spoiled foods, instead of tossing them away. The Safeway manager, swayed by her dynamic arguments, agreed to leave discarded food in a box beside the dumpster.

Soon, my mother persuaded other grocery stores to follow suit. But discarding the food into separate boxes was not the end goal—someone had to do something with it.

Simon and I became my mother's Salvage Brigade. We accompanied her to the backs of the grocery stores and helped her to collect the unwanted food. We loaded the cardboard boxes that contained bruised bananas, apples, squashes, and eggplants into the trunk of our station wagon. Mom didn't trust the supermarkets to comply fully with her demands, and so— once we had collected the boxes of old produce—she sent Simon into the dumpster to scavenge for more perfectly good food: expired jars of mayonnaise, dented cans of beans and corn, and bruised fruits and vegetables.

I helped push Simon's legs over the edge of the dumpster as he scrambled up the side and dropped down into the smelly abyss. Once, he got stuck in the deep piles of garbage and couldn't pull himself out. Mom marched inside and returned with two Safeway employees. "My boy is stuck in your dumpster," she said, without a hint of embarrassment, as though it was a result of their poor service. "Help him out now."

A few weeks later, as Simon struggled to eject himself from the dumpster behind the IGA, he saw three of his friends approach on bikes. "This is humiliating," he said. "Claudia, don't you dare tell them I'm in here." He cowered in the bottom of the dumpster and waited until his friends left.

"You're being ridiculous," Mom admonished us. "There is nothing shameful about rescuing perfectly useable food."

We didn't just rescue this food—we ate it. "I can't believe someone threw this away," Mom marveled as she sliced the mold off of carrots and carved out the slimy sections of salvaged zucchinis. She tossed the edible scraps into a pot or pan and mixed it into a stew. "In America, they throw away perfectly fine food," she scoffed, proud of her resourcefulness and her culinary creativity. Though the stews tasted good, I could never shake the feeling that I was eating somebody else's garbage.

Mom also had a finely tuned antenna for bargains. She rarely paid full price for anything. And she wasn't shy about asking others what they paid, either. She frequented the neighborhood's secondhand stores, pounced on grocery store specials, and organized her schedule around end-of-the-month sales at Seattle's major department stores.

Month-end sales were the only occasions when Mom seemed capable of being punctual. "No time to finish your breakfast, we've got to get to the month-end before the stores open," she instructed, grabbing the children closest to the door and propelling them to the car.

She was not the only one who anticipated these monthly events. Hordes of people crowded into the entry area of the Bon Marche, pressed up against each other. When the doors were unlocked, we swarmed in. Mom grew physically excited at month-ends. She found the race for bargains to be exhilarating. When I came along, I tried to imitate Mom's style. I ran my hands quickly through the clothing racks, pulled garments from under piles, checked price tags, and showed her the good items. If I found a bargain, she smiled and praised me.

When Mom found something she liked, she maximized her discovery, often returning home with at least a half-dozen versions of the same sweater or pants, in every color available. Month-ends sales were one of the few times that she was willing to buy new garments rather than hand-me-down or thrift store items. She distributed them to us (according to size and assigned color) and gave extras to our friends who visited the house.

My father, Danny, Simon, Greg Miller, Brian Dodd, Nick Farley, Waldo, and Zeo all received the same wool cable knit sweater one winter, as did all the men who visited the house to do repairs that winter, and the mailman. Mom was as generous as she was thrifty, always thinking broadly and inclusively about who might benefit from a particular deal or sale. It didn't need to be a holiday for her to buy these clothes to give to people. When she gave away this clothing to friends and even the mailman, once again everybody considered her to be very generous and thoughtful.

One spring day in 1965, Mia and I were in the checkout line of the Madison Park IGA grocery store with Mom. As the clerk rang up our ten containers of Neapolitan ice cream—and nothing else—the manager marched over to us and interrupted the transaction.

"Mrs. Chotzen how dare you!" he hissed. "You only come to our store to shop the sales!" Other customers turned to watch the confrontation, but my mother didn't respond. She handed me one bag, gave the second bag to Mia, then turned on her heel and walked out of the store.

She didn't say a word until we were all in the car. "Why would anyone shop for an item that wasn't on sale?" she asked. I remember this encounter as one of the first times I had a glimmer of realization that not everybody thought my mother's ways were admirable.

If bargain buys and scavenging were two pillars of my mother's thrift empire, bartering was the third. Though her photography work did generate an income, it was also profitable as a swappable asset. Mom never paid for a service without attempting to trade for it first. She was an accomplished photographer and a formidable bargainer, so her efforts were often successful.

Our music teachers, carpenters, physical therapists, and doctors were selected on the basis of their willingness to trade services. Some of them were quite skilled and likable. Dr. Seward, our dentist, was not. For starters, I didn't understand how we could trust a dentist who had bad teeth; Dr. Seward's teeth were brown and cracked, and Leah and I wondered whether they were rotting. His office sat in the midst of a dilapidated Seattle neighborhood, and beige paint peeled from the dingy office walls. The dental equipment in his office was old, often broken, and covered in a thick layer of dust.

Every time Leah and I visited Dr. Seward, he discovered more cavities in our mouths—even when we had carefully followed his instructions about brushing. Twice a year, just like clockwork, he drilled holes in our mouths and filled them up with silver. We had more fillings than any of our friends, much to my mother's disappointment. "It's a good thing we have a dentist willing to work for photographs," she said. "Or all that silver would cost us a fortune."

Mom found a local orthodontist with a large family and took enough pictures to earn us several years of orthodontic credit. Her trades with the orthodontist covered the expense for braces for Danny, Naomi, and Leah. In sixth grade, when my time came, I took the bus from school to his downtown office, getting braces on my top teeth. "The bottoms aren't quite ready," he explained. "We'll do those in a few months."

A few months later, though, Mom's photography credit had been exhausted. She offered to take new portraits for the orthodontist's family, but he was no longer interested. "My kids aren't that cute anymore," he said. "And some of them are away at college." He removed my braces and, pointing to my mouth, informed Mom, "If you ever want to pay money, we can finish the job."

"I don't think so," Mom said.

* * *

Mia loved animals. My mother, always happy to add a little extra activity to our household, indulged her passion. In addition to Tasha, our family dog, Mia had a bird, a fish, two guinea pigs, and an orange kitten she named Rascal. True to her seven-year-old promises, Mia tended to all of her pets. She fed them, played with them, cleaned their cages, and even nursed them back to health when they were hurt or ailing. Rascal was the first kitten to ever grow into a cat in our household; all of the other kittens had run away, but Mia made sure that Rascal was content and cared for properly. She even fed him milk out of Joey's old baby bottle. Joey thought this was hilarious. "The kitty cat is the youngest Joey," he shouted gleefully.

In June of 1965, just after I had finished sixth grade, Mia, and Phoebe Miller and I went off to a new sleep-away camp. This was far preferable to Camp Solomon Schechter—it had horses. Mia and Phoebe were both horse fanatics. Mom traded pictures so that the three of us could attend. We had a great time at Flying Horseshoe Ranch. We rode horses until dark, then spent most of the evening lovingly brushing them. I had to physically pull Mia away from the stables to get her to go to dinner, bed, or any non-horse-related activity.

On the last day of camp, Mom brought Naomi, Simon, Charlotte, and Joey with her to pick us up. Naomi helped Mom snap photographs of the campers and horses for the camp owners to use in their brochures and advertising. Simon and Charlotte got to take turns riding a horse around the property, and even Joey—clad in an adorable red cowboy hat and a tiny pair of cowboy boots—got to sit on the horse's back and squeal with delight. At the end of the afternoon, we piled into the car and drove home.

As I hauled my duffle bag upstairs to my room, I glanced out the window and saw a shirtless stranger in our yard. He had brown skin—he was either Native American or Mexican, I thought—and a heavy mane of black hair cascaded down his back.

"How do you like him?" Mom beamed. She was right behind me, lugging Mia's bag. "His name is Ray. He's building us a patio." She glanced at her watch and dropped Mia's bag on the top of the landing. "I think I'd better go fix him a snack," she said eagerly, bounding back down the stairs and toward the kitchen.

Mom loved having Ray around; he spent the entire summer at our house. "He's an artisan," she told my father, who nodded in quiet agreement. "We've hired a real artisan."

Ray hand-painted dozens of plain red bricks with yellow, green, blue, and orange glazes. He fired the bricks in a kiln, and then he arranged them, creating a large patio with the image of a huge, orange sun in the center—a striking design.

At first, he worked shirtless and barefoot; his skin looked like tanned leather and his chiseled arms gleamed in the summer sunshine. As the summer progressed, and the weather grew warmer, Ray removed his shorts and worked naked. My mother, ecstatic, mirrored his nudity.

I stole glances from my upstairs bedroom window, peering over the top of the books I was reading, as Mom and Ray covered the emerging patio with articles of their discarded clothing. My mother offered him canned lemonade, sliced apples and oranges, and prepared sandwiches for him. She giggled and fawned over his work, and she took dozens of pictures of Ray in her studio—his long hair draped over his bare back.

I rarely spoke to Ray all summer—partly because I was mortified and partly because my mother was so protective of their time together. "Not now, I'm working," she would say when Charlotte or Joey approached the patio to inquire about lunch. She gestured to her Rolleiflex camera, perched atop her discarded underwear.

Later that summer, I went away to my third and final unsuccessful attempt to make friends with Camp Solomon Schechter. When I returned, Ray and Mom were just as I had left them—naked and flirting—although significant progress had been made on the patio.

I was twelve, soon to enter junior high; my mother's pervasive nudity and flagrant flirtation made me very uncomfortable. My view of the world was finally expanding beyond the narrow frame of our own household. The families in the books I read and the families of friends I visited never came remotely close to resembling mine. And in none of them were their mothers naked—never! Not even once.

In addition, I felt like my father was being humiliated. He arrived home from work at least once a week to the sight of my mother and Ray sitting naked, side-by-side in the early evening sunlight, laughing.

Dad was much more modest than my mother; he would never have wandered the house nude, but he admired my mother's uninhibited spirit. He generally viewed her nudity and flirtations as prime examples of her best qualities. "Carla is a real bohemian," he proudly declared more than once to the rest of the Friday Night Group.

As far as I could tell, Ray's presence failed to raise my father's blood pressure. Ray often joined us for dinner, sometimes still naked, and grinning at my mother. My father smiled and grinned right along with them.

One night in August, Dad arrived home and found a vase filled with flowers on the dining room table. "Ray bought them for me," Mom announced, throwing her arms around Dad. "Aren't they beautiful?" My father emphatically agreed. But to me, it sounded as though she was saying, "Isn't Ray beautiful?"

When Ray finished the patio, my mother suggested, "We should find more reasons to have an artisan around." My father pointed out how expensive the patio had been—a rare lapse in my mother's relentless thriftiness—and commented that additional yard work might not be practical for the time being.

* * *

It wasn't just my mother's inability to keep her clothes on that now made me self-conscious. Her cost-saving techniques that dictated how I dressed also were a huge concern.

Less than a month after the start of junior high school, I arrived home to find Mom proudly hovering over a large box of used bowling shoes. "They were a great bargain," she exclaimed gleefully. They were also bowling shoes.

There were various sizes—including pairs that were the right sizes for Simon, Mia, and Charlotte. And, unfortunately, for me. The shoes were red and white leather, with the size numbers in bold black ink on the back of each heel.

"You'll wear them to school," Mom declared.

"I won't," I said.

"They're perfectly good shoes," she said. "You'll wear them, just like your brothers and sisters."

"They're ugly, Mom. They're hideous. And they have a huge number 5 on the back. Everyone will laugh at me."

"Nonsense," she said.

"Please don't make me wear them," I begged.

"Not another word of this! You're lucky to have shoes. You'll wear them, and you won't complain again!"

Trudging down the hallways of Meany Junior High in my ugly bowling shoes, I was aware of kids laughing behind my back. I was convinced that I would never make friends. The timing was awful: I was at a new school, with new classes, new teachers, and—most importantly—new classmates. In addition, for the first time in my life, I was attending school with other white kids.

Meany drew from a broad range of elementary schools, including those in the whiter Capitol Hill and Montlake neighborhoods. Additionally, some of the white students had been bussed in from other districts as part of Seattle's school integration plan.

I was accustomed to looking different than my Black friends, who had marveled over my white-girl hair. Now, it turned out, my wavy hair was not as fashionable as the long, straight locks of my new white classmates. They used Goody rollers at night and cropped their bangs. They wore Maybelline makeup and shaved their legs. I wanted to fit in and to look like them.

The bowling shoes were the first of many arguments that I lost with my mom that fall. A fight over my hair came next. My request for hair rollers was firmly denied, although I was permitted to tie ribbons over the rubber bands of my pigtails. Makeup was the next losing battle, followed by leg shaving—both practices had always been forbidden in our household, and my desperate efforts at reform were met with rejection. "In Germany, we didn't shave our bodies—not our legs and not under our arms—and we won't do it here in America, either. It's always better to be natural," my mother preached.

My mom's definition of "natural" felt embarrassingly unnatural within the walls of Meany Junior High School. I needed straight hair, makeup, and smooth legs, not to mention coordinated sweater sets, kilted plaid wool skirts with oversized safety pins, immaculate white blouses, colored knee socks, and brown and white saddle shoes.

My request for new clothes was refused as emphatically as my other pleas for fashion support. "You have too many clothes as it is," Mom said.

She was right. The cedar closet was crammed with hand-me-down clothes in colors of rust-orange, brown, and green. I had more dresses, skirts, and blouses than I knew what to do with—but not one of them came close to being stylish or fashionable. Curious about how many days I could wear a different outfit to school, I decided to wear a different dress or skirt to school every day. The other girls might make fun of my fashion, but I could at least deny them the privilege of mocking the same outfit twice. I managed to do this for two months. I hoped that this experiment would help me to determine my favorite items from my vast wardrobe, but I faced the unfortunate truth: I had worn everything, and I had no favorites.

In spite of all this, I made friends. I still had my longtime friends from Madrona Elementary School, and I made friends with many of our new classmates. No one would have guessed that all of us were twelve. I was still very small and could have been mistaken for nine; a few of them looked sixteen. Six or seven of us became good friends, we spent many nights and weekends at each other's homes. Two of those girls I met in the early days of seventh grade at Meany Junior High school are still my lifelong friends: Lila and Vanessa. Lila was an artist and a kind, bright and thoughtful seventh grader; she lived in the Madrona neighborhood, not far from our house. Vanessa was enthusiastic, already very interested in boys, and interested in world politics, too.

Both Lila and Vanessa liked to visit my home. "There are always so many fun things going on here," Lila said. "It's busy and safe and I never have to take care of anybody." She was the oldest of four kids and she shouldered a lot of the family responsibility in her home, much like Naomi did in ours, so it was always a relief for her to get away for the evening.

Looking back at Lila's memories of being in my home now that we are both adults with children and grandchildren, her comment that my home was "safe" feels especially ironic. And sad. We were both twelve/thirteen years old. My mother was still coming to my bed to molest me at night. But this was something I never talked about; I lived with it as if it was just a normal part of childhood. It was certainly a *routine* part of my childhood, but never *normal*. Years later when we were adults, Lila revealed that her father was an alcoholic who was physically and emotionally abusive to her mother and to her and her three siblings during her entire childhood. I don't remember being aware of any of this when I spent time at her house. I just remember that her family ordered pizza for dinner, a huge treat because in our house we never ordered pizza. As adults, Lila told me that along with being like a second mother to her younger siblings, she tried to shield them from her father's violence. But she felt powerless to do so. Just the way I yearned to protect my younger siblings from my mother's emotional and sexual abuse, somehow believing that if she came to my bed, she wouldn't visit theirs. It astounded me that even though Lila and I were best friends through junior high and high school, we never talked about our dark family secrets.

Vanessa loved visiting my house, too. "You have so many beautiful things," she said. "Old-fashioned furniture and oriental rugs, and so many books. It feels very European and educated."

"I don't know," I said. I thought of the Millers, who spent much more time reading than we did, though it was true that my parents had an impressive collection of books.

"Your house is elegant," Vanessa said. "And your brothers and sisters are so awesome. You're all so nice to each other, and everyone knows how to play basketball."

That was true. We played basketball on our patio under the fir trees all the time. Vanessa had no idea how to shoot a basket; even little Joey at three years old had a better shot than she did.

Vanessa was most fascinated by the food that we ate. I gave her a bite of dark, European chocolate that Aunt Ilse had brought on her last visit, and Vanessa's mouth fell open in astonishment.

"That is the most delicious thing I've ever tasted in my whole life," she raved.

She wanted more, but I had to explain that this was a very rare treat, even for us. It might be months before Ilse visited again and brought more of it.

"Next time she comes from New York, you need to call me right away," Vanessa insisted.

If Mom was home for dinner, she'd spend the duration of it telling us about her work with Seattle CORE. Their latest project, Voluntary Racial Transfer, was now being seen as a feeble effort. The schools across town that had received Black students had made no efforts to make them feel welcome or comfortable. CORE had given up negotiating with the Seattle School Board.

"Voluntary Racial Transfer is too small and slow to make a difference," my mom announced to the Friday Night Group one evening. "We're moving on to direct action. Seattle CORE has made education its highest priority."

There were talks of a school boycott, although Mom would not say if or when it might occur. "It's controversial," was all she would tell us. "You'll know more soon."

On other nights, she and my father lamented the unfortunate parallels between American discrimination against Blacks and the Nazis' persecution of the Jews. "We immigrated to get away from this kind of hate," my father said. "It has got to be stopped."

In History class, we were due to study recent European history just before Christmas break. My teacher, Mrs. Nawrot, knew that I was a child of German Jewish immigrants, and she pulled me aside after class one day.

"Claudia," she said, "we're going to be watching educational films that show Hitler and the Nazis. If you don't want to watch these films, I understand. If you want me to, I'll excuse you from class on those days, and you can go to the library until the films are over."

I thanked her for giving me the choice and told her that I'd think about it.

I was touched by her thoughtfulness, and I wondered whether I should accept her offer and go to the library. The pictures I had carried in my mind since the second grade of my relatives and millions of others being murdered in the gas chambers and made into lampshades and soap, were terrifying.

At the same time, I was curious to see how the images in these films matched the ones that had grown so vivid to me. I wanted to see how Hitler looked and sounded in person.

I decided to watch, without consulting my parents on the matter. The first thing that struck me, as I sat in my history classroom and stared at the screen, was that the films were all in black and white, whereas the images of Hitler, concentration camps, and gas chambers in my head were in overwhelming color. We watched Hitler give impassioned speeches in German—the same familiar language that my parents spoke at home and with their friends, the same language I was studying at Meany Junior High. We saw Nazi soldiers marching, kicking their boots high in the air, giving the "Heil Hitler!" salute that I know Mom had been forced to give when she was a schoolgirl.

I looked down the rows of my classmates. Many were napping, doodling, or whispering to each other. To them, this was just another boring history lesson—somebody else's problem from long ago. A surge of loneliness swept through me as I realized that they couldn't possibly understand the terror and sorrow that this particular lesson had brought to my parents and their families.

* * *

In mid-February 1966, Mom came home happy. The CORE Executive Board had officially recommended a boycott of Seattle schools to protest Seattle's failure to effectively implement school integration. The citywide boycott would be held on March 31st and April 1st. My mother had been named the boycott's lead coordinator; planning was to begin immediately.

The decision to boycott was controversial. CORE had more than 150 members, but it was also a busy organization; other projects included direct action against a grocery store that refused to hire Blacks, negotiations with the Chamber of

Commerce to secure more downtown employment for Black citizens, a rent strike against Central Area slumlords, and food and clothing drives for the Blacks in Mississippi whose public assistance had been cut.

Even those CORE members who were focused on achieving better school integration had serious misgivings about supporting a student boycott. Some of them worried about using an underage population to send a message, while others objected to the concept of encouraging truancy.

The solution, my mother explained, was to offer students an education that would be superior to what they would be missing in public schools.

"We're calling them Freedom Schools," my mother told me, her eyes gleaming. "For two days, you'll attend a Freedom School. You'll learn all the things the public schools won't teach you."

My mother and her CORE colleagues started preparing to ensure that the Freedom Schools would offer students a high-quality experience, that they wouldn't just be a place to warehouse children during the two-day walkout. She organized meetings to set the curriculum—which varied according to student age—and recruited an army of qualified volunteer staff. Each Freedom School would have two volunteer co-principals—one Black and one white—as well as a team of volunteer teachers. After they recruited eighty-five teachers, these volunteers were enrolled in a special training program to learn about the details of the boycott and the Freedom School curriculum. The Freedom School teaching philosophy focused on "fostering dialogue," rather than lecturing to students.

Mom worked to secure Freedom School sites—many of them churches and synagogues whose leaders supported integration efforts. CORE arranged to rent chartered buses to transport students to the school; a whole team of volunteers labored over the comprehensive transportation plan. It was vital that all students have the opportunity to join the boycott.

I accompanied Mom around the Central Area as she canvassed door-to-door, asking Black families for a few minutes of their time so that she could persuade them to participate in the boycott. Sometimes, if the kids were old enough to be curious or have opinions, I would talk to them while Mom conversed with the parents. I told them about the importance of boycotting and described the exciting learning opportunities that the Freedom Schools presented us. "It will be a fun and powerful way to send a message to our Seattle school board," I told the kids.

Money was raised to purchase pencils, paper, glue, as well as milk and juice. Ten thousand flyers were mailed to recruit participants. "Do You Want Action on School Integration?" they asked. "Join the Boycott of Seattle Schools. Send Your Children to Freedom Schools." The flyer included a response coupon that could be mailed back to CORE: "I will send my children to Freedom School, March 31–April 1."

The pledge coupons made their way back to the CORE office by the hundreds, although some high school students and their parents expressed hesitation. Several high schools were administering exams during the boycott days. One afternoon in early March, Naomi and Danny burst through the front door together, breathing fire.

"They made an announcement to the whole school that anyone absent on March 31st and April 1st would be listed as 'unexcused,'" Naomi complained.

"And because they're calling it 'unexcused' nobody can make up the exams that they miss on those days. We'll have to take zeroes on the test," Danny explained, furious.

There was no question what Naomi and Danny would do. My mother would never have allowed them to skip the boycott. And they wouldn't have wanted to.

Their friends were a different matter. "Everyone I know supports CORE and the work they're doing," Naomi told me as we tucked Joey into bed. "But my friends are worried about their grades and attendance records."

Less than a week before the boycott, Mom organized a meeting to coordinate final arrangements. Despite the RSVP coupon on the flyers, it was hard to determine how many students would actually attend. And even though 85 volunteer teachers had signed up to help teach, the boycott felt it needed fifteen more volunteers to adequately staff the classrooms. A group of ministers promised to discuss the boycott at their church services that Sunday to help with the final push for participants. Lawyers were preparing a statement that argued that the boycott was not in violation of school policies.

I felt so excited when I showed up to school on Monday. In just three short days, I would attend a Freedom School instead. My assigned seats would be vacant, my name would be followed by a silence at every roll call, and everyone would know that I was taking a stand for equality.

The planned boycott was hardly a secret. The Seattle newspapers ran daily coverage of the preparations, expectations, and reactions; two television stations scheduled special programs to cover the boycott on Thursday and Friday. The Greater Seattle Council of Churches lent its public support to the cause, and many individual churches urged their members to volunteer or participate.

According to Mom, support had been expected from the Black churches in the Central Area, but she and her CORE colleagues were pleasantly surprised to find that white religious leaders, too, including a local Archbishop of the Catholic Church, were backing the boycott.

Not all of the Seattle clergy was so supportive. Some voiced their belief in school integration but spoke out against the boycott. One prominent minister told the newspaper that the boycott organizers were using children as pawns, and a local rabbi made the front page of the Seattle Times when he called for a conference and suggested that the matter could be resolved with discussion.

"A conference?" my father scoffed, before tossing the paper down on the table in disgust. "Where has he been? Does he think they haven't tried that a hundred times before?"

When I left school on Wednesday, I could barely contain my excitement. I woke early Thursday morning to assist with the last-minute preparations. Our house was already full of people, on their way in and out of the front door.

The turnout was better than expected. More than three thousand students flocked to the Freedom Schools that Thursday morning. Volunteers had to scramble to find additional space for the overflow crowd, and they secured three more locations at the last minute.

The adult volunteers were young and old, white and Black, male and female. They were activists, parents, and ministers, as well as various community members who had felt compelled by the call to action. They stayed busy all day: at lunchtime, more than 500 McDonald's hamburgers were picked up for the students who had forgotten to bring sack lunches.

We middle school students met at the Mt. Zion Baptist Church Freedom School where a Black minister taught us about African American history. He began with the slave ships from Africa, continued through slavery on American plantations, the Blacks' part in the Civil War and its aftermath, and eventually outlined the major civil rights struggles of the last several decades. We watched a film about civil rights and participated in a discussion about what we might want to do when we grew up.

Several prominent members of the Seattle community dropped by to visit and take part in the celebratory boycott spirit. A lawyer taught us about the legal history of the civil rights struggle, and a professor from the University of Washington spoke about the African Diaspora.

Friday was even more successful; nearly 4,000 students participated, and the enthusiasm and energy were infectious. Of the 4,000 students, approximately 70% were Black. And in some Central Area schools, more than 50% of the student body had been absent. We were elated. We had sent a strong, powerful message.

That evening, the leaders of the boycott gathered in our living room for an evaluation meeting. The room was so crowded that my siblings and I had to listen from the dining room.

Boycott leaders from CORE and NAACP reported on the overall event; teachers and volunteers from each Freedom School spoke about the successes and challenges at their particular site. "I think we have sent a clear sign to the Seattle School Board that segregation will no longer be tolerated," my mother announced. There were murmurs of agreement, but no wild shouting.

Finally, the meeting wrapped up. And then the celebration began. My mother encouraged us to join in the fun. "Come celebrate with us, my wonderful activists," she exclaimed.

More volunteers arrived at the house, bringing food, and sharing stories from the past two days. There was laughter, hugging, and a great deal of toasting. My brothers, sisters, and I did our best to host—refilling glasses and pointing out the way to the bathroom. Everyone enjoyed telling us how impressive our mother was, and what an involved and socially committed family she had raised. "You should be very, very proud of your beautiful mother," one tall man told me, patting my shoulder with such enthusiasm that it hurt a little.

When I returned to school on Monday, there was a buzz in the air. Everything felt exciting and hopeful. I tried to bring both my white friends and my Black friends together at my lunchtime cafeteria table, and I noticed a few similar efforts around the cafeteria. "Cathy, come here," I beckoned to Cathy Winter. "Sit with us!" Cathy hesitated for a second, but then she sat down right between Vanessa and me. "You were at the Freedom School, weren't you?" she asked. Vanessa nodded.

Over the next few weeks, as the excitement of the boycott gradually faded, our focus retuned to more typical seventh grade concerns—the social scene. We had dances at Meany where the whole seventh grade gathered; we danced to Motown hits like The Temptations, Martha and the Vandellas, and Marvin Gaye, and joined together in line dances, with lots of clapping and repetitive moves.

* * *

After a summer of swimming, hiking and spending lots of time with my new seventh grade girlfriends, eighth grade began. Now I was the only Chotzen representative at Meany Junior High. Leah had started at Garfield High School, where Naomi and Danny were beginning their senior year.

I was studying German, which made my grandparents, Omi and Opi, very happy. They began to write me long letters in German. Though my command of the language wasn't good enough for me to respond eloquently—or even to understand everything they were writing—I saved the letters so that I could reply as soon as I was capable.

I had new teachers in most of my other subjects, including History. Eighth graders focused on American History and our teacher, Mr. Scott, was very enthusiastic about the subject. Our first assignment of the year was an essay entitled "Why Study American History?" I began my essay this way:

"If we gain an understanding of our past, it will help us to build on the happenings of our past, and to learn from them so that we can be wiser with our future, and so that we have a more stable one. Thus, we will not make the same mistakes as those did before us."

Mr. Scott was pleased by my answer, which held a lot of similarities to the arguments for studying American History that he had made in class. I had learned from Naomi and Danny that it was smart to tell teachers what they wanted to hear, and I thought Mr. Scott had some good points about learning from the past. History was one of my favorite subjects.

Math was another favorite. I loved algebra and my math teacher, Miss Healy. There were so many real-life problems I didn't know how to solve, like how to make sure our family had enough money and how to keep Dad from getting angry and how to make the world fair for people of all races and ethnicities. Algebra was easy by comparison, and I liked figuring out equations.

When the University of Washington announced a contest specifically for Seattle eighth grade math students, Miss Healy told me that she and the other math teachers had picked me to represent Meany Junior High School. After some meetings with the principal and other teachers, however, she delivered some bad news.

"We're sending Mark Edwards," she informed me. "I argued that you have better marks on your assignments, but no school has ever sent a girl. It would be highly unusual, and if you lost, we would feel pretty silly."

I was very hurt, angry, and disappointed, but I told her that I understood. That was something else I had learned from Naomi and Danny—that teachers liked it when you told them that you understood. "Teachers are very self-conscious," Naomi confided.

At Garfield High School, the twins were immensely popular—our upbringing had made it easy for them to connect with students of all races and backgrounds. Danny was president of the Garfield High Student Body, and girls seemed to flock to him everywhere he went.

"I was the first of many women who will want to eat this boy up with kisses," Mom announced, stroking Danny's face.

"Get off me," he snapped. He pushed her hands away.

"Don't push your mother," Dad barked, jumping out of his dinner chair.

"He didn't push her. He just wants her to stop suffocating him," Naomi said, leaping into the argument.

"I don't understand why they're so angry at me," my mother complained later, as I helped her clear the dishes. "They're such beautiful people, and I just want to love them."

The twins were angry a lot of the time, and so was Leah. They all seemed to have no patience for my mother, whose every move irritated and infuriated them. All three of them constantly yelled and swore at her when she gave them instructions about what to do or how to be more helpful. Leah dealt with her anger alone, in her room, and the twins seemed to stay away from the house more and more with each passing week, though they always completed their chores and other familial obligations.

"I'm just busy," Naomi snapped at me, when I asked why she spent so few of her weekends with us.

She wasn't lying. Naomi was a consummate overachiever: in addition to her schoolwork, her babysitting, and her significant household responsibilities, she also participated in ski patrol, moot court competitions, and all-city student council. Through these activities, she had befriended several girls from other schools, including Seattle's private high schools and the more affluent public schools on Mercer Island and in Bellevue. She was constantly rushing off to parties, borrowing the car to drive into the suburbs.

"Sometimes," she confided in me, "I think the girls only invite me everywhere because they're hoping I'll bring Danny. Everybody wants to meet him."

Naomi's new friends came from families steeped in the traditions of prestigious East Coast colleges. Even before their junior year was over, these girls had set to work on their applications. My parents didn't understand all the fuss, but Naomi was inspired. She wrote to East Coast colleges and requested their catalogues. She read the catalogues, considered her options, and arranged meetings with alumnae from the schools that interested her: Wellesley, Vassar, Sarah Lawrence, Smith, and Mt. Holyoke.

When the subject of colleges came up at our dinner table, my parents made it clear that they were not interested in sending Naomi across the country. "We have a perfectly good university here," my father insisted.

"The family simply can't do without Naomi Girl," my mother announced. "She'll stay close to home because family is the most important thing."

But for Naomi, the University of Washington didn't offer any of the allure that emanated from those private, faraway colleges. She conducted her research and applications in secret, and she swore Danny and me to secrecy. She strategically scheduled the meetings with alumnae so that they always followed one of her extracurricular commitments. "Sorry I'm so late," she'd say, when she arrived home from one of the secret meetings. "The all-city student council meeting took forever, and then there was traffic."

She joined us for dinner, washed the dishes, bathed Charlotte and Joey and helped to put them to bed, and then set to work on homework. Once that was done, and everyone else had gone to bed, she moved on to her college applications.

"I have to escape, Claud," she whispered to me, when I snuck into her room to check on her one night. "It's not that I don't love the family. I love the family more than anything. But there's so much work for me to do at home. If I don't go far away, I'll be ensnared forever."

She obsessed over her applications and essays and rewrote them constantly until she was convinced that they were perfect. She was revising her Sarah Lawrence essay for the third time when she realized that she had missed the application deadline. "I'm going out," she told me. And she rushed out the door without explanation, just as I had seen Mom do so many times.

The next day, our mother received a telegram from the Sarah Lawrence College Dean of Admissions. "Dear Mrs.

Chotzen," it said. "We are happy to grant Naomi an extension of two weeks on her application, and we hope that your health improves soon."

"What in the world is this?" my mother demanded.

I expected fireworks, or at least a small explosion. But Naomi smiled and didn't answer, and my mother left the kitchen to greet photography customers who had arrived at the front door.

"I told them I was sick, and that Naomi was taking care of seven younger siblings and the household and her schoolwork, then I signed it Carla Chotzen," she told me later. "It's not that far from the truth."

I was having a good year at Meany Junior High. In December, the Meany Junior High newspaper, Meany News and Views, published a list of "Perfect Parts." Students had voted on superlatives for a number of important categories. I was singled out among eighth grade girls for "Best Personality" and "Friendliness." Lila was recognized for "Best Eyes," which I thought was nice and true.

A week later, the same school newspaper named me the "Ideal Eighth Grade Girl." They interviewed me for the article and printed my picture right beside that of Benson Wong, the Ideal Eighth Grade Boy.

Most of my friends were very excited for me. "Your quotes are so good," they said. "You sound smart, and your picture looks pretty." But a few of my Black friends complained that neither of the Ideal Eighth Graders and few of the superlative winners had been Black students. "All this talk about integration, but it just means that Negroes are being overshadowed again," my friend Yvonne grumbled.

I didn't want the Blacks to be overshadowed. I tried my best to integrate the Civil Rights Movement into my education at every possible opportunity, as if I was still attending a Freedom School. For history class, I wrote reports on Black Power and prominent Black leaders. I titled them, "Which Way for the

Negro Now?" and "Black Power: A Demand or Plea?" and "Stokely Carmichael: Beginner of Black Power." When we were asked to profile five key figures from a single American revolution, most of my classmates focused on the Revolutionary War or the Civil War. I profiled Carmichael, Martin Luther King, Jr., Floyd McKissick, Roy Wilkins, and Whitney Young.

Black Power was a big topic of conversation among Friday Nighters, too. Some people felt excluded by the movement, while others argued that it might be the necessary next step. "You don't have to be Negro to see that we're not getting anywhere with cooperative tactics," Dora Miller complained.

"We are getting somewhere," my mother said. "Just not as quickly as some of the leaders want."

When Naomi's acceptance arrived from Sarah Lawrence, my parents were stunned. They set the letter on the kitchen table and hovered over it, staring down like it was some strange, unfamiliar organism.

"Why would you want to go so far away?" my mother asked, seeming to imply that this constituted some sort of betrayal.

The feeling was doubled when Swarthmore College sent Danny a letter accepting him.

"You too, Danny Boy?" my dad asked, clearly crestfallen.

"I want to be near Naomi," Danny explained.

"The University of Washington is a great school," my father declared, shaking his head in puzzlement. "I don't see why you'd work so hard to remove yourselves from family life."

But I was proud of Naomi and Danny and excited for them about their acceptances. I wished they would wait a little while to leave. Maybe four years, I thought, so that I could go with them.

My parents gradually came around to the idea of East Coast colleges, but my father was resolute in his opposition to financial aid.

"It will help," Naomi tried to convince him. "It will ease the burden on the family."

But Dad was proud. He equated financial aid with charity, and he had never accepted charity in his life. He had immigrated to America with nothing, founded his own business, and supported a family of ten. And damn it, no expensive East Coast college was going to make him feel poor.

"Let me write to them," he said. "I'll write to the colleges." He sat down with a pen and paper and painstakingly listed every asset the family possessed—including our sofas, tables, and chairs. "How much do we think nine beds are worth?" he shouted into kitchen, but nobody knew the answer.

"Mine tucks away under Claudia's," Charlotte reminded him.

Their college acceptances had arrived at about the same time that the twins turned eighteen. Birthdays had always been a reason for celebration in our household, but this one was filled with anxiety. Danny was now eligible for the draft. The risk of being drafted and sent to Vietnam was real. My parents took Danny to see a draft counselor to check if there was a way he could get Conscientious Objector status, a Selective Service designation for young men who were morally or religiously opposed to war of all kinds.

"It's not going to work for Danny. He's not against all wars, just the Vietnam War," Dad reported to us when they returned from their meeting with the draft counselor. "I told them I would have fought against the Nazis," Danny admitted.

Muhammad Ali had been sent to prison the previous year for refusing to serve. He wasn't considered a conscientious objector either—he just hated the idea of this particular war. Danny liked to quote the statement Muhammed Ali had made to the press, "I ain't got no quarrel with the Viet Cong."

Stokely Carmichael didn't have any quarrel with the Viet Cong either. Later that spring, he made a much-publicized visit to Seattle. Carmichael was the leader of SNCC (Student

Nonviolent Coordinating Committee), and a leading advocate of Black Power. SNCC had its roots in student activism, and they wanted Carmichael to speak at the Garfield High School auditorium.

The Seattle School Board was not cooperative. Citing Carmichael's status as a controversial figure, it suggested that he could speak at Garfield only if SNCC would allow rebuttal speakers to represent an opposing point of view.

Carmichael refused to share the stage with another speaker, so preparations for the event suddenly stalled. SNCC and the School Board had reached a stalemate.

"An opposing point of view!" Mom scoffed. "Maybe the school board wants to find a segregationist to speak to our students?"

The Central Area community shared her outrage. Carmichael was immensely popular among Blacks who were eager to see him in person. Ultimately, the School Board backed down and consented to let Carmichael speak without rebuttal. They did hold firm on another point. Carmichael had requested a "Negro-only audience," but the School Board refused to dictate who could attend.

My mother was unimpressed by the School Board's stance. "They're cowards," she pronounced. "They're afraid of what will happen if a room full of Negroes gets together without any white supervision."

I skipped my last afternoon class and walked over to Garfield with two friends to hear Carmichael.

Carmichael took the stage, and the crowd cheered with excitement. He was an impassioned, angry, powerful speaker. He paced the stage, shouted, and pumped his fist.

"Black America is the white man's colony, held in place by its fear of the master class, and its doubts about itself," he declared.

He worked his way through American history, criticizing and name-calling every white historical figure or leader.

Christopher Columbus was a "dumb honky," George Washington was a "honky who had slaves," and Abraham Lincoln was "another honky." He labeled President Lyndon Johnson "a buffoon."

Carmichael railed against the war in Vietnam and yelled, "To hell with the laws of the United States! Black Power is legitimate!" He incited the audience to chant against the Vietnam War. "Hell no, we won't go!" we shouted in unison.

He wound himself into a frenzy of passion. "Black leaders have been for so long worrying about what white people are saying that they don't know what Black people are saying. Black Power doesn't mean that we're anti-white; it means that we are busy tending to our real work, organizing Black people that are poor. Black Power is a Black Declaration of Independence!"

That really got the crowd going. People roared and cheered all around me, standing up and shoving their chairs aside. I stood with them, impassioned by Carmichael's sentiments, and charged by his call to action.

But I also felt uncertain that I was welcome in this auditorium. My skin was white. Carmichael hadn't even wanted any white people here in the first place. As I looked around and saw many of my lifelong friends shouting, "Be Black and be proud," I didn't know whether to join their voices or to slip towards an exit. I looked around for Naomi, Danny, Mom, or Leah, but I couldn't spot them in the frenzied crowd.

"Stop trying to be white," Carmichael screamed to the audience. And my friends—the ones who had grown up pressing their hair and envying my light skin—yelled back in agreement.

"Seize your power! Be Black and be proud!"

The crowd's response was deafening.

The next day, my friend Cathy arrived at school with her hair in an Afro. "It's called a 'natural;' I'm not going to press it anymore," she said.

She looked beautiful with her Afro. "I like it," I told her.

A few days later, Cathy lingered at the lunch table while I finished my sandwich. "Claudia, I'm confused," she admitted to me in a soft voice. "I don't know if I'm white or Negro, and I feel like I have to choose." I had spent countless days and nights at Cathy's home. Her mom was white, and her dad was Black.

Cathy hesitated a little, and then pushed on. "And if I have to choose, I'm choosing Negro. Or Black like Stokely says. With everything that's happening, and after listening to Stokely Carmichael, that's what I've got to be. I'm going to be Black, and my friends have to be Black. So, I don't think I can be seen with you anymore."

I felt devastated, but I told Cathy that I understood. I truly did understand because the times were so intense, and there was nothing we could do about all that was happening around us. Over the next few weeks, I noticed all the Black students isolating themselves from their non-Black peers. Even though the school district continued to bus in white students, Meany Junior High School became more segregated every day.

Nationally, CORE announced that they would no longer be defined as a "multiracial organization." Instead, it would officially dedicate itself to promoting a Black Power agenda. When my mother and her Seattle CORE cohorts heard the news, they held an emergency chapter meeting. The Seattle chair—a respected Black leader—criticized the national changes and proposed that the Seattle chapter should continue to abide by its own guidelines. A few days later, Black CORE members demanded the Seattle chair's resignation.

"He was thrown out," my mother said. She had arrived home in a rage. "They voted him out. And they're dividing the work along racial lines. They're going to focus their work on their own community, and they think people like me should stick to fighting prejudice among whites. They're segregating the organization!"

* * *

In late August, we staged our annual family holiday photo
at the train station. Naomi and Danny climbed aboard a parked
train, leaned out of the door, and waved. The other eight of us
gathered on the platform, staring up at them and waving back.

Charlotte began to cry. "I don't want them to go!" she
wailed.

"They're not actually leaving," I reminded her. "This is just
a photo shoot."

But two weeks later they did leave. We all escorted them to
the airport and watched them board their plane: they would fly
together as far as New York, then Danny would take a train to
Philadelphia, and Naomi would take the short train ride to
Sarah Lawrence, just outside of New York City. Returning to
our Madrona house, their absence suddenly felt glaring and
irreparable.

I had done a lot of growing during the previous summer;
after years of being the tiniest girl in the class, I finally looked
like a young woman. My friends were very excited about my
transformation. When I turned up at Meany for the first day of
ninth grade my friend, Yvonne, let out a deafening howl.

"Claudia!" she shouted. "Look at you! Look at what
happened, honey! You got breasts!"

Though I was embarrassed by Yvonne's public
announcement about my recent developments, I did feel older.
The weight of Naomi and Danny's departure settled itself upon
my shoulders. Suddenly, the responsibility of being a Chotzen
was immense.

"Who's going to clean the kitchen without Danny and
Naomi?" Mia asked. To me the space they had left was much
vaster than the sum of their considerable household chores. I
wondered who was going to set the example for the younger
kids, and who was going to remember all the details that my

mother forgot. After Leah, I was the oldest sibling left; I had two very big pairs of shoes to fill.

Naomi hit the ground running from the second she arrived at Sarah Lawrence. She liked to stay busy, and within weeks she had secured several different student jobs. One of them—operating the college switchboard—even required her to be up at dawn every morning. Still, she wrote to me, she felt out of place at a prestigious East Coast College. She missed the family, worried about what we would do without her, and feared that her professors and peers would discover her as an imposter or a fraud. She wrote and phoned us often to complain about her roommate, or about the ridiculous sign-out procedures for her dormitory.

At Swarthmore, Danny struggled with his transition. He was uncomfortable at his suburban college campus, and painfully aware that his Black friends in Seattle were being drafted into the military to fight in Vietnam. He felt like a traitor, traipsing across manicured lawns to attend seminars with distinguished professors while his former classmates were fighting racism at home and facing war overseas. He was desperate to divorce himself from the cloistered world of academia and engage with real issues and real people. Several of his friends from the Central Area had been drafted and deployed, and the rest were mired in the increasingly hostile fight for civil rights. And Danny? He was supposed to be studying Chaucer.

A dislocated shoulder—a lingering football injury—had blessed him with a 4-F exemption, labeling him physically unfit to serve in the military. But while Danny was relieved at his deferment, he said it only made him feel more detached and isolated from the world's real turmoil. "I got out on a technicality," he complained. "Most young people don't have bum shoulders as an excuse."

In early October of 1967, Danny wrote home to tell us and that he and a few friends would be travelling to Washington

DC later that month to participate in a large-scale protest against the Vietnam War.

My mother wasted no time in booking a plane ticket. "I can visit Danny at school, see my sister in Virginia, protest the war, and then visit Naomi at Sarah Lawrence and other relatives in New York City," she explained breathlessly.

Going to the east coast and participating in a demonstration sounded too exciting to miss. I pleaded with Mom until she agreed to take me with her. I was eager to participate in the protest, curious to see Washington, D.C. and New York, and excited to miss a few days of ninth grade for such an important cause. Mostly, though, I missed Danny and Naomi. Danny's letters—in which he made no attempt to conceal his loneliness and alienation—broke my heart, and it was painful to live at home with an incomplete family. I was desperate to see them both.

Mom agreed to let me go with her to the east coast, and two weeks later I took my first airplane flight from Seattle to New York with my mom. We then took the train to Philadelphia to collect Danny at Swarthmore. He rushed straight into my arms and squeezed me tight. "I'm so glad you came," he told me. The three of us boarded another train to Virginia, where my mom's sister, Ruth, lived, just outside of Washington D.C.

Aunt Ruth and her family were happy for the rare chance to see us, but they were puzzled that we had travelled so far to protest a war that they felt ambivalent about. My cousins asked me why I would let my mother drag me along to a peace march. When I explained how excited I was, and that protest and dissent were admirable forms of patriotism, they rolled their eyes.

On the morning of the protest, Saturday, October 21, 1967, Aunt Ruth dropped us near the Washington Monument; we had walked to the Lincoln Memorial by noon. The size of the crowd was astounding. Everywhere there were sign-toting demonstrators, huddled together in massive groups. Scattered amongst the banners and signs were lettered placards that designated the different marching contingents. We followed Danny to "Contingent F," which was made up of various college delegations, including a group of Danny's friends from Swarthmore.

A bandstand was set up in the shadow of the huge, white-stone statue of Abraham Lincoln. Dick Gregory and Dr. Benjamin Spock talked about ending the war; Peter, Paul and Mary sang "Where Have All the Flowers Gone." All of us draped our arms around each other's shoulders, swayed, and sang along. My mom captured the scene with her Rolleiflex and her 8mm movie camera.

We were scheduled to leave the Lincoln Memorial to begin the march to the Pentagon at 1 p.m., but both the main and alternate routes were blocked. Finally, by four in the afternoon, we began to walk. We marched in rows of fifteen across, laughing and singing. I felt a sense of pride and purpose; I was there to send a message to the government. Surrounded by thousands of like-minded protestors, we wouldn't go unnoticed. I collected leaflets and political buttons to bring back to my friends at home who I knew would be envious of my exciting day.

We walked arm in arm for almost two miles, crossing the Potomac River. When we reached the grounds of the Pentagon, our sense of purpose and order dissolved into utter confusion; some people seemed to think that the march was over, while others were sure it had only just begun. An announcement rang out over a loudspeaker: "All those participating in direct action are on their own." I had no idea what this meant, but it suddenly sounded ominous.

"Are we participating in direct action?" I asked.

"Of course," my mother said. "Why else are we here?"

A sudden burst of motion swept me forward. Military Police had formed a human barricade, two rows deep, around the Pentagon building. Hundreds of demonstrators responded by running directly at these soldiers—they broke through their lines and tried to reach the Pentagon. As the surging mob pushed against me, I realized that I wasn't really sure what constituted a non-violent march—were these protestors within the bounds of peacefulness, or were they violating some kind of law?

Without any control, I found myself being forced forward until I was stumbling involuntarily up the Pentagon steps. I felt a very uncomfortable burning sensation in my throat, nose, and eyes. I clamped my eyes shut, still being pushed forward, and I grabbed Danny's arm for balance. The words "tear gas" rang out all around me. A piece of torn fabric found its way into my hand. "Use this to cover your nose and mouth," Mom instructed. I was terrified.

When I blinked my eyes open, I was standing face-to-face with the Military Police and their bayonets. They glared at us threateningly, and I dropped Mom and Danny's hands.

"I'm going back," I told them.

"No, you're not," my mother said.

"I am. I really am. I don't want to do this. It burns," I insisted. The soldiers with their bayonets were mere feet away, and I had no control over what our fellow protestors might do to provoke them. I was terrified, and shocked that my very own government was spraying me with tear gas—I had done nothing violent or illegal. I was being patriotic!

"If you go back, then you're on your own," Mom told me. She had no intention of going anywhere but further up the Pentagon steps.

I was desperate. Mom pointed to a grove of trees behind the crowd and brusquely suggested that I could wait for her there. I nodded and frantically pushed my way against the tide of humanity until I reached the back of the mob.

Wiping my eyes and surveying the scene in front of me, I realized that I was not the only protestor who had lost my zeal in the face of tear gas. Several of us had fled to the back of the horde, and many more groups changed direction and walked by me, too tired to push forward any longer. I was immensely relieved when my mother finally appeared from the thinning crowd. I was ready to go home, wash the tear gas from my face, and watch the rest of the protest on TV.

But instead of heading out, Mom insisted that I join her back at the front of the demonstration. Danny and his friends were in the thick of things, and she didn't want me to miss the chance to join them. "It's peaceful," she reassured me. "At the front it's peaceful. Did you come all this way to sit under a tree?"

I let my mom grab my arm and lead me back into the fray, where we were immediately sprayed again with tear gas. We pushed our way right up to a line of soldiers; fifteen or twenty demonstrators, including Danny, sat at their feet. We sat with them, our legs crossed, and our heads tilted up towards them.

As the day grew darker, I found that we had outlasted most of the other protestors. Lawyers from the ACLU shouted at the thinning crowd over bullhorns, explaining our rights to us in case we were arrested. At 6:45 p.m. we were told that our permit to demonstrate would expire in just fifteen minutes. I watched my mother carefully, nervously trying to guess what she would do—if she insisted upon staying past the approved time, I worried that we might get ourselves into real trouble.

Ten minutes later, we heard another announcement: the permit had been extended until noon the next day. Anyone who left the premises, however, would not be allowed to return. For Mom and Danny, the decision was easy: we would spend the night.

"We've come this far," Danny said, squeezing my hand. He could tell that the chaos, tear gas, and armed soldiers made me nervous, but he seemed energized by the day's events. "It's so good to be back in the world," he sighed. I felt safer being with Danny than I did with my mom.

We huddled around a small bonfire made from picket signs and sang songs. It was a chilly October evening, and other bonfires flickered to life all across the grounds. We took turns wandering to the road, where there was food brought in by activist organizations.

I had curled up on the ground and dozed off when the soldiers descended. I awoke to shouts of "hold the line!" and felt swift kicks from soldiers' boots thud against my back and legs. Danny was pulling me to my feet as we were assaulted again with the terrible sting of tear gas. I felt immediately nauseous. Federal marshals wearing white helmets were clubbing indiscriminately at the protestors and screams rang out all around me. I swiveled around, terrified that I might be attacked from behind at any moment. Protestors around us were outraged, screaming that girls were receiving some of the most brutal beatings.

Amidst the chaos, I heard warnings, advice, and calls to action blare over the portable loudspeaker. A former Green Beret broadcasted his belief that soldiers' training only taught them how to kill. Another man announced that he had seen a federal marshal repeatedly beat an already-fallen nineteen-year-old boy over the head. I looked towards my mother, but she didn't seem to hear the loudspeaker at all—I wondered whether it was sensory overload or her apparent fearlessness that enabled her to ignore these harrowing bits of information.

I pleaded with my mother, urging her to leave with me. It was nearly midnight when she finally agreed to take me home. Danny decided to stay behind with his college friends, so Mom and I wound our way through the crowds until we were off the grounds of the Pentagon.

On our way to find a taxi, we entered a restaurant to use the bathroom. The owner, a middle-aged white man, was shouting at a group of Black would-be customers to get out of his restaurant. "Fucking n****** get out!" he yelled. Mom quickly grabbed my shoulders and steered me out of the doorway.

I had never heard such hateful racial language before. It added to my shocked condition, already overloaded from being teargassed, kicked, and seeing people beaten. We hurried away from the restaurant and down the street, our bladders still bursting. It was well into the middle of the night when we arrived back at my cousins' house in Virginia. I fell asleep immediately.

Danny stayed at the Pentagon all night. When he met up with us the following afternoon, he informed us that the brutality had only intensified. His group had marched to the White House at 6 a.m. to wake up President Johnson with chants such as "Hey, Hey, LBJ, how many kids did you kill today?" When they reached Lafayette Park, he said, two girls from his group had picked flowers, which provoked immediate beatings from nearby police. Danny watched as the boy beside him received a blow so severe that his skull cracked open.

News reporters had instructed Danny's group to record the names of any violent officers, but the policemen were one step ahead: they had removed their badges and name tags so that they could not be identified. It had never occurred to me that American police officers would actually plan to beat citizens, and that they would take precautionary steps to protect themselves against just retribution. Weren't the police supposed to set the standard for legal and ethical behavior, I asked? Mom and Danny just shook their heads sadly.

The next day we returned to Swarthmore. We joined the students for a heated discussion about whether or not we could reasonably classify the protest as non-violent. Had we successfully pulled off the peaceful demonstration that we had sought, or had we been goaded into violating the conditions we had hoped to follow?

As we all shared our confrontations with military and police brutality, I felt a great sadness and disappointment in my country. Early on the day of the protest, when we stood together at the bottom of the Lincoln Memorial, I had felt so hopeful that our voices would ring out clearly and persuasively in favor of peace. Now, I felt defeated and powerless against a government that I had grown up believing in. I was heartbroken.

At the time, I had no idea that the demonstration I had participated in would come to be known as a defining moment in the 1960s peace movement—the historic "March on the Pentagon." The crowd of protestors was estimated at 100,000, and more draft cards were burned at this peace march than at any other anti-war protest in U.S. history. Six hundred and eighty-one protesters had been arrested (another record), and dozens were beaten as they were pushed off the Pentagon's steps. On Sunday, October 22, 1967, *The New York Times* featured one photo with the caption, "U.S. marshals clubbing antiwar demonstrators who tried to storm the Pentagon yesterday," and another photo of Secretary of Defense Robert McNamara observing the demonstration from a window in the Pentagon. The violence, chronicled in novelist Norman Mailer's firsthand account, *The Armies of the Night*, focused the world's attention on the peace effort as never before.

Years later, I discovered several contact sheets of black and white photographs my mother had taken during the March on the Pentagon. Included are pictures my mom took in the dying light of the late afternoon when we reached the Pentagon and encountered more than 2,500 rifle-wielding soldiers blocking our way. Several pictures captured a lone girl standing inches from the soldiers' sheathed bayonets, she was trying to have a dialogue with them, offering the soldiers a flower, trying to convince them to throw down their guns and join us. A similar photograph, taken in the same moments by French photojournalist Marc Riboud, became a defining image of the Vietnam antiwar era, reprinted in newspapers around the world. To this day, it remains a seminal 1960's image, is featured in museum exhibitions, and appears regularly in print.

Danny couldn't go with us to New York because he had school assignments and other commitments. My mother and I both cried as we said goodbye to him—my mother had been crying a lot during our return visit to Swarthmore.

Danny took me aside. "You'll like New York," he told me. "It's tough, but that's because it's the real world. The real world is brutal, but that's how it's supposed to be."

I did like New York, but not because it was brutal; it was fun. When we got in, we headed straight for Sarah Lawrence College, and it was such a relief to throw my arms around Naomi. She asked us all about the protest and told us that she had planted herself next to the tickertape machine in the Sarah Lawrence newspaper office, following every bit of news about the march.

We stayed in Manhattan at Aunt Ilse's Upper West Side apartment. My mother's parents, Omi and Opi, came from Buffalo to visit too. Opi argued constantly with my mother about the Peace March, which he called "pointless," and the war in Vietnam, which he called "crucial."

"What you are doing is irresponsible," he admonished my mother. "If you succeed in stopping the war, Communism will be free to spread. Communism is dangerous."

"What's dangerous is standing idly by while our government wages a misguided war," Mom shot back.

* * *

Back home in Seattle, Mom leapt into life with her customary vigor. The Monday after we returned from the East Coast, she had ten photography sittings in a single day. I wrote a report for my ninth grade English class about what I had experienced. I explained how I felt encouraged by the sense of community that had sprung up on the grounds of the Pentagon—by the songs and signs and bonfires. Once back home, I forgot how terrified I had been during the protest, and instead I was proud of my participation.

Naomi and Danny both wrote to me, to tell me how happy it made them to see me. *"Seeing you made me realize that I don't know you as a teenager. You were a little girl when I left,"* Naomi wrote. She had only been gone to college for two months, but I felt like she was right. Between my new position as the second-oldest sibling and my trip to Washington, DC, I felt like I had grown up since she had left for college.

Danny thanked me for visiting. *"Before you came, I just didn't feel quite right about being at college,"* he said. *"I felt more like a family deserter than anything else. But after sharing Swarthmore with you for a day, I feel like our whole family is going here together with me—like miles don't mean anything to the Chotzen family. Even though we might not be able to eat dinner together, we're still living together all the time."*

Just two weeks after Mom and I had returned from our trip, Danny wrote me again, for my fifteenth birthday. His birthday letter was about the privilege of being my brother and what a sweet sister I had been to him, and he sent it from Swarthmore via Special Delivery. I was at school when the mailman delivered it to our door, but I was still delighted to know that Mom had signed for a special delivery letter with my name on it.

Mia, who was nine, presented me with three marigolds, which she had planted in a bean pot. Mom told me that she had taken Mia to the Epiphany Church Thrift Shop at Mia's request; Mia had spent a full hour scouring the shop before she settled on the bean pot.

Joey, who had just turned five, had also picked out a present for me: a bundle of autumn leaves that he had scooped up outside on his way home from kindergarten. He helped me set the table for dinner; his teacher had just taught him the difference between right and left, and now he was eager to learn which side the fork and knife went on, respectively.

"Only forty-two more days until Naomi and Danny come home for the winter break," Simon reported cheerfully. "I've been counting."

At dinner, Uncle Norbert steered the discussion around to Omi's health. He wanted to know how she had looked during our recent visit to New York.

"Not well," my mother answered. "Not strong. But she has never been strong."

Omi must have been particularly not strong, though, because in late November she passed away.

Mom flew out to Buffalo to tend to my grieving grandfather. "He shouldn't be alone," she said.

The March on the Pentagon was a highlight of Danny's freshman year. His classes and schoolwork felt increasingly more irrelevant. Everything important was happening outside of college, he said. Danny's letters didn't hide how troubled and tortured he felt. He was depressed at Swarthmore and wanted to drop out. He wrote to me saying he was in a "daze." He also admitted that he had been smoking lots of marijuana. He wrote to my parents, describing the feeling of being stoned. *"You should sell psychedelic hair ribbons at your company,"* he urged my father.

His candor made my father extremely anxious. "He's in a fog. He needs to see a psychiatrist," my father grumbled. Dad wrote him back, offering stern advice, *"What's wrong with you? Get on your feet and get going!"*

One afternoon, Danny telephoned to tell my parents that he was on an LSD trip. He wanted to report to them everything that he was feeling, seeing, and experiencing. I watched their faces turn from concern to anger to panic as they passed the phone back and forth and listened.

They wrote him warning him that he was sabotaging his leadership potential and ruining his life, and they complained about him weekly to the Friday Night Group, who all shook their heads sadly.

"I'm sorry that I'm failing," Danny wrote in a letter to the whole family. He wasn't failing his classes, but I knew that he felt like he was failing in his mission to save the world, an expectation that was ingrained in all of us.

Danny's letters and phone calls had us all worried. My father even went so far as suggesting having him committed to a mental hospital.

What Danny was experiencing at Swarthmore was mirrored in Seattle. My friends worked harder and harder to zone out; smoking pot and hashish or ingesting mescaline and LSD was a common diversion for them.

Ironically, the pervasive drug culture that my parents were so critical about with Danny infiltrated the Friday Night group. I remember the night when someone rolled a joint and passed it around the room. I watched my father take a hit and pass the joint to my mother. "We've never been stoned before," she giggled excitedly. She passed it along to Dora Miller, who took a hit and handed the joint to Brian Dodd.

Later that winter, a few Friday Nighters tried LSD, but my parents opted not to partake. "I didn't even like the marijuana," my father confided to me.

Mom and Dad were keener about substance-free paths to mind expansion. I joined my mom at a lecture and film about psychic surgeons in the Philippines—healers who claimed that they could reach into patients' stomachs and other parts of their bodies and remove cancerous tumors without ever making an incision. The film was filled with testimonials from patients who had been healed in this way, and after the film a few members of the audience rose to offer similar endorsements.

As we left, my mom wrote her name and address on a mailing list. "Let me know as soon as one of these psychic healers visits Seattle," she told the host.

A few weeks later, she invited a psychic/hypnotist named Jack Schwarz to attend the Friday Night Group to teach us about how the mind could control the body. Jack showed us a large wooden board with rusty nails sticking out of it and removed his shirt. He lay on the board, face-up, his back stretched across the nails. He instructed Greg Miller, who probably weighed 200 pounds, to stand on his chest and stomach.

We could hear the nails puncturing the skin on Jack's back. When he stood up, we saw blood oozing from half-a-dozen puncture wounds. Then, we watched in amazement as—within the hour—the bloody holes closed up and healed. By the time Jack left later that evening, the wounds had transformed into tiny scabs.

After that demonstration, several of the Friday Nighters rushed to make hypnosis appointments with him. Mom—who had already enjoyed one of his hypnosis sessions—made an appointment for me. "He can help you defeat your fear of the dark," she urged.

She drove me to a downtown hotel room and led me inside. Jack sat me in a chair and dangled a chain with a gold watch on it in front of my eyes. "You're entering a dark cave," he narrated in a deep, mysterious voice. "You walk into the cave farther and farther, away from this hotel room. You walk into the blackness of the cave...."

I was resistant and refused to give myself over to his control.

"What if I hold your hand, Claudia?" Mom wanted to know. "Relax. You're safe here."

Jack tried three times, then gave up in frustration. It didn't work. I didn't want it to. So many things felt out of control in my life; I was determined to keep my mind clear.

* * *

Though Mom made multiple visits to Buffalo that winter, she refused to let her mother's death slow her down. She rose before 6 a.m. to work in her darkroom, fit in at least five or six photography sittings a day, continued to attend meetings and rallies and wrote impassioned letters to the superintendent of Seattle Public Schools. She increased her commitments by signing up for a police task force on community relations and a Model Cities Arts Committee, adding those to her busy schedule of CORE, League of Women Voters, and Urban League meetings.

"I don't like to see a committee that doesn't include me," she explained to the Friday Night Group, which still met weekly in our living room. When I was at home on Friday Nights, I involved myself more in the conversations—especially the ones about civil rights and the Vietnam War. I didn't want to believe that problems of an unjust war and civil inequity were unsolvable, but I could sense that I was losing hope.

"We have no choice but to keep fighting and believing that we will make a difference," Mom insisted.

At home, Mom kept us up to date not only about her many activities, but also on her perspective on the challenges of being a white civil rights advocate amidst the burgeoning Black Power movement.

"I may be imagining things, but I have the feeling that my Negro friends aren't quite as chummy as they used to be," Mom remarked. "I guess it just isn't fashionable now for them to be too friendly with whites."

However, Mom was very successful in becoming quite "chummy" with one particular Black man: a musician she had met at a Model Cities Arts Committee meeting. Jerome Cray had come to Seattle from either Vancouver or Los Angeles, depending on which version of the story I heard at different times.

Jerome was 33—ten years younger than my mother. He had arrived in town with a group of five musician buddies—all of them African American—who were in need of a place to live and opportunities to perform their jazz. "They play serious jazz,"

Mom explained admiringly, even though her knowledge of jazz was minimal at best.

I first heard Mom mention Jerome at a Friday Night Group gathering, when she asked John Verrall whether her "musician friend" might be able to come audition for him at the University of Washington. "He's wonderful," she promised. "Negro, bearded, gentle."

"I'm not sure what opportunities I'd be able to find for him," John answered. "But I'd be happy to meet him and hear him play."

Mom spent an entire Saturday making calls to friends and acquaintances, trying to find Jerome and his jazz group a rent-free home. "They're wonderful artists," she said into the phone, over and over again. "They can pay in music, but the rent should be free. Jerome is a gifted composer, and the Jerome Cray Ensemble plays serious jazz."

It didn't take long before Jerome Cray and his highly touted jazz ensemble were in our home. The first time Mom brought them in was to provide musical entertainment for the Friday Night Group. Jerome was tall and muscular, with a beard and a shaved head. His skin was the lightest complexion out of all the men in his ensemble. They shook everybody's hand, then one of the musicians took over the piano, while another borrowed Leah's cello. The rest took out their instruments from the cases they were carrying. Jerome brought out his saxophone.

"They'll just play through the evening as background to our conversation," Mom explained. But the music was loud, and the other Friday Nighters grew frustrated trying to make their voices heard over the music.

"Maybe we can manage without any accompaniment next week," Brian Dodd suggested.

"I don't think so," Mom replied.

Jerome Cray soon became a regular dinner guest in our home, and he often brought his jazz buddies over to eat with us, too. The thick, pungent smoke smell of marijuana pervaded the house.

"They always smell like marijuana. I think Mom lets them smoke it in our house," Leah said.

My mother loved having Jerome around. "He has such beautiful aspirations," she gushed. "He reminds me of Nick Farley." She flirted openly with Jerome at the dinner table and barely seemed to notice my father's presence.

Jerome seldom spoke to any of us, ate a lot, and watched my mother with a wry smile as she doted on him. "It's so nice to have a handsome, creative guest," she commented.

Once, she even announced that we were ready for dinner before my father had returned home from work. "I think we're all here," she declared.

"No, we're not," I corrected her. "Daddy will be home soon. We have to wait."

"Oops," she said, looking directly at Jerome and giggling.

Mom began to cook meals she had never served us before. "They're Jerome's favorites," she explained. Some mornings, Jerome even managed to join us for breakfast.

"Jerome and his friends still haven't found anywhere to live for free," Mom complained, clearly distressed with the community's lack of generosity. "Somebody needs to buy them a house."

Remarkably, my father, who was usually so cautious about how we spent our money, raised no objections when my mother decided that she should be that "somebody"—at least in part. She found a big red rundown house on a corner less than a mile from our family home. She put down the earnest money so that the men could secure the property while they searched for other sponsors, and she promised to help them round up the rest of the necessary funds. She even offered to make the insurance payments for them.

"The Red House isn't just a residence," she explained. "It's a neighborhood community home. The first of its kind. We're using it as a pilot for the Model Cities program."

She wrote to a local arts non-profit group, urging them to fund Jerome's residency in Seattle.

"Jerome Cray is a rare individual," the letter began. *"Magnetic—Jerome is able to make immediate and direct contact with other beings, in groups or individually, Black or white, rich or poor, young or old. By contacting the essence of the other person, he is able to maintain that hold to make the other a better person."*

"A leader among his people and among all people, Jerome Cray will be a rare contribution to the cultural life of Seattle, speaking of culture in the broader human sense. His dream—to pull our country out of the morass of complacency and wake 'em up. The strident quality of his music crystallizes the strident quality of most of our lives in this competitive society, at the same time pointing the way to a resolution of these discords. Physical aspect of the dream—a warm, feeling place where this can happen.

Jerome Cray is truly avant-garde, projecting himself and all of us to a larger home in the universe."

Certainly, on a very personal level, Jerome Cray and my mom had succeeded in lowering the simmering tension in Seattle between Blacks and whites. She spent most of her daytimes at the Red House, where she claimed to be fighting for justice and culture. But when she dragged us along with her after school—as she did at least once a week—I didn't see much evidence of a righteous struggle. The whole living room of the Red House was packed with instruments and musicians. They smoked and drank and laughed and seemed to be enjoying themselves immensely—nobody seemed very concerned about advancing civil rights or enhancing Seattle's cultural climate.

Mom instructed us to stay downstairs in the living room, while she and Jerome disappeared upstairs to relax. "Listen to the musicians," she urged us. "Observe their essence. Make friends with them. Don't interrupt me," as she disappeared up the stairs in a fit of giggles.

"She's not even bothering to sneak around," Leah complained to me. "She's flaunting her affair in everyone's face and Dad doesn't even seem to be upset by it."

One late afternoon, while a few of us sat in the living room of the Red House waiting for Mom to finish her upstairs "relaxing," Joey cut his hand on a rusty nail that protruded from the wall. Joey began to cry, and blood covered his palm.

"I'll get Mom," I decided. I left Joey with Mia, who wrapped his hand in her jacket. I darted up the stairs, which creaked and bounced under the weight of my hasty footsteps.

At the landing, I looked down the long hallway with several big wooden doors—all of them closed. "Mom," I shouted. "It's Claudia."

"In here," she yelled back, from inside one of the rooms. I pushed open the door to find her and Jerome lying naked together on top of the unmade bed, wrapped in an embrace. "What is it?" Mom asked. Jerome did not look up, but he kept his arm draped limply across my mother's waist. Seeing them together, intertwined like that, made me sick to my stomach.

When I told her about Joey's hand, she asked, "How bad is it?"

"He's bleeding a lot," I said.

She sighed. "OK. I'll be down in ten minutes, and I will take you all home."

That night, after cleaning Joey's cut and providing dinner, Mom headed out again. "I have meetings," she explained. She came home late that night, which was getting to be common, usually far beyond the time when her political meetings normally ended. Sometimes she never came home at all. Instead, she floated through the front door the next morning, laughing and kissing each of us while my father helped us get ready for school.

"Hello," she would greet us cheerfully. "What can I do to help?" She looked dreamy, blissful, and just the tiniest bit self-conscious.

Dad barely reacted. At least in front of us, he never yelled, swore, or complained. He returned home from work, kissed my mother if she was home, changed out of his dress shirt, and joined us at the dinner table, where he always praised my mother's cooking—even the meals that she had prepared especially for Jerome.

One evening, when Mom was out, I finally decided to talk to my father about Mom. I lingered in the doorway of his study, where he sat at his desk paying bills. I trembled with apprehension as I approached him.

Unable to look at Dad, I fixed my gaze on the metal elephant statue on his desk. The statue was about a foot tall, with real ivory tusks and a textured black and greenish tint that looked like wrinkled elephant skin. It had come from Dad's childhood home in Germany; it was one of the few household items that his parents had managed to bring to America.

I stared into the elephant's right eye as I tried to summon my courage.

"Daddy, why don't you kick Jerome out of our house?" I asked, trying hard to stifle my tears. "How can you let Mom do this to you? How can you stand it?"

My father said nothing at first, then let out a deep, heavy exhale.

"Claudie Girl," he said, "do you really want to talk about this?"

I choked back more tears and nodded yes.

"I love Carla," he said. "I love her so much, and all I can do is hope that she gets it out of her system." He paused. "There is nothing else I can do. I can't make her want to stay here all the time. I just have to be patient and wait and hope that she will come back to me."

I wanted him to fight for her like the romantic heroes in books and movies. I remained silent, devastated with disappointment.

"Well, at least we know where she is," he added. "That's something to be glad about. We can find her when we need her."

That was true. More than once, I had walked over to the Red House in search of Mom. Dad sent me when he needed to talk to her; apparently, he could tolerate Jerome's presence in our home, but he was unwilling to set foot in the Red House to bring Mom home.

At night, the Red House was now packed with more than musicians. Boys my age, mostly Black but some white and Asian kids too, had started to hang out there, along with females of all races and ages. They sat on couches or leaned against the wall. Cigarettes, weed, and alcohol were everywhere, and kids as young as nine and ten had learned to seek it out as a place to sniff glue and get stoned. Everyone was loaded. The air was always thick with jazz and smoke.

And somewhere—usually upstairs in that same bedroom— I would find Mom. "Isn't it so lively here?" she would gush as she followed me down the creaky stairs.

I wrote to Danny at Swarthmore to complain about Jerome, but he had already heard about him from Mom herself. *"Mom called him her 'new attachment,'"* Danny wrote back. *"She sent me one letter asking me if I knew a wholesale source for grass for Jerome and his friends, then she sent me another letter saying I should ignore that request."*

Danny and Naomi told me that Mom had written both of them to say that she looked forward to their next visit. She had been doing some critical thinking questioning the value of monogamy, and she was eager to debate it with her two oldest children.

I couldn't focus on school. Mom's affair occupied my every thought. Sometimes I had to excuse myself from class to visit the bathroom, where I sat in a stall and cried. Mostly, I wept for

Dad. It made me despondent to see him act so helpless, and I hated myself for feeling so disappointed in him.

On one such occasion I was discovered by Mrs. Nawrot. She had been my seventh grade history teacher, and now she also taught my ninth grade history class.

"Claudia, what's wrong?" She asked, kneeling on the tile floor next to the stall door.

"I can't tell you," I answered between stifled sobs.

"Something at home?" She pressed.

Her sympathy made me cry even harder.

"I can't tell you," I told Mrs. Nawrot again. The secret was too distressing, and I would feel disloyal to my family if I shared it. I could not betray them. Yet it was Mom who was actually betraying our family.

I missed the twins so much that it made me ache. My mother was behaving like a love-drunk teenager, and my friends were changing in ways I had never expected. As my Black friends became angrier and more outspoken, my white friends worked harder and harder to zone everything out. I was sure that everything would be better if Danny and Naomi were nearby to offer guidance and perspective.

My mother's affair with Jerome was never discussed at the Friday Night Group who continued to meet regularly at our home. At the end of one gathering, as everyone was collecting their coats and umbrellas, Brian Dodd pulled me aside.

"Claudia," he said. "I think you should come to Quaker meetings with me. You are searching for strength and peace. This will help you."

I agreed to try it out and thanked him for the suggestion.

"This Sunday," he said. "I'll pick you up."

On Sunday morning, Brian and Rita picked me up and drove me to my first Quaker meeting, at the University Friends Meeting House near the University District.

The meeting had no set agenda. Anyone who was moved to speak was encouraged to do so, and no one argued or even responded directly. Instead, everyone listened appreciatively, and then sat in silence until the next meeting attendee was inspired to share.

The lack of direct conversation was startling to me. No one had to fight to get a point across, or even to be heard. Every statement—every act of sharing—was silently affirmed.

At the end of the meeting, Brian and Rita drove me back to their home in Leschi, to the house I had lived in for the first ten years of my life. It didn't feel like my home anymore, but it was still warm and familiar. Rita set to work on a painting while Brian and I sat together and talked. He asked me what I thought of the meeting, and whether any of the attendees had shared thoughts that I wanted to discuss. In fact, they had. Brian and I talked for two hours about how to maintain hope during trying times, and about why there was so much violence in the world.

When he drove me home, he smiled at me. "Thank you for joining, Claudia," he said. "If you'd like to attend again next Sunday, we'd be happy to drive you."

For the rest of ninth grade, Sunday mornings were reserved for Quaker meetings with Brian and Rita. Each week, when the Friday Night Group dispersed, Brian would grin at me. "I'll see you at 9 o'clock," he'd say, before taking Rita's arm and heading out the front door.

As it turned out, I was not the only Friday Night teenager to bond with one of the adults. One Friday night I came home from Lila's house and heard the adults arguing loudly. Their discussions were often passionate, but I had never heard this kind of tense and angry conversation before. I paused behind the door to listen.

"How can you let Nick do that? Aren't you going to go after them?" John Verrall demanded to the Millers. He sounded furious.

"Nick has always been a free spirit," my mother said, defending Nick. "He is very charming, and he has loved a great many women."

"Well, that's fine when they're grownups," Polly added, sounding as agitated as her husband. "I like Nick, too, but for God's sake he's sixty years old. I would never let him anywhere near my daughter if I had one."

"You have to go get her," John Verrall added. "Go to California. Bring her back home."

"No, she went of her own free will," Dora said. "We're not worried about her. Nick will be good to her, a perfect lover."

I couldn't believe what I was hearing. Nick Farley, the Friday Night member who always seemed to be flirting with my mother—when he wasn't bringing a new wife around—had apparently run off with my lifelong friend, Justine, who was fifteen. And now she was in California, living with Nick Farley as her lover?

Paralyzed with shock, I stood behind the door. I couldn't understand how my parents and the Millers didn't see how bizarre this was. How could they think it was fine that a girl my age had run off with any man—let alone a man in his sixties, and especially with Nick Farley?

"We live in a new era, a time where these things just happen," Dora Miller said, defending not just her daughter, but also her own parenting. "Why should we chase them down? This will be good for her. Every girl needs a first lover. Every teenager needs to experience the thrill of a lover."

This extreme permissiveness, this abdication of accountability by the adults in my life, shocked me. First, my mom had been so flagrant and open about her affair in front of my dad and our whole family, and now my mom and her closest friends didn't see anything wrong with a fifteen-year-old girl running off with a man 45 years older. I wondered if the whole world had gone mad.

* * *

And then, in a moment, things went from bad to worse.

On April 4, 1968, Martin Luther King Jr. was assassinated. I was on a city bus at 5 p.m. on the way to the downtown library to research a project for school. One of the passengers heard the news on her transistor radio and screamed. "They killed Dr. King! They killed Dr. King!" I felt as though I had been kicked in the stomach, and it took me several minutes to catch my breath. Several people near the front began crying hysterically.

In the Central Area, as all over the country, racial tension boiled over. When I entered the grocery store to buy milk, I could feel the torrid hatred in my fellow customers' glances. I was a white girl in their Black neighborhood. It didn't matter that I had lived there all my life—I was now both a stranger and an enemy.

The incidents in our own neighborhood mirrored what was happening around the country. Stores and shops took a beating as angry people took to the streets. Brenner Brothers' Bakery shut down after its windows were smashed. Two neighborhood hardware stores locked their doors and sent their employees home. A local drugstore and an all-night grocery quickly installed iron bars on their doors and windows, hoping to stay in business. A dry cleaner was firebombed, as was the local firehouse. Several other businesses burned to the ground.

One of Simon's friends told him that he had started selling Molotov Cocktails—homemade bombs created by filling a glass bottle with gasoline, then stuffing in a rag and lighting it like a wick. "Everyone's buying them," Simon's friend told him. "Except for people making their own."

Armed robberies were commonplace—not just in the shops, but on the residential streets, too. We avoided walking as much as possible. And when my parents drove us to school, angry African American kids hurled rocks at the windows of our station wagon. It was terrifying to drive through our neighborhood; we were afraid to leave the house and would cower in the car. A thick layer of broken glass and debris covered our Madrona community. The air was filled with black smoke and sirens. The closest burning building was never far away. It was like living in a warzone.

The Black Panthers set up their Seattle headquarters in a nearby storefront, and some of Naomi, Danny, and Leah's old friends—kids we'd grown up with—guarded the door with guns.

The Panthers did their marching drills on the playground of Madrona Elementary, where they trained the Black students. They paraded down 34th Avenue, with their firearms held high, offering a visual display of their official motto: "Power is in the barrel of a gun."

My mother tried her best to be a voice for racial harmony. She attended more meetings than ever, held urgent conversations with local civil rights leaders in our kitchen, wrote letters to the Seattle school superintendent, and continued to meet Jerome at the Red House at every possible opportunity.

Two weeks after Dr. King's assassination, Floyd McKissick, the national leader of CORE, was scheduled to come to Seattle. My parents offered to host the reception in our home, and the Seattle chapter agreed.

We all spent an entire weekend preparing to host this major event—scrubbing every surface of the house and helping my mother to set out snacks, beverages, and napkins. "This is an important opportunity," she said. "It's an honor to host this reception, and it's a chance for us to demonstrate how essential we are to the movement." She inspected the house several times, clearing off piles of her customers' black and white photos from the surfaces of the buffet and dining room table.

When McKissick arrived, he cut his own path through the crowd, past my parents' outstretched hands, and into my father's study. He sequestered himself there for the remainder of the evening, and never came out while his armed bodyguards stood by the door and prohibited any white guests—including my parents—from entering.

My mother tried to greet a Seattle CORE leader, Dwayne Hall. He shot her a nasty look and turned away. All evening, I watched as my parents and their white friends were completely ignored by our Black guests.

"*McKissick's not my guy*," Mom wrote to the Naomi and Danny afterward. "*Such is the new life. I don't like it entirely.*"

"*Dan-Man, I'm having trouble with young Negroes' hostility!*" Dad expressed in a letter to Danny. "*Dwayne Hall just about spit into Mom's face at the McKissick party when she reached out to welcome him.*"

"*My fear*," Mom wrote, "*is that America is ripe for Armageddon, whites arming against blacks as in the days of Nat Turner and the slave revolt.*" But my mother's relationship with Jerome, who was African American, did not seem to have cooled. She was still seeing him on a regular basis, and we all knew about it.

If Mom was affronted by Floyd McKissick's hostility in her own home, it was nothing compared to the devastating news she received a few days later. When she arrived at her regular CORE meeting, she was forcibly escorted back to the parking lot. CORE had officially decided to restrict its membership to Black citizens. Mom was out.

She sat in our living room, staring into the study where McKissick had insulated himself earlier that same week. It seemed impossible that only two years earlier we had hosted the celebration party for the school boycott—the boycott my mom had played a key role in organizing—in this same room.

"No more white women," they had told her. "No more white anybody." She had dedicated so much of her life to fighting for civil rights, and now the movement was kicking her out.

That night, Mom went to bed early. She didn't sit with us at dinner; she didn't leave to see Jerome. No one tried to cheer her up. We understood her sadness, and we mourned along with her.

"For Sale" and "For Rent" signs sprang up around the Central Area. The number of white families in the neighborhood, never very high, was shrinking quickly. Fear pervaded our homelife like never before. Joey, Mia, Charlotte, and Simon walked to Madrona Elementary School as a group, hoping there would be safety in numbers. Simon enrolled in Judo classes, hoping to protect his younger siblings from bullies, but he couldn't learn quickly enough.

One night in March, Joey went missing. Normally my mother would have barely noticed, but Madrona no longer felt as safe as it once had. At quarter to nine, when it had been dark for hours, she called around to the neighbors, asking if they had seen him. "Is Joey playing at your house just now?" she asked, trying to sound casual. When the phone calls didn't unearth Joey, my mother sent Simon out to look for him. After scouring the neighborhood for an hour, Simon found our littlest brother in a triplex on the corner, having his portrait painted by an art student named Ted. "If you're going to wander the neighborhood alone," my mom suggested to my five-year-old brother, "try doing it before dark."

But it was dangerous before dark, too. One afternoon Leah and I were attacked in Madrona Park, just across the street from our house, by a group of Black teenage girls we didn't know. When one of the girls shoved me without provocation, Leah leapt to my defense. "Leave her alone," she shouted. "You walk away, and we'll walk away too!"

But the girls didn't want to walk away. They shoved Leah, too, and then they began to throw punches. We fought back, but we were outnumbered five to two. By the time the girls walked away, we were badly beaten and bruised.

My parents had raised us in the Central Area to teach us that race didn't matter, but now that lesson was being drowned out by violence at every turn. Family friends who lived in other neighborhoods and my mom's photography customers were reluctant to visit us.

The atmosphere unnerved my parents who were hauntingly reminded of their final years in Germany. My mother recalled how she and her fellow Jewish classmates had been kicked out of school when she was eleven. My father remembered returning home from his first job in Berlin after college to find that his friends would no longer speak to him. I listened to my parents, terrified that we were having an analogous experience. Already, my Black friends refused to look me in the eye when I passed them in the hallways or cafeteria.

When Bobby Kennedy was shot in early June, the violence escalated another notch. A paint shop, a supermarket, and the home of a state senator in our neighborhood were firebombed.

The twins returned home from college for the summer to a different community than the one they had left that fall. Danny lingered glumly around the house for less than a week and then left for California, where he planned to live with two of his longtime friends from Garfield High. "I don't want to be here," he told me. "Everything about it feels wrong." Naomi dealt with the violence happening all around us by being her usual industrious self. She taught swim classes and worked as lifeguard at Madison Park on Lake Washington—a rare feat of routine normality amidst our mostly terrifying days.

Even the air felt hotter. Charlotte, Mia, and I left all eight windows in our bedroom open every night, trying to get a cross breeze. Howling sirens, raucous parties on Madrona Beach, and drunken fights kept me awake, but my sisters were able to tune out the chaos and sleep. Lying awake, alert, listening to the sounds of the night while they dozed, I felt like I was my family's protector.

One night I heard explosions, followed by sirens. I ran to the window and saw flames erupt from the boats at Yaba Marina, just down the road on Lake Washington Boulevard.

The next morning, I read in the newspaper that the marina had been targeted because wealthy, white Bellevue residents including the governor, Dan Evans, reportedly moored their boats there.

And then our house was threatened, too. A Black friend of Mom's warned her that plans had been made to firebomb the homes of all remaining Central Area white families. "We're on the list," Mom reported.

I stayed awake every night, expecting a Molotov cocktail to soar through an open window and land near our beds. I kept track of where our pets slept, ready to grab them at a moment's notice as we fled from the growing flames. I knew that Mia would be inconsolable if her cat Rascal or our new puppy, Sabra, were left behind. I watched my sisters toss and turn in their sleep, glancing back and forth between them and the open windows just to be sure that they were safe. I was awake and on guard—in a constant state of terror and alertness.

The few white families that remained in the neighborhood were making plans to leave. Finally, I asked the question that was most on my mind. "When are we going to move?"

My parents shook their heads. "We're not," they told me. "We haven't even discussed it. This is our home."

I argued and begged them to reconsider. "We're not safe here. I can't sleep because somebody has to watch Mia and Charlotte and Joey. Please, let's sell the house and find a new neighborhood."

It drove my mother crazy. "Enough," she said. "If you want out, you can go spend some time with Danny in California. Have some loyalty to your neighborhood."

It wasn't the solution I wanted, but I missed Danny, and I took the opportunity even though I was very worried about leaving Simon, Mia, Charlotte, and Joey at home without me there to guard them.

Danny met me at the San Francisco airport, and we hitchhiked to Nick Farley's house. Standing next to Danny on the side of the road, with our thumbs stretched out towards the passing cars, I felt like I was seeing him in a whole new light.

We started to talk—to really confide in one another—and we didn't stop for days. Danny described how hard it had been for him to leave the family and travel three thousand miles away for college. He spoke about his frustrations with Mom and Dad—that they expressed only disappointment, and not empathy, when he shared that he was having difficulty feeling happy at his insular, bucolic college.

I had been frustrated with them, too, I told him. I was resentful of Mom's ongoing affair with Jerome, and I was angry with Dad for enduring the humiliation so passively. And I was angry with both of them for their stubborn refusal to leave Madrona, when routines that should be simple in daily life grew more and more dangerous. Interestingly, anger about being the victim of incest didn't enter my mind. I was still unconscious about the abuse because it had been such a regular, 'normalized' part of my life.

When I returned to Seattle after two weeks with Danny, I felt stronger and more confident.

"Did you straighten your brother out?" My parents wanted to know.

"He doesn't need straightening out," I replied irritably. "He just needs support." Then I broke the news that Danny had decided to stay in California instead of returning to Swarthmore for his second year. Later the Dean wrote to tell him that he would be welcome back any time. The Dean cited a benefit concert Danny had organized as a tremendous accomplishment and called him "a great asset to the Swarthmore community."

"If he's such an asset, he ought to go back there," my father complained.

As the sweltering summer of 1968 ended, Mom's trips to the Red House became less frequent. Simon had heard that Jerome Cray was now living with a woman named Teri and that they just had a baby together.

I resumed my nightly watch over my younger brothers and sisters as the world outside our windows continued to fracture and crumble.

And then, one night, the Red House was firebombed. "It burned to the ground," Mom informed us at breakfast. I expected her to be angry, but mostly she just sounded defeated.

Jerome Cray and the Jerome Cray Ensemble disappeared. They had arrived in our lives with great noise and fanfare, but they vanished in the wind.

Months later, I sat with my father beside the Leschi tennis courts, waiting for our turn to play. Simon and my mother—our doubles partners—lingered by the parking lot, where Mom flirted with a stranger.

Dad and I sat in silence, watching her. I was sure that he, too, was thinking of Jerome.

"Daddy," I asked. "How could you let her do that, with Jerome? How could you let her parade that in your face? You let him sit like a king at our own dinner table."

His eyes filled with tears.

"Claudie Weibly," he said. "You almost had another sibling."

"A brother or a sister?" I wanted to know, but Dad shook his head.

"It doesn't matter. I don't know. It wouldn't have been my child." He turned his eyes to the ground and continued. "Your mother believed she was pregnant with Jerome's baby. She wasn't pregnant, but if she had been, that child would have needed a father and a family. It would have needed brothers and sisters. Carla needed a husband to raise it alongside her."

I stared at him, absorbing his words.

"It would have been humiliating and everyone would have known that it wasn't my child. But what choice would I have had?"

Four years later, Jerome Cray's presence resurfaced in my life when I was nineteen and attending the University of

Washington. I rented a room in a house in the Montlake area, near the University. For weeks, I was plagued by vivid nightmares of firebombs and Black Panther marches, of shoving my way through crowds of stoned musicians and teenagers, of memories of the Red House. Every night I slept fitfully and woke up terrified.

One afternoon, when chatting with the professor who owned the house, he reeled off a partial list of the odd and interesting tenants who had lived there.

"A few years back, there was a jazz musician," he recalled. "A Black guy. Real tall. Played the saxophone. Stayed in the same room where you stay. Name of Jerome Cray."

I moved out immediately.

* * *

As the summer of 1968 ended, high school beckoned. In an attempt to attract more white students to Garfield High School, the school board had started a "Magnet Program," a special arts program, offering pottery, painting, drawing, and dance classes. I had planned to attend Garfield anyway, but I was excited about the new arts program. I was particularly thrilled by the opportunity to integrate my love for dance as part of my regular school day schedule.

As it turned out, the handful of white transfer students that the program attracted actually increased racial tension. Magnet classes were held in an empty elementary school across the football field from the main high school building, away from the main campus. For some reason, the new magnet arts program only attracted white students. There was nothing diverse or integrated about white students attending art classes in a separate building, and the magnet students were easy, obvious targets for our angry Black peers.

My Black girl classmates no longer pressed their hair, nor did they admire mine. Instead, a few had adopted the practice of grabbing onto white girls' hair in the bathrooms and hallways of Garfield and chopping it off with scissors and knives.

Leah and I pinned our hair up under bandanas. We stopped wearing jewelry; long earrings would get forcefully yanked from white girls' earlobes. And since it wasn't safe to carry a purse at school, we kept our money in our tights, down around our ankles.

Every day was an experience in terror and survival. Our actual classes were a joke. Education was no longer a priority. Chaos reigned. Integration had devolved into disintegration.

Despite the best efforts of the administrators and teachers, much of the action was unfolding in the school hallways and outside the building. Most classes were at least half-empty, and those teachers that tried to press on were faced with constant challenges. Screams rang from the hallways, uninvited guests stormed into lectures. A lesson on *Macbeth* was interrupted when a student collapsed from a drug overdose. Another English teacher was assaulted in the middle of class and carted away to the hospital, his head split and bleeding.

And the violence wasn't just coming from students. Angry Black adults routinely stormed in from the streets, marching through hallways and classrooms while they looked for white teachers, white students, white anybody to attack.

Many of the Black friends I had grown up with at Leschi, Madrona, and Meany JHS stopped speaking to me completely. A few still acknowledged me—at least insofar as they nodded at me in the hallways or spared me from the beatings that were happening. We were no longer friends—they would have been labeled traitors if they had sat with me at lunch or chatted with me in the bathrooms—but our history of friendship still lingered, like a thin protective shield.

But though I was an occasional beneficiary of these long-ago friendships, I had no power to protect my white friends from abuse. When I saw a group of my Black classmates from elementary school assaulting my good friend Lila, I tried to intervene.

Doug Jones, whose pet crow had often perched outside my third grade window, glared at me. "Shut up Chotzen," he said. "Get out of here, or you'll be next." I cowered as they hit Lila with sticks, dumped the contents of her purse onto the pavement, and made off with her watch.

I banded together with my small group of friends at Garfield to weather the chaos and violence. We escorted each other to class, stood guard for one another in the bathroom, and spoke honestly about the terror we felt every time we arrived at school and our despair that the struggle for the civil rights movement had crumbled into more violence and hatred.

"I'm depressed," Vanessa confessed to me. "My mom is worried about me." I was depressed, too, although my mother was unaware, and consequently unconcerned.

After ballet class one afternoon, Vanessa reported that she had tried a new kind of therapy. "It's helping," she said. "You should try it."

It was through an organization called Personal Counselors—or P.C. for short. Its philosophy centered on one-to-one peer counseling (or "co-counseling") experiences in which participants expressed themselves to an equal, rather than to a professional. Each person paired off and took turns as the "client" or the "counselor," alternating between expressing their deepest feelings and listening patiently.

Vanessa, Lila and I started Personal Counseling classes in downtown Seattle together, and we learned this new technique. P.C. gave me an outlet to express my fear and sadness, but it could not protect me from the dangers of Garfield High School.

At home, Mom busied herself with photography. "I'm doing better than ever," she insisted. "At least five sittings a day." She also made daily visits to Group Health Hospital to see Gertie Nussbaum, her longtime friend and our family's grocery shopper. Gertie had cancer.

The minimum age for visitors at Group Health Hospital was fourteen, which meant that only Leah and I were old enough to accompany Mom. I was nervous the first time I came along—I had never set foot in a hospital before. I followed my mother into the lobby, past the reception desk, into the elevator, up to the fourth floor, and down the corridor to Gertie's hospital room. There were two beds and two patients in the room; another very sick-looking woman lay in the bed by the door, while Gertie's bed was by the window that looked down onto 15th Avenue.

My mother leaned down and embraced Gertie. She kissed her face, as though she was not at all concerned about all the tubes and machines and smells of disease that seemed overwhelming to me. I was terrified of getting too close to Gertie, but Mom didn't seem to be afraid at all. She spoke to Gertie in a calm, reassuring voice and wiped her forehead with a cool cloth. She refilled her glass with water and ice cubes and kissed her again. I had never seen her so tender and nurturing, not even with the babies in our family.

"It's scary, isn't it?" Leah asked me when I got home. She had accompanied Mom on a hospital visit earlier that week. "Hospitals are awful. All those strange machines, and that smell."

I murmured my agreement, but mostly I couldn't stop thinking about the unfamiliar gentleness with which Mom had treated her dying friend.

Most days that fall, Mom visited the hospital alone. Occasionally she brought me or Leah or Dad along, though Dad's business was enjoying a thriving autumn, which meant that he was out of town often.

He was gone on November 7th, my sixteenth birthday. He left me a rhyming poem, written on free stationary from the Knight's Inn Motel in Yakima.

It is bad when a Dad

Is away on the day
When his girl does unfurl
In the mean sweet sixteen
It is good when understood
That the Dad has had
Much regret, and did fret
That the love for his dove
He had to state a day late.

Gertie died a few days after my birthday. I grieved with the rest of our family, but the somber sadness of cancer was mostly drowned out by the deafening danger of Garfield High School. I felt lucky to make it home unscathed—but our Madrona streets felt equally terrifying. It was heartbreaking to watch my teachers and classmates give up, knowing that nothing could be learned or taught anymore.

The school administration could not protect us either, though they tried. The lunchroom and bathrooms—where the most assaults occurred—were locked up. Armed guards were stationed in the hallways, and police patrolled the perimeter of the Garfield campus. Students and teachers were required to show identification before entering the building.

I missed traditional academics, but at least I had dance. To attend my magnet dance classes, I had to cross the football field, leave the campus boundaries, and enter an old building that had once served as Horace Mann Elementary School. The walk was short, but scary. Drug addicts, pimps, and other rough-looking people lined the fence, waiting to prey on passersby. My classmates and I were careful to walk in a group. I loved dance class—it allowed me a temporary escape from the pervasive violence around us, while I focused on the precision of "pliés" and "relevés".

On a Thursday in May, I stayed after class to talk with my ballet teacher about a summer dance program at the University of Washington. "Don't wait for me," I told my friends. I didn't want to make them late for class.

After talking with my teacher, I removed my ballet slippers and dropped them into my dance bag, laced up my sneakers, and slipped a T-shirt on over my leotard. I left the building cautiously, nervous about walking back to the high school building alone.

Just after I left the building an arm flew out of nowhere and grabbed me tightly around the neck. I could smell the stench of stale alcohol, and I felt the blade of a knife pressing into my T-shirt and against my side. I stole a look at the man's face. He was a young, light-skinned Black man, with frizzy, almost reddish hair.

He grabbed me around my chest and pulled me behind the building, with the knife still digging into my side.

"Hey man," I said, hoping to reason with him. "Cool it. I can give you some money if you want."

His eyes were wild and bloodshot, and his face had a dazed, stoned look. I had seen those eyes and that expression on many of my friends, and I guessed that he had mixed too many drugs with too much alcohol.

"Take my bag," I told him. "You can have my bag. There's money in it. I don't have anything else valuable. I'll give it to you." I thought if I kept talking or gave him what he wanted, he wouldn't stab me.

I heard a car pull into the parking lot, just around the corner of the building. "If you let me go, you can have it," I continued. Waiting until I heard the car door open and close, I screamed at the top of my lungs and pushed my dance bag towards him. The man loosened his grip on my neck to reach for the bag. I twisted my body away from the knife and out of his grasp, bolted around the corner and ran straight into Jim, the pottery teacher.

"Are you okay?" he exclaimed.

"He has a knife," were the only words I could spit out.

I ran on, away from the building, while Jim shouted for help. I turned back to see my attacker heading away from the school, pursued by Jim and two other teachers who had run out of the classrooms.

Later, after I had described the man to the police, still scared, I trudged home.

When I told my parents what had happened, they listened with concern.

An hour later, Charlotte turned up with her nose bleeding and broken. Three teenagers had beaten her up on her way home from third grade. "I won't go back to school," she insisted from behind a mask of bloody tissues. "I'm never going back."

My father swore in German, while my mother paced around the kitchen frantically. "Carla, we have to move," Dad said, finally. "We cannot live here any longer." Mom let out a deep, sad sigh, and then she agreed.

Bellevue

1969–1971

R arely had I seen my parents act so decisively and as much in unison. Before the school year ended, they had bought a house on the other side of Lake Washington, in Bellevue. Though it was only nine miles from our Madrona home—a twenty-minute drive across a floating bridge—Bellevue was a vastly different world from the Central Area neighborhoods in which I had spent my first sixteen years. It was an upscale suburban community, a picturesque collection of lakeside homes, flanked by manicured lawns, American flags, and private docks. And it seemed that everyone was white.

As kids, we had spent our childhoods pointing across the lake, scoffing at "rich, white Bellevue" and its cloistered inhabitants who lived in a homogenous bubble, seemingly insulated from the struggles for diversity, civil rights, and integration that consumed our lives. The place we had denigrated would now be our refuge, our safe haven.

Although I had begged my parents to find a less dangerous alternative to our neighborhood and schools, their decision to move to Bellevue seemed extreme. Lila and Vanessa were also fleeing Garfield High School, but they were heading to safer schools within Seattle.

"What happened to fighting for integration?" I demanded of my parents. "Did you just give up on that?

My mother looked tired, defeated. "We're moving so the family can be safe," she said. "I won't discuss it anymore."

Our new home in Bellevue was right on the lake. We had our own boat dock, but unlike most of our neighbors, we had no boat to go along with it. Still, the dock was great for swimming, sunbathing, and hanging out.

Our Bellevue home was smaller than the Madrona one had been. "It's because Bellevue is expensive," my father explained.

"It's because three of our children are no longer living with us," my mother countered.

The ground floor had the kitchen and a dining room that opened onto a patio that overlooked the lake. Two bedrooms were also downstairs: one that Simon and Joey shared, and another for Charlotte and Mia. My mother's darkroom was in the basement. Upstairs, we had a large family room, a bathroom, my parents' bedroom, and a bedroom just for me.

There were no rooms designated for Leah or the twins. "I guess Mom doesn't want me to visit often," Leah observed.

I wondered why I was the only family member who had been assigned a bedroom of my very own. Was this an effort to appease me because I had been so vocal in accusing my parents of hypocrisy in this move to Bellevue? Or was my private bedroom part of an unspoken plan to keep me accessible for Mom's night visits?

After hearing about the move, Naomi and Danny were very upset. Danny had moved back to Seattle and taken up residence in the Dodd's basement, in the same Leschi house we used to live in. He played the saxophone all night with a group of musician friends. He rarely surfaced during the day; when he did, he was sullen and angry. Naomi was only home for a short time before leaving for Washington, D. C. to work as an intern in Ralph Nader's office. Leah had gone to Israel immediately after her graduation from Garfield; she planned to spend a year there taking classes and working on a kibbutz before starting college.

My younger siblings didn't voice the same fierce opposition to the move, though they did seem somewhat disoriented by

Bellevue's unfamiliar atmosphere. Mia kept herself busy by tending to our animals. "It must be very strange and hard for them to move somewhere so new and different," she mused, with a hint of her own panic in her voice.

She had a new pet to care for, a rabbit she named Duchess. My father helped Mia build a large pen outside in the yard. Duchess quickly became Mia's favorite companion; when the rest of us headed down the steps to dangle our feet in the lake, Mia exited the front door to sit with her black and white bunny. That summer, if we ever needed to find Mia, Duchess' pen was always the first (and usually the only) place to look.

Simon seemed to adjust to the move better than the rest of us. He loved the lake, and he appreciated the outdoor space that the suburbs afforded. "There's so much room to play sports," he observed. He was thirteen, social, and eager to start eighth grade and make new friends.

I rejected the family move to Bellevue so strongly that I wondered if I could live in Seattle with one of my friends' families. I wanted to be in Seattle to continue the co-counseling my friends and I were finding so helpful; I managed to stay away from home as often as possible that first Bellevue summer. Lila invited me to join her family for a week-long vacation on nearby Vashon Island. I accepted, which made my mother furious.

"If you love your family, you need to treat us like your top priority. It's terrible of you to keep breaking away." When I returned from my week with Lila's family, Mom yelled at me for abandoning my younger brothers and sisters, and for avoiding my household responsibilities.

In order to find a sense of peace in the new house, I started spending every night outside, sleeping on the deck which looked out to Lake Washington. Under the night sky, I was lulled to sleep by the gentle cadence of waves lapping against the shore. On some summer nights the weather was clear, and I could see stars, too. I continued to sleep on the deck when the

school year started. Maybe, in an unconscious way, I was
avoiding my mother's bedroom visits.

As the weather turned cooler, and the autumn rain fell, I
pushed my sleeping bag under the slight overhang of the roof,
covered it with a tarp, and drifted off to the rhythmic sound of
raindrops splashing against the deck, the dock, and the lake.

* * *

I was unprepared for the culture shock of my junior year at
Bellevue High School. My new girl classmates dressed as
though they had stepped right off the pages of Seventeen
Magazine; they had straightened, glossy hair with bangs and
perfectly assembled outfits in the latest trendy styles. I wore
leotards and long flowered skirts that practically screamed
"Dancer" and "Not From Here."

When my classmates learned that I had transferred from
Garfield High School, they peppered me with questions. "Did
you carry a knife for protection?" they wanted to know. Most
of them had never spent time with anyone different than
themselves; their knowledge of Seattle's Central Area was
limited to reports about violence that they had read in the
newspapers or seen on TV.

My new routine demanded none of the obsessive vigilance
or defensive tactics that had dominated my life at Garfield, but
I was surprised to discover that I missed the vitality of living in
the inner city. At Bellevue High School, cars, dating, parties,
and shopping seemed to occupy my classmates' minds more
than the dramatic changes happening in the rest of the world.
At school, I felt distant and lonely.

My parents bought me a used Buick to help with driving the
younger kids to school and to their after-school activities. It also
helped me to get back and forth to Seattle. Dance classes and
co-counseling sessions in Seattle kept me connected to familiar
activities that I loved. I could forget about culture shock once I

began to dance. And in my counseling sessions, I felt that I was beginning to find a sense of my own strength and a nascent feeling of control over my own life. Most days, as soon as school ended, after picking up and distributing my younger siblings, I headed to a dance class. Personal Counseling was the other buoy that kept me afloat during those first few months in Bellevue.

My parents saw how important P.C. was to me, and they helped me pay for classes, which cost $20 for an eight-week session. I was grateful to them for their help and support. I believed that I was learning to be a better daughter, sister, and friend through P.C., as well as a more confident version of myself.

The more our friends saw how much happier Vanessa, Lila and I were becoming, the more curious they became about P.C. By the end of September, more friends had also enrolled in classes at Personal Counselors. In addition to the classes, which we attended one night each week, Vanessa's parents offered their home as a site for our own weekly, teen group counseling sessions. Six of us met at Vanessa's house every Saturday morning, and Vanessa's mother, Joanne, led the group.

Sharing our deepest feelings was a vulnerable and rewarding experience. Vanessa's stepfather, Bill, was always in the next room preparing snacks for us to enjoy as soon as we finished.

Saturdays quickly became the highlight of my week. After a week apart, my friends and I would gather, counsel, and then spend the remainder of the day together. After lunch at Vanessa's, we would drive to the street fair in the University District and then swing by Volunteer Park for late afternoon rock concerts. We didn't get stoned. P.C. made us feel more hopeful; we didn't want to do anything to counteract those good feelings.

In the evenings, I often returned with Vanessa to her home to join her family for dinner. Bill and Joanne were always delighted to see me, eager to hear about everything that was on my mind. Bill had a huge, robust laugh; he would throw his head back and laugh so fully that it was impossible not to laugh along with him. He was a big teaser, but always in a playful way.

Their home was quiet and organized and relaxing. Nobody expected me to clean up or do chores—and when I offered, they refused to let me help. "You're a guest," Joanne said. But she treated me more like a member of the family, like a daughter. "It's so good to see both of our girls," she'd exclaim when Vanessa and I walked through the door together.

"Are you sure you don't want to stay the night here?" she would ask whenever I gathered my things and prepared to drive back over the Lake Washington Floating Bridge to Bellevue. Often, I did decide to stay.

Bill and Joanne also took P.C. classes and co-counseled regularly themselves, and they observed its positive effects on Vanessa and her friends, and me, in particular. "When I met you," Bill once told me, "you looked like a beaten dog. Your head hung down. You had so little confidence. Now you smile more, and you laugh more often, and there's a new kind of strength emerging from you. Joanne and I talk about it sometimes, about how we feel like there's an entirely different young person in our home. It makes us so happy and proud."

Bill's observations shocked me. I was unaware that I had appeared so pathetic. For the first time in my life, I was feeling welcomed, cared about and loved by another set of adults. They felt like a lifeline to me.

* * *

At home, the winter rain and cold finally drove me off the deck and into my bedroom, where I felt more vulnerable.

Mia worried about the cold weather too, though it was Duchess the rabbit that evoked her concern. She pleaded with my mother to let her bring Duchess inside, but Mom refused to have an indoor rabbit. "The bunny will be fine outside," she insisted. "Bunnies are used to living outside. That's where they belong."

I was grateful to have the privacy of my own bedroom, although Mom reminded me that too much privacy wasn't healthy or fair to the rest of the family. "Families shouldn't have secrets," she said. "That's what makes us a family."

When Mom noticed that the door to my room was closed, she would open it. "I'm getting dressed," I'd occasionally protest.

"I'm your mother," she'd retort; "You should always be happy to see me."

I persisted and asked her to please knock on my door before opening it.

"That's ridiculous," my mother responded. "We are not a family of knockers. I don't knock on the neighbors' doors when I want to visit. Why should I knock on my own daughter's door?"

She had already made me feel guilty for spending so much time away from the family. Now I was being made to feel that my desire for privacy was selfish or self-centered. I didn't really know why I wanted to spend more time away from her, but it worried me that I was hurting her feelings. She was my mom. I wanted her love and approval.

I wrote her a note apologizing for my need for privacy. For sixteen years, I had been conditioned to having her invade every aspect of my life. There were no boundaries in our family.

A few times I came home and noticed that my diary wasn't where I had left it. I suspected that my mother had read it. I wrote about this—and to her—in my diary: "*Are you reading what I'm writing here, Mom? Please, please, please don't! I feel guilty for accusing you. I feel guilty for having angry feelings about you right now.*"

I felt most confused about her frequent early morning visits. In our new Bellevue home, she no longer climbed on top of me and had orgasms. Now she came into my bedroom before it was light, slipping into my bed while I was still asleep. I would emerge from my dreams to find her naked body pressed up against me. "Good morning," she breathed, as her hands moved under my pajama shirt and fondled my breasts.

I froze like I had done all my life.

"I love to cuddle with you to wake you up," she whispered. "Isn't this the nicest way to start the day? You have the softest skin, and I love your smooth breasts. You are so feminine."

A voice was screaming inside me—a new one that had never been there before, or perhaps one that I had never been able to hear before. *Get the fuck away from me! Take your fucking hands off my body.*

It was the angriest I had ever felt, and it scared me. I focused all my energy on shutting the voice up, on staying silent, to not confront her. But sometimes, the anger slipped out of me. "Get off me, Mom," I blurted more than once. "Get your hands off me." Or sometimes just a simple "Leave me alone!" It was not a powerful voice; I was still afraid to stand up to her.

On the few occasions when I did speak up, she recoiled as though I had struck her. A sad, wounded expression spread across her face. Naked, she climbed out of the bed and stepped away. "How can you yell at me that way? I just stopped by to love you. I just want to show you how much I love you."

Immediately guilt would overwhelm me. I felt terrible for hurting her feelings, and I always apologized before she left the room.

One Sunday morning, I awoke not to my mother's hands on me, but to a shriek of anguish. I jumped out of bed and yelled downstairs. When no one answered, I rushed out of my room, and realized the cries were coming from outside.

Mia sat near the lake cradling Duchess' frozen body in her arms. She shook with deep, heaving sobs and pressed the lifeless rabbit against her trembling chest. Duchess' eyes were wide open and blank, and a thin glaze of ice covered her black and white fur. I kneeled beside Mia and took her in my arms, holding her as tightly as she held her dead rabbit, as she cried and cried and cried.

* * *

My father had saved three thousand dollars for each of us in a college fund and often told us, "A good education is the most important gift we can give our children."

In the fall of 1969, barely a month into my junior year of high school, I asked my parents for a private discussion.

"I want to use my college savings for P.C.," I told them.

"We help pay for your P.C. classes," Dad said. "And you do counseling with your friends on the weekends, which is good and free."

"I want to have private sessions with Mary McCabe, who is one of the leaders of P.C.," I told them.

"You go to so many sessions already," Mom pointed out.

"Not private sessions," I told them. "Vanessa goes, and she's really transformed." It was true. All my friends were growing happier and more confident, but Vanessa's outlook on the world had evolved to the point of being positively hopeful. The way she walked, the way she spoke, the way she laughed— everything about her was lighter and more optimistic.

Dad sighed. "How much do they cost?"

"They're not cheap," I said. "I'd like to use my college savings."

My father's face turned from astonishment to indignation, and my mother shook her head in disbelief. "It is essential that you attend college," my father began.

"I'll still go to college," I said. "If I feel better about myself, if I'm happier and more confident, I'll be ready for college when I go. I don't have any other money to spend on counseling."

My mother stayed silent. This was not her battle.

"Counseling is all very nice," Dad said. "But college is non-negotiable."

"I don't want to spend your savings and drop out, like Danny," I said. "I don't want to go to college and be angry at the world."

My father's irritation seemed to turn inward. He seethed. Neither of my parents acknowledged what I had just said about my brother, but the whole room felt heavier.

I pressed my point. "It's money you saved for me, right, Dad?"

I paused and waited. I studied Dad's face and was glad to see that the anger had passed. Now he looked thoughtful.

"We'll think about it," he offered, which seemed to me like an excuse for him to delay.

But the next evening, Dad found me on the dock and surprised me. "I thought about it all night and today and discussed it with your mother. If it's so important to you, then we want you to use the college fund money to pay for counseling," he said.

As soon as I began my private sessions with Mary, I understood Vanessa's transformation in a new light. Mary was a veteran and expert counselor. From the moment I walked into her office I felt safe. She gave the most astute feedback, and she gently led me to express emotions that were deeper and more painful than anything I had even realized were inside me.

With Mary, I felt truly listened to and supported for the first time in my life. I spent entire sessions working not on my sixteen-year-old worries, but instead mired in furious, wordless sobbing like a terrified baby who was too young to have any words.

"I don't know what is bringing up so much pain," I told Mary. "I don't have specific memories of being hurt, but when I think about being little, I feel so helpless and desperate. And alone. I can't explain it." She told me that it didn't matter, that I didn't need to know or to explain. P.C. wasn't about talking—it was about releasing deep trauma and pain.

Gradually, a vague memory formed of a man—a dangerous and threatening man. "There was a man who hurt me," I told Mary. "I think I was just a baby. I don't know who he was." The memory began to take fuller shape. It was frightening to have these memories and to experience this deep terror. But Mary encouraged me and made me feel safe, and I emerged from my sessions with her feeling cleansed and cared for. She gave me a piece of paper that said, *"I will never be a helpless baby again. I'm a grown young woman in charge of my environment."* I carried it with me in my pocket or purse everywhere I went.

P.C. instilled in me a new, positive energy, and I tried my best to share it with the rest of my family. The Bellevue move had had a tumultuous impact on the Chotzen clan; somehow, in the absence of inner-city chaos and violence, we became moodier and more impatient with one another.

We felt isolated in our Bellevue haven. Simon, Mia and Charlotte no longer saw their friends from Seattle, and even my friends, who had their driver's licenses, rarely crossed the bridge to visit—it was up to me to seek them out. I made a big effort to maintain my Seattle friendships, but for my parents the adjustment to living in Bellevue created an isolation from their former life. The Friday Night Group had ended; they didn't come across the lake for what had been weekly gatherings.

Danny rarely emerged from the Dodd's basement to visit us. When he did come, he was withdrawn and angry. The warmth and honesty we had shared in California two summers earlier was a distant memory; now, his eyes were glazed and empty, and they looked at all of us—me, Simon, my parents, everyone—without love and instead with resentment. He yelled at my parents for abandoning Seattle and called them traitors, and he criticized the rest of us for going along with the move.

He was toughest on Simon, who had idolized him for so many years. "The suburbs are making you soft," he shouted, and swung his twenty-year-old fists against Simon's skinny, thirteen-year-old frame. After Danny had beat Simon up on two or three visits, Simon gave up on trying to connect with his big brother. When he heard Danny's voice at the front door, he locked himself in the bathroom and waited until he was gone.

My parents were distressed by Danny's angry behavior, and they, too, were more irritable and short-tempered. Dad swore at himself for every little mistake, and he chased Simon around the house in a violent rage at even the smallest provocation.

While I was concerned that Simon was being bullied by both Danny and Dad, I was most worried about Danny. His hostility toward the family and how he was distancing himself from everyone while living in the Dodd's basement and rarely surfacing, made me fear for his mental health. In my journal I wrote an account of a detailed and disturbing dream I had about Danny, replete with drugs and police. And it ended with fears I didn't want to share with anyone—that Danny might even be suicidal.

* * *

Later that winter, my parents left on a vacation to Carmel, California. Since I was sixteen, they left me in charge. As was their practice when they left town, they instructed me not to call them.

"We don't want to be bothered," Dad said. "We're going to get some rest."

"Make good decisions," was the sole advice Mom gave me.

Taking care of Simon, Mia, Charlotte, and Joey was no small undertaking. Every morning, I poked my head into their rooms to make sure that all four of them were awake and getting ready for school. (Invariably, someone—usually Joey—was still in bed.) I fixed breakfast, loaded all five of us into the car, dropped Joey and Charlotte off at Surrey Downs Elementary School, then drove Mia and Simon to Bellevue Junior High, and then headed to Bellevue High School for my own classes. When my school day ended, I picked my four siblings up. I drove Charlotte to gymnastics practice, Simon to basketball practice, Mia to the library, and Joey to the Bellevue Boys Club. By then, it was time to pick everyone up again, starting with Charlotte. We drove home together. Then, I cooked dinner, helped Joey and Charlotte with their homework, and got everyone to bed.

It was exhausting work, but I tried to be as patient and loving as possible. I wanted my younger siblings to have a happy, stress-free week.

Late on a rainy Thursday afternoon, when I had collected everyone from their extracurricular activities and we were heading home in the dark, I braked on the slippery pavement as our car descended a steep hill. The car behind us didn't see me slowing down. It slammed hard into the rear of our station wagon and our necks jerked back against seats.

I pulled to the side of the road and took inventory of my passengers. In the backseat, Mia, Charlotte, and Joey looked rattled, but nobody was crying or bleeding. They assured me that they were okay; Simon, sitting beside me in the front, confirmed that he was all right, too.

I stood in the rain to survey the damage: the rear end of our car was seriously dented, but the rest of the car was mostly unscathed. A middle-aged man in a business suit climbed out of the other car and introduced himself to me. He was very apologetic, and he acknowledged that the accident was his fault. "Five kids," he muttered, peering in our car window at my shaken siblings. "What an awful, rainy day. What an awful day. Five kids."

Though I knew that I was one of the "five kids," I tried my best to handle the situation like an experienced driver. I followed the businessman's lead. When he took out a pen and asked me for my name, license plate number, driver's license number, and insurance information, I requested the same information from him.

We shook hands one more time. (He was very fond of shaking hands.) "What an awful day," he said again.

Back at home, I did my best to keep everyone calm while we ate dinner, did our homework, and prepared for bed. I paid special attention to Joey, who had been unusually quiet.

"Did the car accident scare you?" I asked him when I tucked him into bed.

"No," he said, then added with his six-year-old perspective, "It didn't scare me. But it did make me a little frightened."

After everyone was in bed, I called Brian Dodd. He listened patiently as I described the accident, and he pressed me for more details.

"The police station will be closed for the night," he said. "But you should go there tomorrow. You need to file a police report, then contact your parents' insurance company."

He suggested that I call my parents to fill them in, but I worried they would be critical of me for interrupting their vacation and not handling everything on my own. "They don't want to be disturbed," I insisted. "It's my job to handle things while they're gone."

The next morning, after I dropped my brothers and sisters at school, I drove to the Bellevue Police Station. I skipped my morning classes to file a police report. I knew that my parents hated for me to miss school, but I hoped that this was the responsible thing to do. After leaving the police station, I drove home to contact the insurance company. It took several tries to reach the proper person and explain what had happened. By the time I finished, the school day was nearly over.

My parents knew nothing about the accident until they returned home a week later. I told my father about the accident, then led him outside to show him the damage to our station

"I'll follow up with the insurance company tomorrow," he said. I felt disappointed that he never acknowledged how well I had handled the accident.

* * *

While my communication with Danny was challenging, it improved with my two older sisters. That fall of 1969, my correspondence with Naomi and Leah was frequent and brought us closer together. I wrote to both of them often about P.C., the family, my fears about Danny, school, friends, and politics and, most especially, about how much I missed them.

Naomi had taken the year off from Sarah Lawrence College to travel abroad on an international honors program. While in Japan she had discovered solace and guidance in Zen teachings. She wrote to me about Zen, and I wrote back about P.C., and we both agreed that they were means to the same end.

"It doesn't really matter whether it's P.C. or Zen or love that allows you to see the beauty of your being—all that matters is that it happens," I wrote to her, feeling very wise indeed. "This year, I feel closer to you than all the times when you were right here."

Naomi's international program took a break in December, and she came home to visit. She stayed in my room, and we stayed up late into the night talking. She even treated herself to a P.C. session with Mary.

"It's had such a positive impact on you," she said. "I want to learn it for myself."

Leah, meanwhile, was doing a lot of reflecting on our family dynamics, and she wrote to me from Israel with love and admiration that I had often missed growing up together in the same house.

I shared with Leah my new plan to graduate early, and she said that she understood, that she had felt a similar eagerness to be done with high school. Inspired by her positive experience studying in Israel, I decided that I wanted to spend the second semester of my senior year in Israel on an Ulpan program—the same program that Leah was currently enjoying. Leah urged me to plan ahead. *"If you want to graduate early, you'll need to start taking senior classes in your junior year,"* she suggested in a letter.

I wrote to the Bellevue High School principal to make my case for early graduation the following year. I explained the Ulpan program, which entailed half days spent in a classroom studying the language and culture of Israel, and the rest of the day spent working in the fields of an Israeli kibbutz. I also explained how my move from Garfield High to Bellevue High had thrown a wrench in my plans to graduate early, but I thought that it would still be possible if the requirement that I take a second Home Economics class was waived.

I attached a letter from my father, in which he articulated his support for my petition, in his own well-intentioned and slightly peculiar way. To him, the soundest argument for my early graduation was the emotional maturity I exhibited at home. He did his best to paint the picture for the principal:

"Claudia lives at our home occupied by my wife, myself, her 15-year-old brother, her 8-year-old brother, her sister 12 years old, and her sister 10 years old....

Speaking for myself, I have adopted the habit of guarding the voicing of my immediate feelings. If these lack in love and concern Claudia will be quick to point out to me that I am doing damage to the development of my children. I may fume for a moment, but then I usually must admit that she is right.

If anyone in the family has problems, of an emotional nature that is, Claudia is the one they turn to. Claudia is able to demand her parents' undivided attention and even manages to get it at times. She does have an air of outgoing warmth and cheerfulness about her, which gives the younger children the desire to be close to her.

In an intellectual dispute Claudia can hold her own, and, if proved in error, can accept it without grudge or pouting. She is a skilled observer of the psychic interplay within the family and her comments in this regard are usually to the point.

When I wake her up early in the morning her first word will be a warm and loving comment to me, and when I kiss her 'good night' I walk away with the feeling that I must be a pretty good father. Her relationship to her mother is open, frank and close, as one would expect of two women living together, both of great heart and giant potential."

I didn't really know what I was supposed to do about the "giant potential" my father saw in me, but I did feel increasingly cheerful and confident. Only a few months earlier, I had lived in the midst of violent chaos, and I had felt nothing but fear and despair. Perhaps it was the comfort and distance afforded by our new suburban lifestyle, where I had recently seen hopelessness, I now saw heroes.

On a Friday in late December, I went back to Garfield High School to hear one of my new heroes—Cesar Chavez—speak. He stood on the same stage where I had once seen Stokely Carmichael stand, and he spoke with passion and gusto.

I had been nervous to return to Garfield. I was worried that walking the old hallways and seeing old friends would trigger feelings of meekness and loneliness. Instead, I was amazed by how different—how much emotionally stronger—I felt.

It was a good start to the weekend. After the Cesar Chavez speech, a big group of us went to a concert at Eagles Auditorium. I got home late, but I was up early the next morning to drive myself to a Quaker Friends Meeting. I hadn't been attending regularly, but I still tried to go when I could find the time. The Quakers welcomed me warmly, as always, and Brian and Rita came right over to greet me.

"How is Danny?" I asked them, after they had hugged me.

"He's okay," Rita said, unconvincingly. "We don't see him much. We told him that he's welcome to come upstairs and join us anytime. For meals. For visiting. For anything. That he doesn't need a reason. But he doesn't come up much."

Behind me, someone squeezed my arm. "Look at you," he said. "You're nearly as beautiful as your mother."

It was Nick Farley. He asked all about my mother and rambled on and on about the years he had spent adoring her.

"Everyone loves Carla," Brian Dodd said.

"Not like I have," Nick countered.

Nick asked for a ride back to Bellevue to visit my parents. As we drove, I told him about what a difference therapy was making in my life, how I was trying to learn to care for and love myself.

"It's great to love yourself," Nick said. "I'm something of an expert. I've loved myself for as long as anyone can remember. And I've loved your mother since Leah was born, almost for 20 years. In fact, when I held Leah when she was just a few days old, she was completely attracted to me. And Carla was extremely jealous."

The conversation felt incredibly awkward. He was so full of himself, commenting how any woman should feel honored to be loved by him. My friend Justine had lived with him for a while in California, but they were no longer a couple; now she was back in Seattle going to college.

When I led Nick into the house, my mother jumped up from her chair and threw her arms around him.

"Still the belle of the ball," Nick said, kissing her through his enormous beard.

My father embraced him too, grinning broadly.

The four of us sat together at the dining room table talking. Nick's eyes were glued to my mother's body. She was wearing a see-through, slinky dress.

Mom giggled and stroked the hair on Nick's arm. Dad sent quick glances towards Nick and Mom, and then he fixed his gaze outside, on the mimosa tree on the patio, until his eyes darted over again. He didn't look upset: he kept smiling and laughing and telling Nick how good it was to see him.

Nick told us all what a masterful lover he was, and Mom gave a girlish laugh and said, "Yes, I'm sure."

I felt sick to my stomach. My mind was flooded with images of Nick dancing with Mom, Nick massaging Mom's shoulders and running his hands through Mom's hair; and Dad was always there too, tucked away in the corner of the memory, smiling. Images of Justine being lovers with Nick when she was fifteen floated through my brain, disgusting me.

I excused myself from the table and went upstairs to fume. I was sure that I had seen Nick clearly for the very first time—as an arrogant and creepy egotist and womanizer. He used the same behaviors that others used to connect in healthy, meaningful ways—hugs, eye contact, dance, and physical affection—but he twisted them to manipulate people. It made me furious. It wasn't until years later that I was able to clearly realize that my mother manipulated her world—and mine—in a similar way, taking things that are innately wholesome and healthy, distorting them and crossing lines in deviant ways.

More than an hour later, Dad knocked on my door. "You vanished on us," he said. "Didn't you like seeing Nick?"

"Of course," I lied. "I just wasn't feeling well."

* * *

During my spring semester I was finally enjoying my classes at Bellevue High School and forming new friendships with a few of my classmates, finding that we shared a lot of the same interests and values. The whole group of us often gathered on weekend mornings to share breakfast in downtown Bellevue. We carpooled together to classmates' parties and studied together for upcoming exams.

Gerald was my favorite. He was a sweet, quiet, easygoing guy who always asked me how I was before saying anything about himself. His father was a Lutheran minister, and he had one younger sister, whom he adored. We talked a lot about the responsibilities of being an older sibling, and he was always awed by the sheer size of my family. He was very outdoorsy, and he loved to bike—often, when the rest of us carpooled, he would decline a ride and take his bicycle instead. "I'll meet you there," he'd say. "It's a nice day." Even when it wasn't.

He was a photographer, too, and he was very interested in my mother's business. "I'm more into nature photography, not portrait photography," he explained. "But your mom really knows how to apply the same kind of craft to her photos of people. She's incredible." I agreed.

"And your father is such a nice man," he observed. "But then he'll get so angry. So upset. I've never seen a mild-mannered person turn on a dime like that, like a switch has been flipped."

It was true my father's pleasant demeanor was transforming into fury more and more frequently. He was angry at Danny for "squandering so much potential," and he was most easily provoked by Simon, who had always had a tendency towards teasing and being something of a harmless troublemaker. Simon was now a tall and athletic teenager, but he still crumbled like a little boy under the weight of Dad's emotional rage—and his fists.

Although Dad liked to blame his fury on something the boys had done, it was more often instigated by something inward. A word of disapproval from my mother or a little mistake in the kitchen such as spilling flour on the counter would send Dad into an immediate spiral of self-loathing. "You stupid, stupid man," he'd bark at himself, cursing in German and pounding his fists on the counter.

For his 59th birthday in May, I waited until my father opened all his other gifts, and then I gave him mine: a large, heavy cardboard box. I hadn't wrapped it, but I had folded the flaps so that they would stay shut. I hoisted the box onto the table and returned to my chair, waiting.

Dad unfolded the flaps and peered inside the box. He lifted his head and shot me a quizzical look, and then he pulled out the top two plates from stacks of faded white and patterned dinner plates.

"Claudie Weibly, Gott in Himmel, what is this?" He wanted to know.

"They're plates, Daddy," I said.

"I know they're plates. Old plates. We have plates. Why do I want them?" He demanded.

"I got them at Goodwill," I explained. "They're not for eating. They're for breaking. When you get mad, break a plate. Whenever you feel anger coming on, grab a plate and smash it. Smash it on the counter, or on the floor, or against the wall. They weren't expensive."

Joey snorted with laughter. Everyone else was very quiet. Simon looked frightened.

"And here's the other part of the gift," I continued. "I promise to clean up the pieces. So there's really no good reason for you not to smash them whenever you're angry."

Dad pursed his lips tightly, and we all waited. Mia shot me a nervous glance. By raising the subject of Dad's anger during a happy family celebration, I was taking quite a risk.

Finally, Dad grinned. "What a clever idea," he said. And then he laughed, like he had just heard a good joke. At first, only Dad and Joey laughed. But Dad's laughter was infectious. One by one, we all joined in, until the whole family was laughing.

Suddenly Dad stood up, lifted one of the plates high above his head, and hurled it onto the kitchen floor. We flinched at the noise as the plate shattered everywhere. And then I took a broom and swept up the shards.

After that, I'd sometimes come home and find broken remnants of the birthday plates waiting for me on the kitchen floor. Dad kept our agreement and left the mess for me.

The sight of the broken pottery always sent a surge of relief through me. If the plate had taken a beating, I knew that Simon probably hadn't.

But it didn't always work that way. One rainy Saturday afternoon, I had come home from a drizzly bike ride with Gerald and curled up on the couch in the upstairs family room to read. Sabra, our yellow Labrador, dozed on the carpet near me. I heard my father, downstairs in the kitchen, scolding Simon for neglecting his chores.

"Do you think you can just take out the garbage only when you feel that it's convenient?" Dad roared.

Seconds later, Simon came bounding up the stairs, his arms flailing, knocking into paintings on the wall as he bolted through the house. I jumped up. Simon's eyes met mine, his face white with fear as he ran past me and ducked behind the couch in the family room.

Without thinking, I stepped into the doorway, feet planted firmly, as my father reached the top step and came charging towards me. I thought he was going to push me down to get to Simon.

"Get out of my way," he screamed at me. "Get the fucking hell out of my way!"

But I wouldn't move. "You can't do this," I told him. "You can't hit us. You can't hurt Simon anymore."

"Get out of my goddamn way!" Dad yelled again. I knew what it was like to be hit by Dad—even six years after he had hit me for plagiarizing, I hadn't forgotten. My whole body was trembling with fear, but something made me stand firm to protect Simon.

"No," I said. I could feel Simon cowering behind me. "I won't let you do this anymore."

This time my father screamed even louder. "I could kill you! You know I could kill you?" Dad shouted. I did know. "Get out of my way, God damn it!"

I tasted salt and realized that I was crying. Simon had crumpled into a fetal heap behind me, sobbing. Dad's fists twitched, as though he was gearing up to hit me, but abruptly he turned around and stomped down the stairs.

I turned and knelt down by Simon, who was crouched next to Sabra, petting her for comfort. He didn't say anything. He just held on to Sabra and sobbed.

That evening at dinner everything seemed normal. Simon and I exchanged tentative looks across the table. Mia, Joey, and Charlotte had all been out during Dad's outburst, and Mom had been in her darkroom. Apparently none of them had any idea what had occurred that afternoon.

After dinner, I cleared the dishes, the younger kids disappeared into other parts of the house, and my parents remained at the dining room table. Mom was re-touching photographs with an inkpad and a tiny brush: wetting the brush's tip in her mouth, swirling it over the black ink, and dabbing it onto the photograph to cover white dust spots. Next to her, Dad calmly read the latest *Newsweek*, which had just arrived in the mail that day.

I drew in my breath. "Dad, can I talk to you?" I asked.

He raised his eyes slightly. "Yes," he said.

I sat down on the other side of him. "Daddy, what do you want most for your children?" I asked.

"For you to be happy," he said. He was still holding the *Newsweek*, and seemed impatient, as if he hoped this wouldn't take too long.

"Well," I said. "How can we be happy if you hit us?"

He clenched his jaw and glared at me. He seethed. "Do you have any idea what I have been through?" He asked, his voice quaking. It seemed to come from a different part of him, a part I had never seen or heard. "Do you have any idea about the hatred I have for myself that I live with every day?"

I shook my head, scared.

He went on. "Do you know that when I look in the mirror, I hit myself like this?" And suddenly he slapped himself hard across his face. It made a loud noise, and it left a mark. And then he kept hitting himself, alternating cheeks, slapping his own face hard.

My mother didn't even look up from her photographs. She kept her head down and her body rigid, but I watched as tears spilled down her face and onto the photos and mixed with the black ink. I was crying, too.

Dad stopped hitting himself. "Do you have any idea what it's like to be stripped naked in the center of a group of grown men? To have them point at you—at your penis—screaming *'Jew! Filthy Jew! Filthy pig Jew!'* They laughed and screamed at me. *'Dirty filthy Jew!'* I hate who I am."

Nobody said anything. The three of us sat there for more than a minute, quiet. But I couldn't let it go. Much more gingerly this time, I reiterated my point. "How can we ever love ourselves if you hate yourself so much, Daddy? If you beat us? You have to get help."

The next week both of my parents enrolled in classes at Personal Counselors, the co-counseling therapy I was doing. Years later, Simon told me that after that day, Dad never hit him again.

* * *

I filled the summer after my junior year at Bellevue High School with activities. I took an intensive dance program at the University of Washington, taught by an esteemed teacher named Ruthanna Boris. I worked part time at the Bellevue Public Library, and I also worked at my father's downtown Seattle business.

On the mornings when Dad wasn't traveling, we drove together across the Lake Washington Floating Bridge to the Otto Chotzen Company. I had visited often when I was younger, but during junior high and high school, my visits had become less frequent.

When I started work in the summer of 1970, I was greeted by the scent of the worn wood planked floorboards. Curt Nussbaum barely looked up from his typewriter when we entered but he always grunted, "Good morning," and my father and I would respond cheerfully.

And then, my father and I would part ways. He headed into his office, and I trudged off into the warehouse aisles, where I filled orders under the supervision of three other employees: June, Edith, and Tommy.

June was an older African American woman who had worked for the Otto Chotzen Company for more than two decades. Edith, like Curt and my parents, was a Jewish survivor of the war. My father had employed her for a long time, too. Tommy was Curt's son, and had been working there for several years, ever since his high school graduation. Tommy was friendlier than his father, and he told a lot of jokes. These three were experts at running the warehouse: filling orders, packing shipments, keeping track of the inventory. I liked all three of my colleagues, and the time in the warehouse passed quickly.

On the days when I worked at the Otto Chotzen Company, I brought a sack lunch and ate it in the lunchroom, along with Tommy, June, and Edith. Curt never joined us, but my father occasionally would. The whole spirit of the room seemed to lift when he sat down to eat with us—and not in a forced or insincere way. He was good-humored and attentive with the employees—teasing them lightly and asking after their families and loved ones. Just as I had when I was little, I marveled at the way that all eyes turned to him. At home, it seemed that his primary role was to deflect attention to Mom. Here, not only was he the boss, but everyone admired and respected him. One nice word from Walter Chotzen was all it took for June and Edith to spend the whole afternoon grinning and humming.

Dad was in a better mood at home, too; Personal Counselors was having a positive effect on the entire Chotzen clan. My parents had never been the type of people to dip their toes into the water of a new experience; they dove in headfirst, and their commitment to P.C. was no exception.

First, they attended the classes. Then, they set up their own private co-counseling sessions with other adults they had met at class. Then, they took off for a weeklong retreat with Harvey Jackins, the founder of P.C.

When Mom was excited about something new, it became a mandatory activity for the rest of us. And so it was that Simon (who was fourteen), Mia (who was twelve), and even Charlotte (who was ten) were dragged along to Personal Counseling classes and sessions.

Only Joey, eight years old, was excused from the obligation. "It's because I'm already perfect," he boasted. "I don't need to discharge any bad things." He had picked up the jargon from the rest of us.

At home, Mom oversaw family co-counseling sessions. Everyone took turns as the "client" in front of the entire family, or else we paired up and alternated turns. We seemed to be listening to each other in ways we never had before. My father's rages had abated, and he no longer lashed out at Simon. And all of us were more patient and attentive with one another. Now, when someone in the family was upset, someone else would immediately offer a co-counseling session. Dinners, birthdays, homework, visits with the Millers—nothing was sacred; everything was subject to interruption if an impromptu session seemed important.

When Leah and Naomi came home from their international travels, they joined right in the family sessions, and they took classes and workshops led by Mary McCabe and Harvey Jackins.

Naomi took to it especially well. "I'm recovering things," she told me privately. "I'm uncovering really dark memories that are never quite clear. Mary keeps asking me whether Dad molested me, but that's obviously not something he would ever do. I know she's wrong about that."

I confided in her that I had some dark memories, too. It seemed impossible that I could recall events that had transpired when I was a baby, but my memory was strangely specific. I came home from my sessions with Mary describing the details of old Persian rugs and pieces of furniture that my parents had given away when I was one and two-years-old. Their mouths fell open as I recounted long-ago details about our Leschi home. Their amazement and affirmation of these physical details gave me the courage to believe that the other memories I was recovering—including the one with the man who had pressed his hand over my mouth and yelled at me to shut up—had really happened.

"It's not just the old Leschi house that I remember," I told Naomi. "There's another place. Like a loft. With a staircase that retracts up into the loft. It's creepy."

"I remember that, too!" She exclaimed. "The staircase. The scary staircase. I remember watching it retract, and I was up above, and Danny was down below. We were looking at each other as the staircase separated us, and I could tell that he was as terrified as I was."

After finishing her year with the International Honors Program, Naomi had decided to take more time off from college, but she didn't stay around the house long.

"I want to talk about Jerome," she demanded to Mom, just a few days after she arrived. The noisy kitchen went silent. Nobody had mentioned his name aloud since we had moved from Madrona.

"I want to talk about what you did. Let's hear you apologize to your family," Naomi pressed.

"You're being a mean, nasty girl," Mom said, dismissively. She slid gracefully between Joey and Mia so that she could remove a roast from the stove. She did not seem the slightest bit embarrassed.

Naomi didn't mention Jerome again, but every time Mom spoke to her Naomi's answers were tinged with anger.

"Will you be joining us for dinner?" Mom wanted to know.

"I certainly hope not," Naomi responded curtly.

"Don't you dare disrespect your mother," my father yelled at her.

"Don't, Daddy," Naomi complained. "This is between me and Mom."

But, as it turned out, it wasn't just between them. It was Dad, not Mom, who asked Naomi to leave. He did it privately, after dinner one night. Afterwards, Naomi knocked on my door.

"I'm not staying here anymore," she told me. "I have to go, Claud."

"It's hard when the house is so chaotic," I reassured her. "It's hard for me sometimes, and it must be hard to adjust when you've been away."

"It's not that," she said. "I'm not leaving by choice, though I can't say I'm sorry about it. Daddy's booting me out. He doesn't like the way I talk to Mom, and he says he won't have me sleeping under this roof."

She found a job as a caretaker at Fisher Farms, a historic property just outside of Bellevue. The property had never had a caretaker before—at least not one who lived on the premises—but local teenagers had vandalized the farm three times in the previous month. Naomi spoke with the park director and suggested that she move into the small cabin on the edge of the property—that way, she argued, she could keep an eye out for vandals at night, when they were most likely to strike. She moved in right away.

She came by our house often, but she always went back to her cabin to sleep. She told me that she tried to avoid dropping by during family co-counseling sessions: she preferred to have her own sessions with Mary, apart from the family.

"It's hard, though, to predict," she complained. "You never know when you're all going to suddenly launch into a P.C. session. There's no regular schedule. It's like spontaneous counseling all the time."

"I know," I gushed. "We're all doing such a wonderful job of respecting and listening to each other."

Naomi had also signed up for Erhard Seminar Training (promoted and marketed as "est."), a new kind of therapy invented by a man named Werner Erhard. Between P.C. and est, she said, she was starting to have a pretty good handle on her traumatic memories—especially the one with the angry man whose staircase retracted into his loft and separated her from Danny.

When she described the man to me—a bald older man with pasty white skin and white sideburns—it was the same man I had been working on in my sessions with Mary.

And then, one day, Naomi came home from a session with Mary and told me that she had remembered the man's name. "Clark Taylor," she said. "It just popped out of me. Mary asked me who had hurt me, who had caused me trauma when I was a little girl, and suddenly the name just leapt out of me, and I knew that it was right."

I knew it, too, as soon as Naomi said it, I knew that this was the same man who I had been working on in my sessions with Mary. I had been having vivid memories: I was a baby lying on my back in a basket in this man's home, and he was torturing my beloved big brother Danny a few yards away from me. Danny was shrieking and I was howling—baby screams at the top of my lungs. Suddenly Clark was pressing his huge hands over my mouth, screaming at me "Shut UP! Shut up you goddamn baby! Shut up or I'll kill you" until I lost all my breath.

Naomi recounted her memories to me in vivid detail.

"The first time Mom left us with him, she was rushed and late for a photo sitting with photo lights and equipment in the back of the car. She dropped Danny, Leah and me off at his house, somewhere on Queen Anne Hill. Leah was three, and Danny and I were five. You were a baby, and she took you with her in a basket in the car. He ushered us kids to an upstairs room by stairs that could be lowered or drawn up, so that he had total privacy. He settled Leah in for a nap on one side of the apartment. Then he took Danny downstairs to the front yard and told him to play there by himself.

"And then he came back upstairs with me, and retracted the stairs," Naomi said.

The room had high ceilings and thick draperies. Naomi looked out the window and saw Danny standing in the yard below. Their eyes met. She says they both knew something horrible was about to happen.

"I remember him checking on Leah. And he asked me to come over to the bed, and he said, 'Have you ever seen one of these?' I didn't know what he was talking about. Then I noticed that his pants were down around his knees and his penis was hanging out. He was standing and kind of towering over me with his penis and it was white and hairy. I didn't say anything and then he took me up in his arms and laid me on this bedspread. I remember jumping down and him pulling up his pants, kind of irritated, and grabbing me and putting me down again. I remember that I was wearing a little white fitted T-shirt and faded red corduroy pants. He pushed off my tennis shoes very roughly, pulled down my pants and just pushed my legs apart. And then very quickly, with no explanation and no sense of what was happening, he put his entire weight on top of me and started moving against me, and he must have gotten hard right away, because he jammed himself inside me and it was like a knife. I remember screaming and feeling like I couldn't breathe, like I was being suffocated or killed. And there was a wetness. He lay on top of me for a long time. I remember him saying, 'That wasn't so bad, was it?' and 'You'll visit here again.'

"He pushed himself up and said, 'You're a very dirty girl. You're a very, very dirty girl and you must not tell your mother or your father that this happened. They would not want to know what a dirty girl they have.'

"He kept saying that over and over. Because I was crying, Leah woke up and she started to cry. He pulled my pants back up and pulled his pants back up and then he told Leah to shut up. I hurt terribly, but I was afraid he was going to hit Leah or do something to her. I remember him going to her and trying to calm her. I went to the back window and looked down and saw Daniel just standing in the back yard, looking up at me like he was locked outside.

"When Mom returned to pick us up, he told her, 'Naomi was a very good girl.'

"Thank you so much. I don't know how I'm ever going to thank you for babysitting," Mom said.

"We'll do it again," he answered. "Don't worry about it. No problem. I'll watch them anytime."

On the way home, Naomi sat in the back seat. The car had a velvet strap hanging from the side of the seat.

"I remember just gripping it until my hands were white."

Clark was our babysitter for two more years. Naomi recalled that he always kept her separated from her twin brother. She said she would never let him near her again, but she hid behind the drapes in our home, watching and listening as he molested the three of us, including me as a baby. "I would watch from behind the curtains, unable to stop him, and feeling like I was terribly letting you down by not protecting you. If he caught me watching, he would threaten me and ask if I wanted my turn next.

"I remember trying to talk to Mom, and just absolutely not being heard," Naomi said. "I don't know if I had the vocabulary for how overwhelmed I was. The tantrums started then. That's when I developed the duodenal ulcer and had to be hospitalized. I would just literally fly off the handle around Mom. I screamed and screamed and screamed. I wanted him dead. And somehow it was connected to her. I was outraged at her, and it was a rage that stayed in my body and my life for years."

Now I understood how vulnerable and awful Naomi felt when my mother made her pose for Clark Taylor in our family's home, in high heels and nothing else, for the portrait he painted of her. Mom still loved to display that painting in our Bellevue home.

Naomi continued to do therapy that summer with Mary and in est. I continued to work with Mary and to do co-counseling sessions too. Counseling sessions with my family turned out to be full of surprises. I still thought of my little sisters as children, but I quickly realized that they weren't. Charlotte and Mia were ten and twelve, and they were thinking about serious things. They worried about the things they saw Mom and Dad worrying about—about money and the Vietnam War. And they worried about Danny, too.

When my father and I co-counseled together, he delved into his painful memories of the Nazis. I had heard the vague outlines of these stories once or twice, but the details were new to me.

"In Dresden and Hamburg, the bigger cities, every public place hung a 'No Jews' sign outside the entrance," he recalled. "Every place. Shops, restaurants, grocers, theatres, all of it.

"That was when I understood that the end was coming. The end of our life as Germans. And my world crashed down completely when I saw the parade with thousands of men in brown shirts, marching through the streets of Berlin to show their support of the Nazi movement. Thousands. My favorite high school teacher from home walked by me in a brown shirt. He was a storm trooper now.

"And when I lost my job in Berlin, I went home to Ziegenhals. I went to work alongside my father. But my old friends wouldn't speak to me. The children I had played with in childhood would see me coming and cross to the opposite side of the street so as not to encounter me. If they looked at me by mistake, they would turn their heads away quickly. Those were the merciful ones. The ones who ignored me instead of spitting on me.

"It was a very dangerous time," he told me, and his whole body shook.

He told me about smuggling money across the Czech border, and about the sheer terror he felt when the Gestapo came to arrest him. These were memories he had never spoken of before, and I had never known how to ask.

But he wasn't recounting the stories for my benefit; he was recovering experiences that he had buried away.

When it was Mom's turn to be the client, I focused all of my loving attention onto her, just as P.C. had taught me. But as soon as I did—as soon as I looked at her, Mom would begin to cry.

She cried so much that she barely spoke. She would ask me to hold her in my arms and cradle her, and I did. I held her and encouraged her to cry more, to discharge all the awful things that were inside of her. And she did cry more. She continued to cry non-stop.

She told me that our sessions together were extremely helpful, and she even wrote me notes to thank me for leading the family to counseling. *"I always report to friends how your spirit shamed us into trying P.C. We thank you for helping us embark on this new experiment of feeling more deeply."*

* * *

When I went out on dates with a young college student I was seeing that summer, Mom would often wait up for me until I got home. Sometimes she was working at the dining room table, retouching her photographs, but other times she just sat on the stairs near the front door and waited.

The moment I opened the door, she sprang to life, wrapping her arms around me and covering my face and neck with hurried kisses.

"How was your date?" she cooed. "How is your handsome boyfriend? Tell me what you did."

If I responded at all, it was in the vaguest terms possible. I might name a restaurant where we had been or friends we had seen.

"Tell me more," Mom coaxed. "What does it feel like when he kisses you?" She wriggled her hands up under my shirt and cupped my breasts. Her questions and her groping me made me so uncomfortable that each time I came home, I hoped that she would already be asleep.

I would push her hands off and rebuke her, even tell her it was none of her business. But once I was upstairs in my room, I always worried that I had been terribly mean to her. She ran a photography business, had many commitments with a houseful of kids, and she had sacrificed sleep to greet me at the door. I felt guilty about my ingratitude. But it never occurred to me at the time, that it wasn't her love for me she was expressing, but instead she was getting the vicarious thrill she craved about anything to do with sex.

In August, Naomi attended a three-day est retreat. They kept the participants up all night, she said, because sleep deprivation was a useful way to tap into the subconscious. The culmination of the retreat was an event in which each person stepped onto a stage and spoke to the assembled crowd; they could share whatever they wanted—memories, revelations, frustrations, feelings.

Participants were encouraged to invite guests to the closing event. Naomi invited my parents, who were excited to witness a new kind of cutting-edge therapy. "There might be a useful way to fuse it with the teachings of P.C.," Mom suggested to me, while applying her red lipstick.

"Naomi said it's very important that we be there," Dad told me. "She said that she needed your mother and me to come. Perhaps she's going to apologize to Carla for speaking so rudely to her."

When they returned home, later that night, my parents were ashen-faced and reluctant to explain what had happened.

"We went onstage," was all Mom said. "Naomi got onstage, and she announced some revelations, and then we went onstage to embrace her. In front of hundreds of people."

But when I asked what kind of revelation she had announced—even though I had a pretty good idea—Mom changed the subject. "You'll need to scoop up the little ones tomorrow after their tennis lesson," she said.

I wasn't home when Naomi came by the house the next day, but she left me a note, saying that the est retreat had changed her, and that she was eager to talk to me. *I think I'll be by the house more often,* she wrote. *"I've had a breakthrough, and it no longer makes me angry to spend time here."*

The breakthrough, she told me a few days later, had been announcing her Clark Taylor memories to the whole group. After months of struggling with the truth of what had happened to her, she stood up at the culminating ceremony and told the crowd that her parents had left her—repeatedly—with a babysitter who had raped her.

"But then I asked them to stand up. I singled them out, in the crowd," she recalled. "And I said, 'Mom, I forgive you. Dad, I forgive you. I forgive you for leaving me with Clark Taylor, the rapist, the molester.' And they came up onstage to hug me.'"

"I found out more about Clark," she confided. "I saw Tim Miller last week, and he asked me, just right out of the blue, he said, 'Remember Clark Taylor? Did you know that he had a criminal record? And that he was arrested on moral charges?' And I told him that I didn't know that, but that I had been recovering my own traumas with Clark. Tim said that the Miller kids had horrific memories of him too.

"I asked Mom and Dad about what they knew about his criminal record. They admitted that they knew about it, and they even knew that he had lost his Scoutmaster position with the Boy Scouts because of it. They knew those things about him, but they still let him look after us. Because Mom always wants to see the best in everybody, that's what's beautiful about her. I've forgiven them."

Naomi's discovery of forgiveness ate at me from the inside. I was impressed by her ability to examine her childhood trauma and pursue redemption, but I didn't quite know how to do it myself. It was shocking to me that my parents would leave us with a man whose criminal record included charges of sexual abuse of children. Why did Mom's beautiful qualities—her love and trust of perfect strangers—have to take such a dangerous form sometimes?

Naomi said she had forgiven my parents. I told myself that I should forgive them, too, though I wasn't really sure which things, what things, I needed to forgive them for. My mother's abuse of me was still so deeply buried, and so woven into my entire childhood, that I lacked both the recognition and the words for it.

Someday, I thought, in a few years, I'll forgive them for something. Looking back now, as an adult, I realize how unaware I was about the hard work ahead to heal from parents whose irresponsibility continually threatened the health and safety of their own children.

* * *

The principal of Bellevue High School had reached a decision. In a letter sent to our house that September, days before the start of my senior year, he informed my parents (and, more indirectly, me) that I would be permitted to graduate one semester early. I had also broken up with my boyfriend. "I'm sorry to hear that," Mom said. "I thought it was very encouraging that you were learning about the sexual side of yourself." She sounded like Dora Miller; the way Dora had gushed about Justine's relationship with Nick Farley.

Perhaps, I thought, I was more conservative than Mom or Dora when it came to sexuality. It was an odd thought to wrap my head around—I considered liberalness to be an important value, and from what I had learned, it seemed that it was always the younger generation's tendency to be more progressive than their forbearers. But how, I wondered, was one supposed to improve upon the sexual liberalism of Carla Chotzen and Dora Miller?

My mother's loose attitude about experiences with sex surfaced again a few weeks later in a different way. On a Wednesday afternoon, Mom overheard me calling to cancel a co-counseling session at Personal Counselors. I had a paper to write that night, and I knew that counseling would have to wait for another day.

"Don't do that," Mom instructed, waving her arms until I stopped mid-sentence in my conversation with David, the young man I was supposed to co-counsel with. "One of your sisters will take it. Don't cancel! Walter and I are taking a class anyway this evening at P.C."

Charlotte—who was still a month shy of her eleventh birthday—was ordered to fill my spot at the session. "I don't want to do it," Charlotte protested, but she wasn't given a choice.

That night, my parents drove to the P.C. center in downtown Seattle and took Charlotte along to fill in for my appointment with David, which was supposed to happen simultaneously with their class, from 7 to 9 p.m.

Charlotte sat with David, a 21-year-old man she had never met until that night, in a soundproof booth. David told Charlotte that he wanted to work on his sexuality. ("I wasn't even sure what that meant," she told us later, "but it didn't sound like fun.") He asked Charlotte to hug him and hold him—activities that were encouraged as part of the co-counseling process. "I need to feel close to a female body," he explained.

"I didn't want to hug him, but I felt like I had to," Charlotte reported. "He cried a lot and said that he had problems with sexuality. He asked me to touch his face, so I did that. And then he said that he wanted me to kiss him, but I didn't do that."

David's session with Charlotte lasted longer than any of the other sessions. When they finally emerged from their counseling booth, everyone except the class instructor had finished and gone home. Even my parents had left.

"Where's Charlotte?" Mia asked, when they arrived home without her.

"Shit," my mother said. "We forgot her."

"I'll go back to get her," Dad said, slipping into the shoes he had just removed, ready to make the twenty-minute drive from Bellevue to downtown Seattle. Mom stopped him.

"She can find her way home," she said. "She's a big girl."

Charlotte did find her way home. She wisely declined David's invitation to drive her, but she took the instructor up on her offer to drive her home.

"Why did your session go so long?" Mom wanted to know when Charlotte finally came through the door shortly after ten p.m. "We completely forgot you had come along with us."

"He had a lot to say," Charlotte said. "About his sexuality." She told us about the session. I was disgusted, but my mother just nodded. "Yes," she said. "That would take a while. I'm glad you were there for him."

Though Mom regarded Charlotte as a "big girl," I couldn't help but see my four younger siblings as vulnerable. I was struck by the thought that all of them—Simon, Mia, Charlotte, and Joey—really needed a big sister to protect them.

I wasn't even certain I was doing such a great job of being a good sister now while I was still living at home. I was out with friends, or co-counseling, or at dance classes, nearly every night; when I was home it was usually because I needed to study. I was often impatient with Joey, Charlotte, and Mia, all of whom sought out my attention when I really preferred to be alone in my room.

"Will you be home with me some day, Claudia?" Joey asked one night. It was the night before his eighth birthday. I assured him that I would be there the next night to help celebrate.

"This is your last year at home, and the little ones complain that you're never home," Naomi told me over the phone. She had moved back to New York. I felt guilty that my siblings were complaining about me, and I worried that I was starting to resemble my mother, always rushing out to another obligation. But I recalled that Naomi had been the same way when she was seventeen.

In my co-counseling sessions, journal entries, and conversations with Lila, Gerald and Vanessa, I confronted my feelings that I was abandoning my younger siblings, but I also reminded myself that I was not their actual parent, and that I had a right to my own life.

To add to my anxiety, I wasn't sure what I wanted to do with that life—the one that "I had a right to." I had decided not to travel immediately after my graduation; I needed to do more research into programs and places and opportunities. I had applied to a few colleges, and I planned to go to one of them eventually, but an academic setting didn't hold much allure for me.

In December, without any fanfare or ceremony, I graduated from Bellevue High School. My friends congratulated me warmly, but they all had one remaining semester, so they didn't feel much like celebrating.

Aunt Ilse wrote that she was eager to show me New York City, and Naomi and Leah were both on the East Coast. Leah had finished her time in Israel and started classes at Bennington College in Vermont. Naomi was in New York City, working as an intern in the office of Mayor John Lindsay, taking a break before going back to finish at Sarah Lawrence in the fall.

In early March, I flew to the East Coast for a three-week visit. I spent the first two weeks at Aunt Ilse's apartment, where Naomi was also living. Ilse lived on the Upper West Side of

Manhattan, just a block from Riverside Park. Her apartment was furnished with oriental carpets and antique furniture that she and her late husband, Ernst, a dermatologist, had brought from Germany in 1935, when they realized the early signs that their lives there, as Jews, would be in peril. Looking at the old chairs and silver, I felt as though I had a glimpse into my parents' homes in Germany.

Naomi had been staying with Ilse for several months, and she and Ilse welcomed me into their routine. The three of us ate breakfast together. Naomi took the subway to Mayor Lindsay's office, and Ilse walked through Central Park to her job as a German translator at the Goethe Center on 5th Avenue.

Central Park was far more scenic than the subway, so I opted to walk Ilse to work rather than accompany Naomi. We strolled down winding paths, around the reservoir, and up to the steps that led to her building. We exchanged a loving hug before she entered the lobby and took the elevator up to her office.

After that, I had the entire day to myself. I learned the subway system and found free and inexpensive dance and yoga classes all over Manhattan. I tried as many different classes as I could—I wanted to meet new people, see new neighborhoods, and learn new approaches to yoga and dance.

Each evening, I returned to Ilse's apartment and reported on my day's adventures to my aunt and sister. Some nights, I accompanied Naomi to dinners and cocktail parties—events that she had been invited to because of her internship with the mayor's office. On other nights, when Naomi didn't have functions to attend, we bought discounted tickets to dance performances and plays.

Together, the three of us saw several Broadway musicals. My favorite was *Fiddler on the Roof*, with Zero Mostel as the lead. I was deeply moved by the story of Tevye's attempt to preserve his family's traditions in the face of a changing world. It resonated with my own internal tug-of-war between loyalty to my family and my desire to grow up and be independent. Tears rolled down my cheeks during the standing ovation.

There were East Coast colleges that I had planned to visit—colleges where I had already been accepted—but I realized that I wasn't interested in looking at them. I was so much more energized by the bustling city, full of culture and endless opportunities. I had petitioned to finish high school early so that I could experience the world—not so that I could find myself in more classrooms and tied down to more school assignments.

One afternoon, as I left a dance class at a studio in Chelsea, I noticed a flyer on the bulletin board. *"Dance in Greece,"* it announced. The flyer described a dance program located on the island of Paros, ninety-six sea miles from Athens. Intrigued, I wrote down the contact information.

When I got back to Ilse's apartment, I phoned the number on the flyer. A woman named Donna answered. I told her that I was interested in the program. She suggested that we meet the following week to talk. I told her that I was only in New York for a few more days—that I was visiting from Seattle.

"Well then," she said. "We had better meet tomorrow. Bring a leotard in case you want to audition."

The next afternoon, we met at a café near the studio where I had seen the flyer. She bought my tea and a coffee for herself, and we sat and talked about our backgrounds. She was an American dancer who had graduated from Smith College. She had spent two years in Greece, performing and teaching dance, and later she had danced and choreographed professionally in New York. For the past two years, she had taught dance to students on the island of Paros.

"Most of our students are already enrolled in college, and some have even graduated," she said.

"I don't know how I could possibly enjoy college without seeing the world first," I told her. "That's why I want to do this."

We walked down the street to the studio, where I changed into my leotard and auditioned for her. She accepted me into the program immediately. Delighted, I agreed to join her company in Greece that fall.

That night I announced to Naomi and Ilse, "I've figured out my future! But don't tell Mom or Dad," I added. "I need to explain it to them myself."

For the last week of my East Coast adventure, I stayed with Leah in her dorm room at Bennington College. I was her first family visitor, and she was overjoyed to have me. We went everywhere together. I attended parties and classes and club meetings with her, and she introduced me to all her friends.

When I wandered the campus without Leah, as I sometimes did when she was studying or in cello and concert rehearsals, I was constantly mistaken for her. We had similar features and the same dark, long hair, and students, faculty, and staff all greeted me familiarly everywhere I went.

"Please just smile and wave back," Leah implored me when I told her. "I'd hate for them to think I'm rude. Especially my professors!"

I enjoyed my week with Leah so much that I almost reconsidered my decision to postpone college. But I was very excited about the prospect of dancing in Greece, and Leah was equally enthusiastic about my plan.

"I'm so glad I didn't go straight into college," she told me. "Living in Israel was such a wonderful change. I feel like I have so much of the world to explore, and so many people to meet, and very few of them are inside the walls of a school."

At the end of my week at Bennington, I helped one of Leah's friends drive her Volvo to Montreal; my first time driving a stick-shift car. My plane ticket to New York had been one-way, and I needed to find a less expensive way home. In Montreal, I bought a train ticket on the Canadian Pacific line, which took three days to cross Canada before eventually ending in Vancouver, British Columbia. I didn't have enough money for a sleeper car, so I spent the whole time in an upright seat and made friends with other college age kids traveling across Canada. We spent the evenings singing songs, and one morning we woke up to the spectacular peaks of the Canadian Rockies.

I didn't sleep much, and I was very eager to get home to my own bed, which was (among other wonderful qualities) horizontal. When the train pulled into the Vancouver station, I rose and stretched my legs and hauled my large backpack over one shoulder. My plan was to catch a bus from Vancouver to Seattle, then another bus home to Bellevue.

As I came to the end of the passenger cars and scanned the surroundings for a sign directing me towards the bus station, I saw my father. He was standing at the edge of the track, scanning the crowd of passengers, and trying to find me. My heart skipped several beats. I ran to him, shouting "Daddy!" and waving my arms. When he saw me, he opened his arms as wide as they could go and waved exuberantly until I reached him. It moved me to tears to see him there. I hugged him hard.

"How did you know I would be here?" I asked.

"Leah phoned and told Carla that you were taking a train from Montreal to Vancouver," Dad said. "I looked at the train schedule, and then I rescheduled my business trip to Bellingham so that I could drive across the border to meet you."

We climbed into Dad's station wagon, and I chatted all about New York and Bennington for the duration of our four-hour drive home. He had so many questions about Naomi and Leah, about his sister Ilse, and about my impressions and adventures.

When we stopped for dinner, I told him about the dance program in Greece.

"What's the next step?" he asked cautiously.

"Dad, there is no next step." I explained. "I auditioned. They accepted me. I accepted their offer. The next step is to go."

"And college?" He asked.

"I'm not ready yet," I said. "I want to go to Greece and dance. After that, I'll be ready for college."

He reached across the table and grabbed my hand and squeezed it firmly. Tears sprung up in his eyes.

"Claudie-Weibly, I'm so happy for you. I will miss you so much."

* * *

After announcing I was going to Greece, the days flew by; I barely noticed when spring turned to summer. During the week, I was busy working at Dad's warehouse to save money for living on Paros. On the weekends and on the long summer evenings, I attended dance classes, swam in Lake Washington, and hung out with friends and my younger brothers and sisters. I knew I'd miss them a lot when I was gone.

One Saturday in June, Simon surprised me with an invitation.

"Hunter and Jamie are going to sail from Seattle over to Bainbridge Island tomorrow. Why don't you join us?" Hunter and Jamie were cousins who Simon had met through skiing.

"I don't really know them," I said to Simon. "It might feel weird."

"It won't be," he reassured me. "They encouraged me to invite you. Mia, too."

The next day, Mia, Simon and I joined Hunter, Jamie and half a dozen of their friends on a beautiful wooden sailboat. Though they were only fifteen or sixteen, Hunter and Jamie were experienced sailors who guided the boat expertly from the fresh water of Lake Washington through the Ballard locks and out into Puget Sound.

"We're heading to our Aunt Sally's home on Bainbridge Island," Jamie explained. "We can play there for a few hours, then sail back."

I was the oldest one on the boat and felt comfortable, confident, and pretty. My legs were strong from all the dancing I'd been doing and were bronzed from the summer sun. It was hot out, a perfect day to be on the water. We snacked and sipped cold sodas, laughing and enjoying the warm sun and brisk wind.

When we reached Bainbridge Island, Hunter and Jamie skillfully tied up the boat to the end of a long, private dock. An expansive green lawn sloped down to the water's edge. The house itself was farther back, atop a knoll, commanding a sweeping view of Seattle's downtown skyline. A small gazebo was nestled in one corner of the property; Adirondack chairs, deck chairs, and outdoor tables were grouped in different areas. A few hammocks hung between the trees.

Hunter and Jamie gave us a tour of the property, but they didn't bother to visit the house or say hello to their aunt. I didn't even know if she was home.

Mia expressed out loud what I was thinking. "Do you think it's okay that we're here? Just a bunch of kids?" she asked.

"I think so," I replied. "It's their aunt's house. I'm sure they have permission."

We chased each other across the lawn, did cartwheels, and reclined on benches in the shade of the gazebo. I found a peaceful spot under the leafy branches of two trees, climbed into the woven hammock that stretched between them, and lay down, swaying gently in the breeze and looking up at the cloudless cerulean sky.

Simon and Mia spotted me and jumped into the hammock on top of me. It quickly turned into a game. Hunter piled on, then another of his friends, then another, then Jamie, then another.

"Who's on the bottom?" someone from the top of the pile of seven shouted with a laugh.

"Claudia," Simon yelled from his spot near me at the bottom.

And then the hammock collapsed. I felt it in slow motion: the chains snapping under the weight of our bodies, all of us falling together as one, crashing collectively onto the hard ground beneath us. My tailbone hit first, and shock waves reverberated through my entire body. I heard the other kids laughing, but mostly I felt body after body crash down on top of mine. I felt each of them roll clumsily off the pile, off of me, untangle their limbs, then stand up.

But when I tried, I couldn't move. I wanted to ask for help, but I couldn't speak. I could hear them, but I felt far away, as though I was watching them through binoculars.

"Come on Claudia, let me pull you up," Hunter said. I sensed him reaching out his arm to help me up.

I couldn't form the words to respond to him, but even worse, I had no sensation in my legs.

Hunter's voice suddenly turned serious. "Claudia, are you alright?"

The other kids had stopped laughing. It was very quiet. I managed to push out a short sentence: "I can't move." A small voice, from far away; it didn't sound like me. "I can't feel my legs," my voice said. I looked into Hunter's face, which was flushed with worry. Oh god, I thought, I can't move my legs.

Hunter turned to someone. "Stay here while I go find my aunt," he instructed, and then he took off running. Everyone else gathered around me. I heard them talking about me, to me. Mia's face darted in and out of my line of vision, and I could hear Simon's familiar voice, now sounding frightened.

Suddenly, there was a new face close to mine.

"Claudia, this is Aunt Sally," Hunter announced.

Aunt Sally had soft blonde hair, a kind face that seemed to glow with light, and a calming, gentle voice.

"Can you move?" she asked.

"I can't feel my legs," I replied.

"I've called the fire department. They'll be here in a few minutes to help." She covered me with a blanket. "Just stay very still. You're going to be okay."

She squeezed my hand and sat with me while the commotion around us faded at first, and then increased with sirens and screeching brakes.

Firemen and EMTs surrounded me, poking at my body and asking me questions. I heard them talking about me to one another, as though I wasn't there, snippets of conversations. "She can't feel her legs...might be a broken back...could be paralyzed from the waist down.... Let's get her to the hospital."

I was petrified, but I just kept looking into Aunt Sally's eyes, and she kept holding my hand, reassuring me with words and looks.

After they loaded me onto a stretcher and placed me in the back of the ambulance, Aunt Sally climbed in next to me. Just before they closed the ambulance doors, I noticed Mia's face, filled with panic.

"Can Mia come too?" I asked.

Aunt Sally shouted something to the driver, and Mia climbed up to sit beside Aunt Sally.

"She's going to be fine," Aunt Sally told Mia. "The ambulance is taking us to Seattle," she said to me. "I'll be here with you."

The driver called back to her, "We've called ahead to Group Health Hospital. And we've called her parents. They'll meet us there."

The ambulance had priority boarding at the ferry terminal on Bainbridge Island, so we were loaded onto the boat ahead of the passenger cars. Aunt Sally stayed with me in the ambulance during the 35-minute ferry trip to Seattle. She encouraged Mia to step out and get a breath of fresh air.

"We won't go anywhere," she said reassuringly, patting Mia's arm.

When the ferryboat landed in Seattle, the ambulance drove us to Group Health Hospital, where I had been born eighteen years earlier. I was transferred to a gurney and whisked into a curtained cubicle in the emergency room area.

I heard my parents arrive, and Aunt Sally stepped outside the curtain to meet them. I heard her introduce herself ("I'm Hunter and Jamie's aunt, Sally Black.") and explain how the hammock had collapsed under the weight of all those kids piling on top of it.

I listened as my father apologized. "We feel so terrible to bother you like this. We've ruined your day and taken so much of your time. We're very sorry."

Mom joined in. "I can't believe you had to come all the way into Seattle because of Claudia. We really feel just awful about that."

"It's no trouble," Sally told them.

I kept waiting for my parents to step inside the curtain, to see me. Finally, when the doctor returned with X-rays, my parents followed him and Aunt Sally to the side of my gurney. Mia still stood beside me.

"She cracked her tailbone," the doctor told Mom and Dad. "She's lost all feeling below the waist, but it should slowly return to her feet and legs. We don't expect permanent damage, but we will need to keep her here overnight."

The doctor left. Aunt Sally took my hand and squeezed it.

"I think you have something to say to this lovely woman," Mom coaxed me.

"Thank you," I told her. I hoped she knew how much I meant that.

"That's nice," Dad said, sharing a glance with Mom. "But I don't think it's quite enough to just thank her. She's spent hours of her day with you, Claudia. You need to apologize for inconveniencing her like this."

And so I apologized.

Aunt Sally left. "I'm going to have a heart attack when I see that ambulance bill," my father complained as my parents and Mia walked off down the hall.

I spent the night in the hospital. As sensation crept back into my toes and feet and ankles and legs, I was ecstatic with relief.

By morning, I had recovered well enough to go home. Mom picked me up. "I don't have time to tend to you right now," she said. "I've arranged to leave you with Jill and Mike for a while."

Jill and Mike were co-counseling friends of mine, a couple in their 30's, who lived in Bellevue with their three young children. I stayed with them for almost a week. I worried that I was burdening them terribly, but they seemed to enjoy having me in their home. "We're glad to be able to take care of you," Jill reassured me.

A few weeks later, when I had fully recovered, I called Sally Black to thank her and to apologize again.

"May I speak with you candidly?" she asked, then continued. "I was shocked by your parents' behavior. You were lying behind that curtain not knowing if you might be paralyzed, and they were only concerned that I had been inconvenienced. They were worried that you were a bother when they should have worried about whether you were okay. I accept your thanks. But I won't accept your apology. Tell me this, Claudia: what did you do that requires an apology?"

I didn't know how to answer her. I tried to explain that I had been brought up to believe that if you infringed on people's time, then you owed an apology. When we needed new shoes or school supplies, we were a financial burden to Dad; when we needed to be picked up, we were an imposition on Mom's time.

"Please stop thinking of yourself as a burden," Sally said. "Everyone on this planet has a right to live, a right to take up time and space, and a right to feel welcome. And don't ever feel bad about needing help. We all have opportunities to give and receive. Learn how to do both of those things well and think of your life as a gift. Promise me."

I promised.

"Thank you, Claudia," she said. "For allowing me to help you."

Greece, Israel
& Home
Again

1971–1974

O ver the summer I made all the arrangements for my trip to join Donna's dance troupe. I bought several new leotards, new pairs of dance tights, and an extra pair of ballet slippers. Mom shopped with me to find two long, flowered rayon skirts that wouldn't wrinkle when folded into my red backpack. From a travel agent, I purchased a one-way plane ticket to London and another plane ticket from London to Athens.

My father's cousin, Suse Lackner, lived in London; her father and my grandfather had been brothers. Suse and Dad had played together as children in Germany, and she had visited us several times in Seattle. I wrote to Suse, asking her if I could visit her while en route to Greece, and she wrote back inviting me to stay with her and her roommate in their London flat.

In late September of 1971, when my friends had headed off to colleges, I traveled halfway across the world to Greece. My father took me to the airport. I was excited to leave but filled with anxiety about the unknown ahead and very conflicted about leaving my younger brother and sisters.

I arrived in London in the early morning and found my way from the airport on the "tube" to Suse's flat. Suse was in her early sixties, a sturdy woman, with short gray hair and rosy cheeks. Born in Germany, she had studied architecture at the Technical University in Berlin where she met her future husband, Joe, in 1932. Joe and Suse were part of a group of students who organized a resistance movement to fight the Nazis' rise to power. Joe, who wasn't Jewish, was arrested in 1933, and sentenced to two and half years of hard labor. Suse hid in a neighbor's home, then fled to Paris where she wrote for a left-wing newspaper about what was happening with Hitler in Germany. But, she said, "No one wanted to believe it was happening."

When Joe was released from prison in Germany, he and Suse reunited in France and married, but Joe left for Spain to fight in the Spanish Civil War against Franco, where he was captured and imprisoned once again. After the war, they continued to live in France, had a daughter, and made a living teaching languages. After Joe died of cancer in 1961, Suse and her young daughter moved to London where she taught French, Spanish and German at a language school near Regent's Park.

Suse welcomed me into her apartment on Eton College Road in Hampstead. She shared her flat with an older woman named Dodo. Dodo was also Jewish and was a concentration camp survivor. Their small apartment was up two flights of stairs. Coming from our large homes in the United States, the compactness of their living quarters was a new experience for me. The flat had two tiny bedrooms, a miniscule kitchen, and a small sitting room where I slept on the couch. I stored my backpack in the corner of the sitting room. Every night Suse helped me make up the couch with sheets and blankets. I woke to the early morning noises of London traffic, the sounds of cars and the scent of chestnut trees wafting through an open window.

Suse's apartment was filled with small creatures— sculptures of bears and other animals. Recently she had taken up sculpting and was carving marble, alabaster, soapstone, and wood into animal shaped figures and abstracts. She used all kinds of materials but confided, "My heart is in marble."

I went for walks with Suse through the Hampstead neighborhoods and parks, and we took the tube everywhere. She did own a car, a blue Citron 2 CV, or deux chevaux, which she only used on rare occasions. When we did take the car, I laughed about the strange British terms like *bonnet* for the hood and *boot* for the trunk. Suse and Dodo loved having me visit, and I basked in their attention. They argued over which one of them would get me a piece of scrap paper or whose butter knife I'd use at breakfast. When they realized that I didn't own a wristwatch, Dodo rushed into her bedroom and returned with an antique silver one. "Take this. You'll need it when you travel to Greece," she said. Suse lent me her nightgown because I had forgotten to bring one. They lavished me with a kind of motherly care that I wasn't used to, and it eased the loneliness and anxiety I felt about leaving home.

Suse connected me to two other elderly cousins from my father's side of the family who lived in London. One morning I took the subway to the National Gallery to meet Ilse Karger, who was in her late sixties. After touring the museum, she drove me to meet her mother, Margit Freund. Margit greeted us at the door of her apartment and embraced me. She was 87 years old: a tall, regal, beautiful woman. Her eyes shone with delight as she joyfully patted my face and hugged me again. I loved Margit immediately. Because Margit only spoke German, I had to use the little German I remembered from junior high school in order to communicate directly with her.

With Ilse Karger translating from German to English, she and her mother began to fill me in on the history and lineage of my father's family. In order to keep it all straight, I asked for a pen and paper and began to create a family tree, starting with my father's grandparents, Rosalie Orgler and Wilhelm Chotzen. Next to my great-grandparents' names, I noted, *"Wilhelm had eleven sisters and one brother! And Rosalie had a huge family, too. Wilhelm started a spinning mill in Ziegenhals to make thread. Daddy's father, Otto, took over the factory and refitted it to manufacture wooden plugs for beer barrels."*

Rosalie and Wilhelm had eight children: five daughters and three sons, just like in my family. I wrote the names of their eight children in chronological order. Deborah was the oldest; Margit Freund was her daughter. My grandfather, Otto, was fifth from the top. Memories and stories about the Chotzen clan cascaded from Margit and Ilse; they referred to uncles as "Onkel" and aunts as "Tante." "Your grandfather, Otto, had the best sense of humor," they told me. "Tante Olga always smelled good," laughed Margit. "Remember how every young Chotzen female was in love with Onkel Fritz!" chimed in Ilse. One by one, we went down the list, with Margit and Ilse bringing to life relatives I had never met nor even heard of. As Margit commented, "Tante Olga's whole family perished in the war," or, "Tante Hedwig's seven family members were destroyed entirely," I wrote that information next to their names. They told me about my father's sister, Vera, who escaped from Germany to Sweden, and how, for a while Vera received letters from the relatives who had stayed behind. Then, one by one, she no longer received replies from the different family members. Again and again, as they mentioned a family member who "perished in the war" or who died in a concentration camp, I put an asterisk by each of those names. In the upper right-hand corner of my page, I wrote "* = Hitler."

By the end of our visit, the asterisks were everywhere on my family tree. All my life I had heard that six million Jews died in the Holocaust, but in many ways, it was just numbers and words. Suddenly it felt very personal. These were the aunts, uncles, and cousins that my father and his two sisters had grown up with in Germany; the family they had laughed with, shared their holidays with, spent evenings playing board games with. I was shocked to realize how many of my father's family, my relatives, had been exterminated by the Nazis.

While in London, I also met, for the first time, one of my mom's relatives—another Ilse—Ilse Glaser, my mother's aunt, and the only remaining relative of that generation on my mother's side of the family. At my request, Ilse Glaser helped me piece together the family history on my mother's side. That family tree was also filled with "asterisks"—family members murdered by the Nazis.

My parents had seldom talked about the Holocaust when we were growing up. My father had only begun to share a few details of his life in Germany when we had co-counseled together during the previous year. Being away from the routine and habits of my homelife and meeting new extended family members freed me to be inquisitive about a topic that somehow felt off limits in our home environment. Slowly, I began to piece together the personal histories and events that shaped my family, and consequently had shaped me.

Spending time with family members in London was a gentle transition between leaving home and starting my dance program in Greece. I ached from missing my family. I felt responsible for my younger brothers and sisters, and yet was eager to spread my own wings. I knew I had to leave home to start growing up, to create my own life, to be independent, but I felt guilty that I was abandoning the younger siblings I had left behind.

* * *

A week after arriving in London, I hugged Suse and Dodo goodbye, took the subway to Gatwick Airport, and flew to Greece. I arrived in the Athens airport on October 4th, 1971 at 4 a.m. Lugging my large backpack I made my way in the dark into downtown Athens by bus. I wasn't scheduled to meet Donna, director of the "Dance Project in Greece," until the following day when she arrived in Athens on the boat from Paros. I walked under a full moon on the empty city streets to the Plaka, the old neighborhood near the Acropolis, and watched the sun rise over Athens. I bought food from a street vendor for breakfast and climbed up to the Parthenon where I could look over the city and rest near other early morning tourists. While I tried to put up a brave front, it was a difficult day. I was really on my own for the first time. I knew no one. I couldn't speak the language. I was tired from lack of sleep. The city felt huge and hot. I was hauling a heavy backpack. All I wanted was a friend, a bed, and a shower. Finally, I made my way to a youth hostel and fell asleep, feeling frightened, unsafe, and lonely.

Donna, and her husband, Yannis, met me on my second day in Athens. They greeted me with warm smiles; they both embraced me and kissed me on the cheek. I was so relieved to see their friendly faces, to speak English, and to be welcomed by them.

They were in their early thirties, both olive-skinned and good looking. Yannis was Greek and had grown up on Paros. Donna was an American dancer who married him, moved to Paros, and established a dance program on the island for American college students. She was tall and had long, dark hair flowing down her back.

They took me by taxi to the Orion Hotel—a small hotel on a hill above downtown Athens. For the first time in my life, I had a hotel room all to myself, with a view overlooking the Acropolis. The sounds of the busy, sun-washed city—a mixture of rooster and truck noises—filled the warm air. Donna and Yannis took the room next door to mine.

Being in Athens with Donna and Yannis suddenly made everything feel safe instead of scary. They knew their way and spoke the language; what had felt dangerous now felt exciting. They introduced me to Greek yogurt and to loukoumades, small golden pastry puffs drizzled with honey and sprinkled with cinnamon.

That first night we went to dinner with three of their friends—all men. Greek Bazuki music filled the restaurant. The five of them ordered their favorite Greek foods for me to try, and they encouraged me to drink retsina, the Greek wine. That night, I wrote in my journal: "It's so good to be safe and on my way to Paros with Greeks taking care of me. Donna and Yannis are lovely."

The *Ellie*, the ferry from Athens to Paros, sailed only twice a week. On the day we were scheduled to leave, the sea was too rough, and the sailing was cancelled. For the next few days, Donna and Yannis were my guides, inseparable friends, as we explored Athens. The three of us did everything together. They took me to the Acropolis and the markets, they taught me my first words of Greek and how to order meals. I was so relieved and happy to be with them because inside I felt insecure about being young, female, and completely on my own in a new culture so far from home. I needed them to like me, and I could tell they enjoyed my excitement and enthusiasm.

One afternoon, after we had spent the morning on a shopping trip to the Athens flea market, we came back to the hotel to rest. I had taken a shower and was resting on my bed in my clothes. I had locked the door, but someone from the outside had a key. I heard the door being unlocked and opened. I was alarmed to see Yannis come into the room, a finger to his lips, shushing me. I jumped off the bed. "What are you doing here? How did you get a key to my room?"

He came toward me and said in a hushed voice, "Donna is having a nap, and we don't want to disturb her. I wanted to tell you how happy we are to have you here and how much we like you. I just came in to visit with you; how about a hug?" I was alarmed, uncomfortable. I gave him a quick hug and told him he had to leave, that I needed to rest.

"Okay," he said, "I'll take off. Donna and I both love your passion for life. I just wanted to tell you that. Let's have one more hug and I'll go for my walk." I hugged him again and he left.

My mind raced. I was in a state of alarm. *How did he get the key to my room? What made him think he could just let himself in? Clearly, he hadn't told Donna he was coming to my room. And what should I do now?* Donna and Yannis were my hosts in Greece. She was my new dance teacher. *Should I tell her Yannis had shown up in my room? What if I did tell her, would I have to leave the program and go home?* I had just come all this way and I hadn't even started the program.

Sifting through my confusion, I decided the best thing to do would be to stay aloof, to hold back on the warmth and friendliness. And I wondered if I had done something wrong— been too friendly, misread the cues, given off some wrong sign of interest to Yannis.

We sailed to Paros the next day. On the eight-hour boat trip I tried to avoid Yannis. When he approached me, I walked away from him. Near the end of the trip, he cornered me and apologized. He was very smooth. "I know it was wrong of me to come into your hotel room. Can we be friends again?" It was so hard to know what to do. I was in a totally foreign land; these two people were my hosts, my translators, my link to the unknown. I warned him, "Don't *ever* do anything like that again."

* * *

When the ferry pulled into the port town of Parikia, I was captivated. This was the main village of Paros, with a population of 2000, and it was one of the most beautiful places I had ever seen. Waves crashed against low stonewalls and a promenade curved along the sparkling blue Aegean Sea. White sand beaches stretched in both directions. Restaurants and cafes lined the waterfront. Everything seemed ocean-blue and white. "It has a Turkish and Venetian influence," Donna told me as we left the boat. Narrow streets were paved with stones and all the shops and homes were whitewashed bright. There were no personal cars on the island. "You can visit villages on other parts of the island by bus," Donna informed me. "And there are taxis, motorbikes and donkeys." Paros reminded me of someplace I'd seen before, something from my childhood memory, and it was an eerie recollection—Paros looked like the place where the Light Ladies had shown me brilliant sunshine and orange trees sparkling in the sunlight.

Donna walked me to a small hotel where she said I should stay temporarily until I picked an apartment to rent. She introduced me to two other dance academy students who had arrived a week earlier, both American girls who were about my age, one from Ohio and one who went to Skidmore College in New York.

My new dance-mates took me on a tour of the village and to the agora, the cobble-stoned market street, lined with all kinds of shops. We walked to the outskirts of town to see where our dance classes would be held. Donna's "dance studio" was a large, wooden platform built under a grove of cypress and lemon trees. Donkeys and pigs grazed in pastures around the dance platform. A battery-powered boom box was perched on one side of the platform, music to accompany our movement.

The next day, fourteen dancers gathered for our first class. We were all young women from different parts of the U.S. Soft breezes cooled our skin as Donna led us in a warm-up routine, and then we danced her choreography. I was thrilled to be dancing again and to be dancing outside on a picturesque Greek island surrounded by citrus trees and donkeys!

After class on the second day, Donna took me to see several possible places I could rent. I fell in love with a one-room cottage that was a seven-minute walk outside of town, on a bluff overlooking the ocean. An ancient fig tree shaded the blue door. Inside the apartment there was a small kitchen, a table, a bed, and a large window that looked towards the ocean and framed a pomegranate tree laden with ripe, red fruit. The walls of the apartment were built of stone, plastered and painted with bright white paint. A rocky cliff covered with curly plants was all that lay between the little house and the waves breaking on the beach below. The Greek landlady lived in a separate home on the cliff above this smaller dwelling.

"This place is perfect," I told Donna.

She walked me up to the larger house to introduce me to Marina, the landlady.

On our way up the path, Donna warned me that Marina might not seem very friendly, but she often rented her apartment to students. "The villagers think American girls who travel on their own are whores. No Greek girl would ever be allowed to travel alone," Donna explained.

Too soon, I knew why.

During the fourth night in my new apartment, my small, isolated haven of beauty and peace above the surging waves, I was wrenched awake by the weight of a heavy body of top of me. Yannis!

He had a key to my apartment and had let himself in. "Get off me!" I screamed. I struggled, slugged him, kicked him with every ounce of strength I had. "No one will hear you," Yannis declared as he pushed on top of me with the full force of his weight. I fought him, but he held me down, cursing at me, "There's no point, Marina's house is too far up the hill and she can't hear you over the ocean." He was right, I could scream and fight, but it was useless. I couldn't get him off of me. Finally, I stopped fighting and Yannis did what he wanted—just like my mother had done night upon night, year after year. I remember only the image of a stick going in and out, and the overwhelming, familiar, sensation of hopelessness and defeat. And, just like all those times lying underneath my mother, I left my body.

He raped me. And then he left.

Right after he left the room, I grabbed the container of Ortho-Novum birth control tablets that I had brought on the trip. I swallowed a whole handful of the pills. I knew the dose was supposed to be one a day, but I just had no idea what to do. I hadn't had any reason to start them. This was my first experience with sexual intercourse.

I had wanted to wait until I was deeply in love with a man I trusted completely. Before leaving for Greece, Leah and I had gone to Seattle's Planned Parenthood so that if I felt like I met the right man, I was prepared. Now I was battered and bleeding and terrified. The thought of pregnancy added to my panic. I spent the night crying. My vagina hurt, and my insides ached.

I didn't tell anyone what had happened. I went to my dance classes. I bought fresh produce in the market. I visited with the other girls in the program. I saw Donna every day, and I often saw Yannis at their apartment and around town. He acted as if nothing had happened, and I did the same. I went through the motions of my days, and I felt terrified, desperate, and totally alone. At night, I had trouble sleeping. Before bed, I'd shove the heavy kitchen table up against the blue door. I put a large kitchen knife next to my bed, ready to fight Yannis if he attempted to get in again.

My letters home described the beauty of the island, the joy of dancing, the dazzling, azure ocean, but I was filled with the same silent shame I'd felt as a child. I wondered if Yannis' attack was my fault. Had I been too friendly, too open, too American? I knew what Yannis had done was wrong, but I blamed myself.

I immersed myself in dance to help keep myself from spiraling downward with worry and desolation. I took ballet classes, modern dance classes, stretch and improvisation classes. A thin blue airmail letter from Gerald, my friend and classmate at Bellevue High School, lifted my spirits. Like me, Gerald had decided to travel after high school instead of going to college. About the same time that I left for London and Greece, he left Bellevue to travel through Europe, with vague plans to come see me in Greece. I was elated when his letter announced an actual date for his arrival on Paros!

When the *Ellie* docked at Parikia a week later at the end of October, I was there to meet him. He was wearing a red, nylon windbreaker, and his jacket and sandy hair whipped in the wind, as I waited for him to debark.

Gerald moved into my small apartment and unloaded his backpack, crammed with his camera, film, clothes and books. We shared the bed as friends. The landlady probably clucked that her assumption about American girls was accurate, but I didn't care what she thought. I was thrilled and relieved to have my good friend with me. Gerald's arrival felt like a safe harbor for me.

During the week, while I was busy with dance, Gerald went for runs on the roads and hills outside of town, and he occupied himself with his photography. I introduced him to my dancer friends and to other artists and writers living on Paros, ex-pats from the U.S, Europe, and England. We met these friends for meals at cafes in town and at each other's homes.

On the weekends, Gerald and I explored the island together. We hiked to the nearest town, Naoussa, and rode the bus to remote villages. We visited the "Valley of the Butterflies," sparkling white churches, and monasteries. We shared delicious Greek meals: fresh fish and squid, vine-ripened tomatoes, wine, and my favorite: *ryzogalo*—a comforting, sweet rice pudding sprinkled with cinnamon. We explored all parts of the island, gazing at fields of wheat, barley, olives, citrus fruits, and grapes, and we attended a harvest festival where the grapes were trampled into wine. Gerald photographed everything we saw.

One day we stopped to talk with a farmer named Demetrius who was singing to his donkeys. I had been studying Greek—trading Greek lessons for English lessons with a Greek girl in town—and learning new Greek words every day. I had been practicing conversing with the local people. After we had chatted for a little while, Demetrius invited us to his home. He gestured for me to climb on one of his donkeys and ride it back to his home. Gerald took a picture of me sitting on the donkey wearing my orange, knitted Greek sweater. Demetrius and his wife, Kula, served us hot chocolate, sesame-wine squares, ouzo, nuts, home-made cheese, and fresh rysogalo. They spoke only Greek, and I was amazed at how well I could understand and speak with them. Gerald and I visited with Demetrius and Kula for over two hours. They told us about growing up on Paros, their children, how they made the food and the wine. When Gerald took their photograph outside their home, they were very excited.

I was relieved and happy to have Gerald's companionship, but I was growing more and more worried that Yannis' rape had made me pregnant. My period was late. I hadn't told Gerald about what had happened with Yannis. When my period had not arrived after several more weeks, I finally told him the whole story. Gerald was enraged; he wanted to go find Yannis and tear him apart. I begged him not to say or do anything. I wanted to protect Donna and myself, and I also worried that she'd be angry at me and that I'd have to leave the program. I still felt that somehow, I must be at fault. Gerald's response made me realize that Yannis was completely responsible and helped me begin to shed the familiar sense of shame.

On my nineteenth birthday, my first away from my family, Gerald and I swam in the icy-cold Aegean Sea. The sky was grey, and the sun wasn't very hot, but we were from the Pacific Northwest, and we were excited about swimming outside in November.

Later, I called home from a telephone facility that placed transatlantic phone calls. Mom's voice came crackling across the line. "Gerald and I swam in the ocean for my birthday! Can you believe we could be swimming in November?"

"Oh my, it is your birthday," Mom, replied. "We totally forgot about it." I felt crushed. I was halfway across the world, but my family was still the center of my world. My journal was filled with how much I missed all of them; of how grateful I was for "their steady, constant, solid love." But I was far away, and they were immersed in the daily rhythms of their own busy lives.

The dance program closed for the last two weeks of November, so Gerald and I made plans to travel to Istanbul. We flew on Olympic Airlines from Athens to Istanbul. From the window of our room in Hotel Gungor in downtown Istanbul, we could see the Bosborus Strait, the harbor, and the spiraling towers of the grand Blue Mosque. It was autumn in Istanbul. The weather was crisp and cold. The trees had shed their leaves and the branches were bare and brown. As we walked the streets together, we inhaled the scent of smoking fish on the waterfront, ate roasted chestnuts, and admired the mountains of tangerines piled high on carts. We explored the bazaars, visited mosques and the Topkapi museum, ate Turkish food and even experienced real Turkish baths. One night I dreamed that my period came but woke to find that it hadn't.

When we returned to Athens, Gerald helped me find a Greek medical doctor who spoke English. I had to face reality and get a pregnancy test. It had been six weeks since Yannis had raped me. I was near tears when I explained what had happened to Dr. Zerris, who was clearly judgmental about the fact that I had had sex. His exam added insult to injury; it was a cold, intimidating experience, resurrecting both shame and fear. But the news was a huge relief—I wasn't pregnant. In the elevator after the exam, Gerald held me while I quietly cried. "You're okay now," he told me. I wiped my eyes as we left the building and entered Omonia Square. I squeezed Gerald's arm tightly, with gratefulness for his caring and his comfort.

When we returned to Paros a few days later, a pile of wonderful air letters awaited me at the post office. Letters from my sisters and brothers, my parents, and my friends made me ache with homesickness. It was the end of November, and Gerald was preparing to head home to Seattle to be with his family for the Christmas holidays. I desperately wanted to go back with him, but I knew that wasn't an option. I wasn't expected home until spring. My parents would disapprove if I came home for a short visit and then returned to Paros, and they'd be really disapproving if I quit the program early.

Gerald and I had lived together for six weeks. When he left in early December, I started to slide back into that sense of isolation I'd felt before his arrival. I was incredibly sad, but one thing was different. I noticed that many of the people around me were genuinely concerned about me, aware that Gerald's departure was difficult for me, that I was a little morose. Greek townspeople and the Paros American/European community checked on me, invited me to parties and meals, and several of them invited me to live with them. Not enjoying living alone, I moved in with a friend from the dance program, Twinkie. She was twenty years old, from Georgia, a shy slender girl with huge green eyes. Her house was small, outside of town, had no electricity and had a hole in the ground that sufficed as a toilet. Winter storms came with torrents of rain and wind. The *Ellie* couldn't sail for several weeks—which meant no mail from home. The weather turned very cold. Our home had no heating and no fireplace, so I dressed in layers of tights, two pairs of socks, four shirts, and two sweaters in an effort to keep warm.

I missed my family, and I missed the familiar Hanukkah celebration. Mom wrote to me, "*It is the third night of Hanukkah, and I just put things at the foot of each bed. I thought of you and of what to put at the foot of your bed. I saw a lovely brown scooped-neck top that I thought would suit you perfectly, but I didn't buy it because you were not here to grace it. I thought of you as I fingered it gently. Dry clean only, the tag said. I'd rather lick you clean like a kitty. You were always a delightful little girl.*" I cried at my mother's expression of love. Many of her letters expressed wanting to touch me or caress me. *"Claudie-girl. Can you feel my hands touching your skin? Fingering your eyes. I'm closing them to rest. I love you. Your friend. Your mother/Carla."* This was the way she had always expressed her love for me, and I still believed it was a wonderful closeness that we shared. I still revered her. In my journal I wrote, *"Mommy, last year you slipped into my bed with me each morning—the best gentle hello to the world possible. What closeness—sharing our warm nude bodies close together. Our sleeping smells mingling. Sometimes I'd feel hostile and then we'd argue. Other times 7:30 and needing to get ready for school came too quickly."* I thought our physical closeness was *beautiful* because she had had always told me it was. I was still unconscious that this behavior between a mother and her child was abnormal and inappropriate. My early training was so pervasive, and so strong, that it was almost thirty more years before I could speak the word that described the reality of my relationship with my mother: incest.

Dance classes ended in late December. We had three weeks off before the next session began, and Twinkie and I decided to travel together to Israel. I'd had been interested in visiting Israel since learning about my relatives who had perished in the Holocaust. I wanted to connect with my cultural roots. We bought $30 student tickets on a flight from Athens to Tel Aviv. I planned to return to the island in a few weeks.

The last days on Paros were difficult: I was sick with some kind of flu and vomited for several days. Just as I was starting to feel better from whatever virus I had, my period came, three months late. Finally. Maybe the stress was abating.

Once again, I left Paros on the *Ellie,* choosing the identical seats Gerald and I had sat on when we left for our trip to Istanbul—this time Twinkie slept next to me. The Ellie docked in Piraeus at 3 a.m. We tried to stay asleep on board while attendants cleaned the seats, but noisy teens and a loud jukebox made it hard to sleep. At 5 a.m. they kicked us off the boat. We loaded our packs on to our backs, and in the cold and dark I guided Twinkie to the subway. We landed in Omonia Square. Athens felt friendly and bright in the Christmas lights. We bought *Time Magazine* at a kiosk. It was December of 1971. On the cover: *Man of the Year: Richard Nixon.* As we spent the day doing errands to prepare for our flight to Israel, I felt confident, radiant, and happy. I loved being in the sparkling big city and I enjoyed speaking Greek with the shopkeepers and other strangers we met.

During my time traveling with Twinkie, I felt safe enough to tell her about being raped by Yannis. I was stunned to discover that she had also been raped by him, and she told me that another girl in our dance program had also had the same traumatic experience. Did Yannis force himself on every young woman who came to the dance school? Did Donna know? Was she complicit? None of us ever went public with what had happened. Maybe we thought we were protecting Donna, maybe we were afraid of being labeled as independent American girls who "asked for it."

* * *

On a January morning in 1972, the plane landed in Tel Aviv at 4 a.m., but the airport was far from asleep at this early hour. People were rushing everywhere. Loudspeakers blared: "Flight 161 leaving for Ceylon at 4:52. All passengers are asked to board immediately." "Flight 73 is at gate 6 in the West Terminal." Twinkie and I found seats at an empty gate and tried to doze until daylight. I felt tired, anxious and uncomfortable, lost and far from home. Greece had become familiar and comfortable; now we were facing a new language and a new culture. I thought, *"The Greeks move slowly, and they save everything to do tomorrow. Israelis push and rush and they certainly don't seem to care about a couple of confused strangers."*

On our first afternoon in Israel, Twinkie and I separated; she boarded a bus to get settled on a kibbutz near Ashkelon in the south of Israel. I took a bus to a kibbutz in Rehovot, located in central Israel, to visit a family friend, Randy, from Portland, Oregon. He had gone to Camp Schechter with Naomi and Danny. Randy had met and married Yael, who was Israeli; they lived on the kibbutz where she was raised.

I realized how much I was looking for the warmth and closeness of family as I knocked on Randy and Yael's door at dinnertime. They were expecting me, and they welcomed me so warmly and with so much love that I almost burst into tears. They took me to dinner in the communal dining room and introduced me to their friends and family. After dinner, they gave me a tour of the kibbutz, with the soft evening light illuminating the citrus and avocado orchards.

"Here is where you can stay as long as you want," they told me as they settled me into a perfect set-up: a small, separate one-room building next to their little house. There was a mattress on the floor; I shared the bathroom and kitchen in their house. "We're so happy to have you. Our home is your home. Help yourself to anything we have." Even though they ate most of their meals in the communal dining hall, their small refrigerator was filled with fresh, delicious fruits and foods. My favorite food—something I had never tasted before—was thick, creamy, "shemenit," a cross between sour cream and yogurt.

Randy woke me every morning at 7 a.m. to pick oranges and grapefruits. Desert sunshine glistened on the wet fruit in the orchards. I loved working in the cool morning air, hearing the birds' songs and feeling the sunshine soak into my skin. Other volunteers of all ages—but mostly young like me—had come from all over the world; there were young adults from Holland, Germany, Sweden, and Australia. The Israelis taught us Hebrew words, and we had lively conversations as we picked the fruit.

In the afternoons I learned how to milk the cows and drive a tractor. I loved what I was doing: I enjoyed the fresh air, the earth, the friendly and hard-working people.

Randy and Yael included me in all parts of their lives. On Friday night they took me to dinner at Yael's grandparents, where thirty-five relatives of three generations gathered every Shabbat to be together. Again, as I had when Randy and Yael had initially welcomed me, I got teary when Yael's grandmother gently welcomed me by warmly squeezing my shoulder.

Randy was very happy living in Israel. Yael's parents, grandparents and friends all lived on the kibbutz, and they had welcomed Randy into the family. He cherished his new wife and his new life—he was a respected, beloved member of the kibbutz, and he liked being away from what he called the "rat race" in America. Yael was only one year older than me, but she was the director of the Children's House, where the younger kids slept and played and had their classes.

Randy and Yael's life on the kibbutz seemed like a utopia to me. They worked hard, but there was no pressure and no competition. Yael was married, yet she saw her mom and sisters and grandmother every day. I envied the kibbutzniks' sense of community and their common purpose: they worked hard for their kibbutz, their country, and their Judaism.

After picking fruit and milking cows for a week, I rode the kibbutz school bus into the nearby city of Rehovot and boarded another bus for Jerusalem. I visited the Wailing Wall. I spent several hours with an older Jewish couple from Montreal; they wished they could share this experience with their children, and I was wishing that I could share it with my parents. We toured the Arab market, Mt. Zion, tombs, and mosques. Suddenly I yearned to know Jewish history and my heritage. I was Jewish, but I knew almost nothing about *being* Jewish. What defined a Jew? So many of my family members had been killed because of their identity, I wanted to know *why*. I needed to find out what Judaism meant to me.

Everyone in Israel observed the Sabbath. On Friday afternoon businesses closed their doors, people headed home to be with their families, and the cities came to a halt. On the kibbutz with Randy and Yael, when I visited the Levines in Haifa (the family we had Passover dinners with), and later when I visited friends at the Hebrew University in Jerusalem, I relished how one reality stopped and another, quieter, slower pace replaced it. This was a time of gratitude, observed with traditions that involved special cleansing, clothing, food, and prayers, and I enjoyed the rituals, especially in contrast to the unpredictability of my family life in Seattle.

Radios always played on loudspeakers on the busses in Israel. On the bus on my way back from visiting the Levines in Haifa, I listened to a news report about new discoveries on an archaeological excavation by the Dead Sea. The Israel Exploration Society believed that the crew was digging up an ancient synagogue. When I reached the kibbutz, Randy and Yael had also heard the report and they were very excited about the news. I told them I wanted to go to the dig to see if I could work on it. I had come to Israel to understand more about my Judaism and digging in the earth seemed, literally, like a good way for me to learn more about my roots.

Hitchhiking from place to place was a way of life in Israel. From the kibbutz to the site of the excavation at Ein Gedi near the Dead Sea was a distance of about 150 miles. On a bright, beautiful morning, I stood on the road outside their kibbutz and stuck out my arm. The first car took me directly to the Egged bus station in Rehovot, the nearest city. In Rehovot I boarded the bus to ride to the city of Ramla, where I planned to hitchhike the rest of the way.

As I stood waiting to get on the bus, a young soldier offered to carry my backpack. His name was Uriel. We sat together and had an easy-going, fun talk on the bus ride to Ramla. Uriel shared fresh fruit with me, and we talked about his life growing up in Israel, his mandatory service in the Israeli army, and "tramping," as he called hitchhiking. At Ramla, we walked together to the road where he was also hitchhiking to Jerusalem.

The first car, driven by another Israeli soldier, picked both of us up. The mountain scenery as we rode up the hill to Jerusalem was lush and green. From Jerusalem I rode in a blue truck with a third Israeli soldier all the way to the Dead Sea. He dropped me on the highway at one end of the huge, windy sea. Another ride took me to the bottom of the road to the Ein Gedi Field School where the excavation was headquartered. The Field School was perched on a hill across the road from the Dead Sea, facing Jordan. It was late in the afternoon, and outlines of jagged cliffs were carved against a pink-grey sky across the vast expanse of water. In the distance I could see the silhouettes of Jordanian soldiers patrolling their border.

* * *

I climbed the hill to the Field School and found the director of the excavation loading tools into a truck behind the school. His name was Dr. Dan Barag, a well-known and respected professor at the Hebrew University's Institute of Archaeology.

When I asked him if I could join his team of workers, he laughed at me.

"Do you have archaeology experience?"

"No, but I'm a hard worker," I replied.

"This is an *extremely* important excavation," he said. "Experienced archaeologists and anthropologists are here from all over the world. Many of them waited one or two years to work here, paid their own expenses, and came great distances to work on this site. People don't just "show up" at this dig. Go home, girl!" He climbed into his truck and drove away.

The next day I found my way to the archaeological site and walked quietly around it. Mustard colored flowers bloomed in the cracks of the rocks. I observed the crew working in the blistering sun; most of them looked to be in their mid-thirties. They were carefully digging in the dirt, labeling pottery, and cleaning corroded green coins.

Again, I spoke to the director and asked if I could work, and again he told me there was no room.

I left the site and returned to the Youth Hostel.

The next day, when I returned a third time, Dr. Barag threw his hands up in the air when he saw me. "You don't quit do you girl? Okay. I will let you work, but you have to follow all of my and Seffi's instructions." Seffi was the other director of the excavation. I assured him that I would do whatever they told me to do. I sent an airletter to Donna on Paros, letting her know that I wouldn't be attending the winter session.

I was teamed with an elderly, white-haired Israeli man, the only other inexperienced excavator on this project. A white beard framed the old man's deeply tanned, weathered face, and his leathery skin was covered with dust and sweat. He wore the blue workpants typical of an Israeli kibbutz, a short-sleeved shirt, and canvas work gloves. His name was Shalom. I was the youngest member of the group, Shalom was the oldest.

We were assigned to dismantle a seven-foot rock wall. Shalom spoke a little English, I spoke a little Hebrew from my days at Herzl Hebrew School, and as we worked, we talked. He was eighty-five, and he was living a lifetime dream as he worked in the dirt. Twenty-five years earlier he had immigrated to Israel from Russia. His heart was devoted to this Jewish land, he had watched the country grow, and now his last dream was to help uncover more of his ancestors' lives. He had saved his vacation time from the last five years on his kibbutz in the north to join a dig.

Shalom knew that the Ein Gedi Dig was more important than any of the excavations being undertaken in Israel at that time. This was the earliest sign of Jewish civilization in the Dead Sea territories. A mosaic floor in beautiful condition had been uncovered, revealing twelve peacocks. The layout seemed to indicate that the site had once been a synagogue, but it still wasn't the definitive proof that the experts, who believed it had been a Fifth Century synagogue of the Byzantine Period, needed.

As I listened to Shalom and others talk of the importance of proving that Jews had lived here first, I realized how intractable and complicated the battle to establish roots in the Holy Land was. I wrote in my journal *"Will anything ever end this perpetual race to establish claims to this land?"* I admired the passion and conviction of Israelis I met, but talk of war, enemies, and land possession permeated every discussion. I wrote, *"I loved getting to know Shalom, but I'd be just as interested in learning about an old Arab man's life with an equal degree of caring and curiosity."* It was a thought I could share with myself in a journal, but probably wise not to express out loud to others.

Now I ate and slept with the group at the Field School. The Field School had dormitory-style rooms, a large dining room, and a presentation room with a screen and a slide projector. The location was beautiful, the Field School overlooked the Dead Sea and was surrounded by desert wilderness trails. Nubian ibexes, a species of wild mountain goats, wandered right up to the doors of our dormitory.

We woke each morning at 4 a.m., with the night still black and cold. We ate a small breakfast of fresh yogurt and tomatoes in the cafeteria, before climbing into the back of open trucks which drove us to the site. By 5 a.m. we began digging. There were sixteen of us, all working together to find buried treasure. The crimson sun rose in front of us over the Dead Sea.

Shalom and I worked for days tearing apart rocks and dirt that had settled over thousands of years. Together we dismantled the wall, loading dirt and stones into a wheelbarrow and dumping the loads in the garbage pile at the edge of the site. I swept my long hair back from my face and tied it with a red bandana to keep my hair out of my eyes. My beige work gloves were coated with dirt, and my skin was covered with the brown dust. When a rock was too large for one of us to lift, we lifted it off the wall together, and then lifted it together into the wheelbarrow. In the early morning the temperature was chilly, but as the sun rose the heat became intense. We looked forward to the ten o'clock break when the wagon carrying jelly sandwiches and ice water arrived, and we could rest and chat with the rest of the crew.

Most nights a group of us slept outside on the ground. I settled into the warmth of my down sleeping bag, my body aching and tired from the hard physical work. The stars were bright against the night sky.

Each day as Shalom and I worked dismantling the rock wall, cries of excitement would fly across the dirt; other members of the crew had discovered bronze coins, or an intact pottery vase, and once even a cloth purse. When someone let out a cry, we all dropped our shovels and brushes and rushed to see the ancient treasure. Work would pause while the directors, Dan and Seffi, figured out the best way to photograph and preserve the find. Then they would give us an on-the-spot lecture describing the significance of the new discovery.

Shalom and I found only dirt and rocks in our wall. Hour after hour we hauled barrels filled with earth and stones to the garbage pile. There weren't even pieces of broken pottery— only crusted layers of rock, and hot, tedious work. While we worked, I asked Shalom to tell me about his life and about Jewish history. As we knocked down the wall, he told me Biblical tales and stories, bringing the land alive. Absorbing his love for this land and listening to him talk made the hot hours pass more quickly. I relished the hard physical work, the healthy farm food, the conversations and jokes and camaraderie with the other members of our group. These people from all parts of the world became a close team, a lively kind of family.

Each day we worked until noon when it was too hot to work any longer. We ate a hearty lunch and spent the afternoon hiking trails to waterfalls or floating on top of the Dead Sea in the dense, salty water. On weekends, Dan and Seffi led us on hikes into the Judean hills to see other ruins. One Saturday Dan led us to see a cave that Shalom had told me about—429 ancient bronze weapons had been found there.

Shalom never joined us on these expeditions. Each day after lunch he retired to his dormitory room. I would see him bent over his books in the afternoon, studying. I asked him one day what he studied. "The Talmud," he replied.

After almost three weeks of digging, only a foot-tall section of the wall remained covering the mosaic floor where Shalom and I were working. Dan approached us, saying, "You're done here." Pointing to a seven-foot wall on the other side of the excavation site, he said, "Start taking down that wall over there."

Shalom's body stiffened, and his hands squeezed the handle of the pick he held. We had worked tirelessly for weeks and were now only a few inches from what we believed to be the floor. Shalom began to argue with the director in Hebrew. I beseeched Dan in English. "We've worked so hard to take this wall down. Couldn't we be the ones to carefully finish the job and see what is underneath?" Dan insisted we leave the spot, saying that we were not experienced enough, that we lacked the technical ability necessary for the final work. Shalom and I continued to plead to allow us to be the ones to complete the job.

Others in the group heard our discussion and came over. They agreed, saying that Shalom and I had worked hard and should be allowed the final uncovering. Dan wasn't hearing it. This started a shouting match. "Teach Shalom and Claudia exactly how you want them to do it," insisted Sarah, who was an archaeology teacher from Hebrew University. "Instruct them and they will do it carefully." Several members of the dig joined in urging Dan to teach us and trust us to do the work.

Finally, Dan relented. He gave us explicit instructions on how to carefully remove the final crust of dirt. When we had finished doing that, under his supervision, using delicate brushes we swept away the final crust from a surface that had not been seen in almost 2000 years. As we brushed away the last layer of dirt, we saw that the mosaic floor did continue! And when we used rags and water to wash the tiles, we saw a design in the tile. Shalom's hands were shaking as together we washed off the final layer of dust. In the same instant we both recognized it—and so did Dan: the tiles were formed perfectly in the shape of a menorah—the seven-branched candelabra of the Jewish people. Shalom began to weep, saying this was the most joyous moment of his life. Dan too was very moved. He confirmed what Shalom had realized: "The menorah indicates that this was a synagogue. The placement of the menorah indicates that this is where the altar was. This is the proof we have been searching for that Jews inhabited this area near the Dead Sea."

By this time, the entire group had pressed around us. What the archeologists hoped to find were the remains of a fifth-century synagogue, proving Jews had inhabited the area around 400 A.D. Finding the menorah in this location provided the indisputable proof.

Yigael Yadin, Israel's leading archaeologist, came from Tel Aviv to the site with a group of newspaper and television reporters the next day. Randy and Yael saw our discovery that night on the television news and read about it in the newspaper. They saved the article for me. "*Fifth-century Ein Gedi Was Totally Jewish, Dig Shows,*" read the headline of the article in The Jerusalem Post.

* * *

In 2000, I returned to Israel with my husband and our two sons, then thirteen and nine years old. This was their first visit to Israel, and my second. It had been twenty-nine years since I had uncovered the mosaic with Shalom. When our tour van pulled up to the Ein Gedi National Antiquities Park, I felt a sense of excitement.

The synagogue had been fully excavated! Nearby, streets and buildings of the ancient Jewish settlement were partially uncovered. Following "my" excavation, which took place from 1970 to 1972, additional excavations were carried out in 1992 and between 1995 and 1999. The synagogue had been restored, and a huge, white, protective tent covered it. The mosaic floor had been preserved and restored. The menorah design I helped to uncover was next to two additional mosaic tile menorahs in front of the altar. The central hall of the synagogue also contained a mosaic floor, decorated with a medallion of birds and with four pairs of peacocks in the corners.

Almost three decades after I had left my sweat and footprints in Israeli soil, my two visits to Ein Gedi were like bookends bracketing intervening years of good fortune. I thought of all that had happened since the excavation—my love for my husband, the life and community we had built together, our two beautiful sons—and I was grateful for my experience in this desert land of searing heat, raging dissent, and ancient mysteries.

* * *

About spending several more weeks at the kibbutz in Rehovot, I said goodbye to Randy and Yael and left their kibbutz. I hitchhiked from the Dead Sea to Eilat, Israel's southernmost city at the northern tip of the Red Sea, where I spent several days enjoying the hot sun and swimming in the warm ocean. I traveled north to spend a few days with my friend Twinkie at her kibbutz near Ashkelon, with spectacular views of the Mediterranean Sea, then on to Jerusalem.

Two of my old friends from Camp Schechter, back when I was ten years old, were studying at Hebrew University in Jerusalem and had invited me to stay with them. Being surrounded by students from all over the world who had come to Israel to go to college, students who were immersed in their scheduled school lives, made me question my own choice to travel instead of starting college. I knew I hadn't been ready to go to college right after high school, that I had wanted to dance and to experience more of the world, but I was feeling a little lost being out in the world all on my own, missing the safety, structure, and security of being in school.

I was nineteen years old and thousands of miles away from my mom, but I was still emotionally entangled with her and seeking her approval from halfway around the world. I wrote her letters professing my adoration, how much I missed her, telling her, "*You're like my best girlfriend. You're a perfect Mommy. I cannot attach words to my love for you, my awakening to you, I just know that I want to keep breathing you into me gently and softly.*"

One February night I went by myself to see the film *Fiddler on the Roof.* As I sat in the theater in Jerusalem and watched the story of Tevye the milkman, his wife Golde, and his five daughters unfold on the screen the characters seemed even more real to me than they had when I'd seen the play the previous spring in New York. The five daughters felt like the five girls in my family. When Chava, the third daughter, was about to leave the family, I felt like Tevye was my father singing to me. I missed my Dad and my whole family so much. I sat silently weeping in the big theater, across the world from my family, desperately homesick and alone.

Compounding my emotional pain was a physical one. I had a persistent aching in one of my back teeth that had become impossible to ignore. A visit to a dentist confirmed that I had an infected molar and needed a root canal and was also suffering from gum disease caused by lack of sleep, worry and trauma.

Back in Athens, on the way back to Paros, I was conflicted. I was homesick, needed dental work, and felt alone, but a voice inside me kept saying that I had to stick it out, that I had to stay away from home for a year, that I had to return to the dance program. Talking to another American who was in the midst of suddenly flying home earlier than he planned, made me reconsider. I had made the best of my trip, had great experiences, but I wanted to go home. What was keeping me? Who was I trying to please?

Rather than take the boat back to Paros, I decided to get on a train to Vienna and find a flight back to the United States. I called a friend on the island, and she agreed to ship all the things I had left—clothes, my dance shoes, and the large pile of letters I had saved. At 5 a.m. two days after leaving Israel, I was sitting on a train, chugging through Yugoslavia to Austria. From Vienna I flew to rainy London where Suse and Dodo warmly welcomed me. I had been gone for over six months. I didn't think I could move another step, see another city, talk to another stranger, or make any more new friends. I never wanted to pick up that battered backpack again.

My flight arrived in New York, at Kennedy Airport, in the middle of the night. Naomi was there to greet me. While I had been in Greece and Israel, she had been in India, living on an Ashram and working in an Ayurvedic Healing Clinic. In December, wearing white Indian pajamas, she had flown back to New York City. On the night I arrived we stayed up all night talking at Aunt Ilse's apartment. I told her about being raped by Yannis and the months of fear, shame and loneliness that followed. We continued to talk for a week, sharing stories of Naomi's experiences in India and mine in Greece and Israel.

Naomi had some big news to tell me. During the winter when I was in Israel, my parents, Leah, and the four youngest kids had spent two weeks camping in Hawaii, blissfully enjoying the sunshine and tropical climate while Seattle was mired in its usual winter weather. The more my father raved about how much he loved the islands, the more the idea crystallized that they could move to Hawaii. When my parents came home, my dad arranged to sell his business to his longtime partner, Curt. My parents were planning a move to Honolulu. I was going home to Seattle, but my family was moving to Hawaii.

* * *

I landed in Seattle on March 12, 1972 and got off the plane filled with excitement to embrace my family. No one was there to meet me. I waited at baggage claim, got my backpack, called home but no one answered. I was leaving the terminal, resigned to taking a bus to Bellevue, when my mother rushed up to me breathlessly and immediately barked out her orders. "Dad's in the car. We can't park at the curb. Hurry up!"

Home felt different, and after just a few weeks I started to feel lost. I had gotten used to living out of my backpack and taking care of myself. Now I found myself overwhelmed in a chaotic environment that I had no control over, living with constant demands from my mother. I needed to reclaim my own life.

I took a scuba class held at Bellevue Community College and applied for a job at the post office. I rented a bedroom in a house in Seattle near the University of Washington and moved out of my parents' home. I enrolled in summer classes in dance and kinesiology at UW and continued on in the fall. I joined a small dance company and performed in local productions.

By spring, 1973 my post office application had worked its way to the top of the list. I passed the physical exam, had a successful interview, and was offered a job as a part-time mail carrier at the Bellevue Post Office.

I loved the work. I liked the other mail carriers and clerks who were so different than the artists, poets, Jewish refugees, and political characters in my parents' universe. I enjoyed the physical challenge of lifting large boxes and heavy bags of mail and driving the trucks.

One day, I thought I was doing customers a big favor when at the end of my route I disposed of a few pieces of junk mail I had forgotten to deliver into the trash cans in the bathroom at the post office, figuring that I was saving them from throwing it out themselves. But when the custodian gave the Postmaster five or six torn up pieces of 3rd class mail I had tossed in the trash, I learned about a different point of view. I thought I was doing a kindness, but apparently, I had committed a federal offense. Luckily, I got off with a stern warning to never do it again.

On the days I was assigned to the route that included my parents' home, I drove down our driveway and personally delivered their mail. When I could, I timed my home delivery so I could take my lunch break with them.

At the end of the summer, while still working part-time at the Bellevue Post Office, I returned to dance and science classes at UW. I rented a bedroom in a friend's home in Montlake, near the university. Eric, an awkward, shy man in his early thirties, rented the bedroom next to mine. One night, I was putting up some posters and photos to make the room feel personal, and I ran out of thumbtacks. I knocked on Eric's door; when he didn't answer, I walked in, searched his desk for thumbtacks, and took some from a small box inside his top desk drawer. I left him a little note thanking him. That evening, Ruth, who owned the house, confronted me. "Eric told me you entered his room without his permission, searched through his desk, and removed some of his thumbtacks. He is extremely upset about it. Eric's room is private. No one in this house has the right to enter your room without your permission, and you never, never have the right to go into his room or any other room in this house without permission."

I was stunned that borrowing a few thumbtacks had prompted such a dramatic reaction. But as I thought about it, I also realized that I had grown up without any sense of boundaries or privacy. My mother had access into every paper, every drawer, and every shelf in my room at any time she wanted. She read letters my friends wrote me. She read my journals that I kept in my desk. I didn't like it, but I never questioned it. In my family, we modeled my mother's behavior—we thought nothing of going into someone else's room, going through their desk or dresser drawers to find whatever we wanted. The world didn't function that way. I needed to learn new rules, new ways of respecting others, a complete revelation to me.

When my second summer at the Bellevue Post Office rolled around, in 1974, my parents were in high gear for their move to Hawaii. They sold their lakefront home in Bellevue and bought a small home in Honolulu. They wanted to be moved in by fall when school started for Mia, Charlotte, and Joey. Simon was moving with them, but he had just finished high school. Naomi was already living in Honolulu having enrolled in a graduate program at the University of Hawaii. Leah was returning to the east coast to finish college. Danny was still living in the basement of a house in Seattle's central area and working as a janitor. I was staying in Seattle.

During that second summer working as a mail carrier, I received a jury summons from the Superior Court of Seattle, telling me to be available for up to two weeks. I was excited about being paid my full post office salary while I served on a jury and was one of the twelve selected for the trial—a criminal case involving alleged child sexual abuse. After opening arguments, the judge closed the courtroom to spectators, and the prosecutors brought in a shy five-year-old girl with long red hair. She testified against the defendant, a thirty-year-old man who appeared very pleasant and clean cut. The little girl related specific, ugly details of what had happened. Her testimony was deeply disturbing. She didn't seem coached, and I didn't believe she could have fabricated the things she described happening to her. The girl's mother also took the stand to explain that although the defendant had been a close family friend, she believed her child and felt a duty to protect her daughter and other neighborhood children.

The trial lasted four days. The entire jury believed the little girl, the victim, was telling the truth. But for all of us, the burden of convicting the accused man "beyond a reasonable doubt" was extremely difficult. We wanted to make the right decision, knowing that a guilty verdict would forever impact the defendant's life. We discussed the testimony and evidence, took preliminary votes, and then discussed the case some more.

We were exhausted, but we continued to listen patiently to each other, hour after hour. I started to feel a sense of closeness with these people who had been strangers a few days earlier. Finally, after a day and a half of deliberation, we reached unanimous agreement that the defendant was guilty.

The bond I felt with the other jurors was similar to what I had experienced before, at the archeological dig in Israel, working at the post office, and choreographing dance performances with other dancers. I thrived in that environment, working with others with a shared purpose to accomplish a common goal.

In hindsight, I find it interesting—but not surprising—that I was unable to make the connection between the child molestation case I served on as a juror and the traumatic events in my own childhood. I was in a state of denial, still adhering to the myth of our perfect family. The mother in the trial had become her daughter's protector; my mother was my perpetrator. My family's secrets remained deeply buried.

But the trial did open my eyes to new possibilities. I had enjoyed thinking about all the evidence, assessing how the lawyers had performed, analyzing what I would have done differently if I had been in their place. My uncle was a judge in the same courthouse where I served on the jury. I met with him a few times to discuss law as a career. He encouraged me, said that I had the passion and intellect to be a lawyer. It was time to try a new path. I gave notice at the post office that August and planned to enroll at The Evergreen State College in Olympia, Washington. Some of my closest high school friends were already students there.

Washington, California, Hawaii & Oregon

1974–1998

In mid-September,1974, I drove my white Plymouth Valiant from Bellevue to Olympia, Washington. The car, a gift from Jill and Mike, the friends who had taken care of me after my hammock accident a few years earlier, had been Jill's mother's car. When her mom died, instead of selling it, they gave it to me. I was told it had a "slant 6" engine but didn't know what that meant. It also had a large hole in the floorboard, which meant that exhaust fumes entered the car near my face; I drove with the windows open so I wouldn't pass out.

Evergreen was one of a handful of new colleges created as a model of alternative education. It had opened in Fall 1972, and it offered programs that were focused on the real world, taught by faculty who endorsed its emphasis on teaching and real life, not on academic research. Students were attracted by its interdisciplinary approach to subjects, and the use of narrative evaluations instead of letter grades. I wanted to take courses that would prepare me for law school. I was almost twenty-two. I had enough credits from the University of Washington to qualify as a sophomore. I stayed with my dear friend Vanessa who had been attending Evergreen for several years.

A week earlier, while camping on the Washington coast with friends, I had studied the Evergreen catalog cover to cover, circling the academic programs that intrigued me the most. I visited Evergreen to interview the faculty teaching the programs I was interested in.

As I parked my car in the campus parking lot, I remember thinking, *I feel like I'm a woman of the world—not a young college student but a grown-up woman coming to check out this college with a clear sense of my purpose and direction.* I felt beautiful, strong, and confident.

My first meeting was with Andrew Hanfman, an older, urbane professor with a European accent. When I introduced myself, he shook my hand warmly, and said, "No need to call me Professor Hanfman. Call me Andrew. Here at Evergreen the students call faculty by our first names." Andrew had been born in Russia, but studied in Germany and Italy, and had lived all over Europe. He had taught at Kenyon College years earlier. What I learned much later was that he had also spent 20 years before joining the Evergreen faculty as an undercover operative for the CIA.

I liked talking with Professor Hanfman, and the course he was teaching seemed interesting, but another program, *Lawmakers/Lawbreakers*, intrigued me the most. Its lead faculty member was Hap Freund, an attorney. The other two faculty members were a woman whose background was in literature and a man who had served time in prison. It was a year-long course about the legal, legislative and prison systems, courts, justice, and racism. The middle quarter was devoted to real life internship experiences in law and justice. The course description in the catalog ended with: *"We are looking for students who have a willingness to work hard, an interest in the law, and a sense of humor."* After my jury duty experience that summer, I felt confident that I wanted to become a lawyer, and the desire to have students who exhibited a "sense of humor" piqued my interest.

That afternoon, I met with Hap. He was thirty-one, bald with thick wild curly dark hair sticking out like wings on the sides of his head, a bushy beard and mustache, and a warm smile. He was wearing a long-sleeved plaid shirt, a vest, Levi's, and cowboy boots. Two or three other students were sitting on pillows on the floor of his seminar room—which was also his office—when I entered; he was speaking with them about the class as I sat down. I remember that I liked his manner with them: respectful and warm, like they were all good friends. These students stayed, talking quietly with each other, while I interviewed Hap at the other end of the room.

I asked him lots of questions about the program, his background as a lawyer, and about the other faculty members, Sandra and Jim. He told me he was passionate about empowering others to know their rights and using the law to help people. When I finished our interview, I was certain this was the program I wanted to study during my first year at Evergreen.

I left Hap's office and headed directly to the Registrar's office to sign up for *Lawmakers/Lawbreakers*. The registrar looked it up and informed me, "Well, we have one small problem; this program is filled, and there is a waiting list of sixty people."

"Sixteen? I asked, thinking I must have misheard her. "Or Sixty?"

"Sixty. You will be number 61 on the wait list."

My heart dropped. I was thrilled about finding such a perfect year-long class, and now it didn't seem like there was any way I could get into the program that I was most excited about. I had no idea this program—or any other program at Evergreen—was so popular. I was way too late signing up. Classes were scheduled to begin in two weeks. "Is there any other way a spot could become available? It doesn't sound like sixty people will suddenly get off the wait list ahead of me."

"There is one way," the registrar said, "but it requires luck and timing. When a registered student withdraws from a program, the professor signs a withdrawal card. Simultaneously another student can be substituted in by the faculty at that time by signing the registration card."

Discouraging news. But having traveled all over Europe by myself, having a strong sense of luck in my life, and having found a way to join the Ein Gedi excavation in Israel when the director originally told me to get lost, I wasn't about to just give up without trying harder.

As I was heading back to Hap's office to ask if he knew of anyone who might be withdrawing from his program, I heard my name being called.

"Claudia? Claudia Chotzen?" I turned to see a guy my age who I didn't immediately recognize. "It's Dean." he told me.

We hadn't seen each other since seventh grade at Herzl Hebrew School—almost a decade earlier. "Dean! What a surprise. Do you go to Evergreen?"

"I'm finishing up my degree. Just got out of this Lawmakers class and got the professor to agree to sponsor me for what I really want to do—a full year journalism internship at the Washington State Legislature."

In his hand, Dean was holding the registration card that Hap had just signed to release him from the program. Dean walked with me back to Hap's office, and Hap signed me into the program in the slot Dean had just vacated. I was thrilled.

During that first quarter at Evergreen, I shared an off-campus apartment with Vanessa. One morning, about a month after classes had started, Hap called, asking me if I wanted to drive up to Seattle with him the next day to visit a friend of his who was in the hospital. I was a bit shocked, and I remember feeling very flustered. He noticed the music I had playing in the background: "Is that the Brandenburg concertos?" "Yes," I replied. It was a warm, friendly, short call. I told him I needed to think about it. I hung up and felt mortified. I liked him a lot. But he was *my teacher.* I didn't want to do anything to mess that up.

I confided to Vanessa about Hap's call, how confused it made me feel. She sat me down and gave me what I remember as "the talk." She told me that at Evergreen, students are friends with their teachers. "It's not like at other colleges," she said. "Teachers and students call each other by their first names, they see each other outside of classes, they even live together in the same houses," she told me. "You aren't doing anything wrong. He's not married, he's single. If you like him, you should get to know him and you should go out with him."

Our first "date" was that one-hour drive to Seattle, a visit to his friend in the hospital, then a visit to a friend of mine who worked at the Earth Shoes store, and our return drive back to Olympia. I asked Hap lots of questions about his life. That was how I treated everybody new to me—male or female. I asked them lots of questions because I was interested and because people always like to be asked about themselves. Learning about others and deflecting attention had always been the way I felt most comfortable. What was different this time was that while Hap shared about himself, he also kept turning the conversation around and asking about me. It was clear that he genuinely wanted to know a lot more about me.

A few weeks later, after a class potluck at his house, a second date followed—a trip out to Hood Canal, a short hike along a river, and a competition between us—with lots of laughter—to see who could spit cherry pits the farthest into the river. Things evolved romantically from that moment. He cooked dinners for me; we took walks with his two dogs; we met at local bars 'by coincidence' to dance; he left poems and flowers at my door.

For my second quarter, I had arranged an internship with the ACLU in Honolulu to interview prostitutes for litigation the ACLU was contemplating. This would allow me to spend the winter in Hawaii to work on a project relevant to the *Lawmakers/Lawbreakers* program and to be near my family. Instead of living at my parents' home, I moved in with Naomi into her large dorm room at the East-West Center at the University of Hawaii, where she was working on a graduate degree. Then, in early February, an opportunity surfaced for Naomi to travel to India for her studies; she asked if I wanted to go with her. It sounded like an exciting and unique opportunity.

I thought I could go with her for a few weeks, then continue my internship when I returned. But my passport was back at my apartment in Olympia. I called Hap, asked if he would be willing to send me my passport, told him how to gain entry into the apartment, and where my passport was. He agreed to get it for me but seemed shocked that I might take off for India. He called back to say he had found it, that he had mailed it to me, but that it would take a few days.

What I didn't know was that he had called my sister Naomi and planned to hand deliver it. On Valentine's Day weekend, Naomi convinced me to go with her to the airport to pick up a friend of hers. She rejected all my excuses to not go with her. Then, as we waited at the gate, Hap walked off the plane—with my passport.

He met my mom for the first time, the unforgettable naked encounter that begins this memoir. And he met my dad, plus my four siblings living in Hawaii. We slept on Simon's apartment living room floor under a light blanket and flew to Maui for the weekend. We found a condo on the ocean that was in the final stages of construction and not yet open. They rented us a room, and we pulled a mattress to the covered lanai and slept listening to the sounds of crashing waves.

We returned to Honolulu, Hap flew home, and I never went to India. In March, when I returned to the Mainland, Hap met me at the Seattle airport. Our romance was loving, respectful, healthy. Hap was as much of a feminist as many of my women friends.

The next fall, Hap was leading a group of 20 students in a yearlong class called Politics of Health Care. I was taking a course in Jewish history, and an intensive writing program in the spring. Several of Hap's students were knitting in his seminars, and Hap asked them to teach him. On my 23rd birthday that year, he gave me one purple wool sock with blue stripes that he had just finished knitting. He finished the second one for my next birthday. Once I had a pair, I wore them often, and when they started to wear out, Hap had them framed; now, 47 years later, they still hang in our bedroom.

That Christmas, we took off together for Guatemala and Mexico, pooling all our money (mostly his) into a hat, and then dividing it back in half. We stayed in a tiny room in Cozumel, rented bikes and rode out to the fancy resort beaches for the day.

When spring break came, we had planned a camping trip to the Oregon coast, but it was the Northwest's gloomy season and rain was forecast all week. At the last minute, Hap suggested a different plan: we drove to the Seattle airport and then flew to Phoenix—the Valley of the Sun. We danced in clubs near Arizona State University in Tempe, went to spring training baseball games, watched the Seattle Supersonics battle the Phoenix Suns, drove up to Flagstaff and the Grand Canyon.

My interest in law school only strengthened. But I never really expected Hap to go with me. I loved our relationship but hadn't thought I'd 'settle down' in a committed relationship until I was in my mid-thirties. During that first year of our courtship, Hap had built a small, beautiful home on eight acres of woods and pasture. He had a great job teaching at Evergreen which he really enjoyed, and colleagues he liked; he was living his dream in the Pacific Northwest. I thought when I finished college and moved away from Olympia, that would be the end of our relationship. When I completed all my required course work for graduation, I had almost a year before I'd leave to start law school. Hap negotiated a leave of absence from his teaching job, and we flew to Spain and rented a small apartment as a base from which to travel.

Four months later, we were back in the USA looking at the law schools that had accepted me. Hap said he wanted to go with me, that he could extend his leave of absence from Evergreen. He told me he could find another job or build another house, but he couldn't ever find another me. And he let me know I was the person, the woman, he had been waiting for and wanted to spend his life with. His willingness to be that clear, direct, open and confident about his love for me reached me at a very deep level.

That August 1978, Hap and his two dogs moved with me to Santa Monica to begin law school. He found a job in Ventura, an hour away, and commuted to work. I had classes on Mondays, Wednesday, and Fridays. Each week I worked hard to get all my studying and written work done by Friday night; every weekend we played together—hikes, biking to Venice Beach, lots of live theater, movies, exploring Los Angeles and taking trips to locations within driving distance of our home.

Neither of us was eager to get married. We didn't see why California needed to approve our relationship to make our love and commitment official. However, our perspective changed in late spring of 1979 when a law school professor and several students were in a deadly car crash. The one survivor, who suffered severe head injuries that impaired his ability to function physically and mentally, was my closest friend in law school.

This tragedy forced us to look at the lifelong commitment we were feeling towards each other, the benefits of being married, and how seriously we wanted others to take our commitment. We announced to our families that in three weeks we were getting married in our backyard in Santa Monica, and then would take a short honeymoon before my second, final year of law school started.

We celebrated our wedding on the summer solstice in 1979, surrounded by fourteen family members and our two dogs. Afterwards, we flew to Salt Lake City, and camped for a few days en route to Idaho where we took a six-day white water raft trip down the Middle Fork of the Salmon River.

In spring, 1980, Justice Herman Lum of the Hawaii Supreme Court offered me a legal clerkship upon my graduation. That August, we moved to Honolulu.

* * *

Hap and I loved the breathtaking beauty of the islands. We moved into in a lovely plantation-style home about a ten-minute drive from our jobs in downtown Honolulu. Graceful branches of an enormous monkey-pod tree spread over the top of our home. In our yard, a giant mango tree was a source of abundant, sweet, mangoes. We filled our non-working hours with swims, hikes, yoga classes, jogs, seeing movies, being with new friends, and walking our dog, Dakota.

While I was an attorney for the Hawaii Supreme Court, Hap found a position with the City of Honolulu that gave him incredible latitude. He ventured into TV production through a series of grants he wrote, created a team of videographers, writers, and producers to create short documentaries on local social issues, and embarked on a new career in television.

When Hap and I moved to Hawaii, my youngest siblings were away at college. But my parents, and two of my sisters, Naomi and Mia, and their husbands, who were also living in Honolulu at that time, were an integral part of our lives. During the week, my parents often visited me at my office and brought me a picnic lunch after their morning group exercise sessions led by Paul Bragg on the beach in Waikiki. On weekends, my father and I sometimes met for lunch. I had never had this much private time with my father; I cherished my conversations and moments with him. He was very proud of me for being an attorney and for my prestigious job working as a law clerk for a Justice on the Hawaii Supreme Court; it made me happy to make him proud.

Often my family gathered for Sunday night dinners at my parents' home. We celebrated birthdays and holidays together, and we hiked together up Mariners Ridge on the weekends. None of us went more than a few days without talking to and seeing each other. I still was convinced that I had the perfect family and that we were "free spirits," uninhibited, and open in expressing our love for each other.

We were free and uninhibited in other ways too. Hap and I joined my entire family for camping trips on Kauai and Maui. Many of my Mainland-based brothers and sisters came too. A home movie taken on one of these family vacations offers a revealing glimpse into my family's behavior. On a hike through a tropical forest, when we came to a secluded mountain stream, all the Chotzens stripped off their clothes and dove naked into freshwater pools. Hap was uncomfortable swimming naked. He was also resistant to lounging naked on the boulders next to the stream, which was how the rest of us ate our picnic lunch.

In the home movie, as I climbed out of the freshwater pool, my mother cupped her hand around my breast. In one continuous motion, I removed her hand and kept moving, making my way over to a rock. I had enough awareness to understand, instinctively, that her hands didn't belong on my breasts, but I responded to her advances casually and mechanically. I remained unconscious about the lack of physical and sexual boundaries that had always pervaded my life.

At home in Honolulu, my mom would show up at our home at all hours of the day and night, without any kind of notice or warning. We repeatedly asked her to call before she came, and to ring the doorbell or knock before entering our home, but she never did. If my mother saw one of our cars in the driveway, she parked, came to our front door, pulled open the screen door, and quietly walked in. If our front door was locked, she would look for some other door or window to gain entry. If she didn't see us in the living room, she tiptoed through the house until she found us, like a thief stealing our privacy.

Sometimes, when we were in bed, we would look up to find her suddenly standing in the doorway, flashing her brilliant smile at us. Hap would shout, "Carla!" I would yell, "Mom! You have to knock! You can't be here." Of course, none of this stopped her. My mother was used to doing whatever she wanted to do. Hap increasingly articulated how bothered he was by my mother's blatant invasion of our privacy.

His frustration was with more than my mother's lack of boundaries. He pointed out her habitual and controlling tardiness, her inflexibility, how everything had to revolve around her and her schedule. He was losing patience, feeling alienated because our boundaries were being crossed all the time.

I, too, during these first seven years that we lived in Honolulu, began to question my mother's behavior in ways I had never done before. All my life, I had idolized her interactions as full of love, closeness, and adventure. Now pregnant and expecting my first child, I was finding my mother's traits more alarming.

One afternoon, a month after our son, Zach, was born, early in 1987, my mom dropped by. "Why don't you go take a little time and go for a swim?" She suggested. "I'll watch the baby."

The afternoon was hot and a quick dip in the ocean sounded perfect. I popped into a bathing suit, grabbed a towel, and walked the block from our house to the beach. I only swam for a few minutes because I didn't want to be away from my new baby for long. Walking up the driveway to the house, I could see my mother sitting on the bench on our deck holding Zach in her arms. As I got closer, I saw that mom's shirt was off, and she was holding Zach to her left breast, trying to breastfeed him.

"What the fuck are you doing?" I reached down, pulled Zach out of her arms, and clasped him tightly to my chest.

"I'm breastfeeding him; he wanted to nurse from me," she responded in a high-pitched, giggly voice that sent chills through me.

"Don't you *ever* do this again!" I screamed at her.

Her eyes narrowed, and she turned on me. All trace of her delirious giggling was gone in an instant. "How dare you yell at me! What's the matter with *you*?" She barked. "There's nothing wrong with this! I was doing a loving thing with my grandson! When did you get so uptight?"

Mom's eyes brimmed with anger and with tears. "How dare you yell at me! I'm leaving. I'm going home now. You have no right to treat me like this!" She grabbed her shirt, got in her car, and sped away, leaving me holding my baby and questioning my own maternal instincts.

I was stunned. Was I overreacting? Was I wrong for attacking her for trying to breastfeed my baby? Was nursing my baby NOT a terrible thing for her to do? The old feelings of being afraid of my mom's disapproval and her lifetime of power over me resurfaced.

The confusion felt familiar. My childhood conditioning had been to never confront my mother. As a child, if I had ever stood up to her or spoken up about what she was doing to me, I feared that no one would believe me, or worse that I would be ostracized from the family. And the family was all I had.

Half an hour later my father called, furious. "What is wrong with you?" he demanded. "Why would you treat your mother like that?"

My mother had arrived home, defended her actions, while vilifying mine. "In other countries grandmothers suckle their grandchildren all the time," she rationalized to him, and which he repeated to me. "You have hurt your mother. She is very upset and angry."

By the time Hap came home I was a mess. My parents had shamed me. I was upset and confused. But there was no doubt or confusion in Hap's mind; Carla's behavior was completely out of line. He was disgusted and alarmed. I hadn't acknowledged my mother's sexual molestation yet, so there was no way that Hap could have known about it at this time.

My maternal instincts to protect my child were powerful, but my lifelong patterns of submission to my mother were warring against them. I sought outside help from a therapist.

Finally, after years of training, after years of being under my mother's spell, I awakened to the realization that Carla's behavior was much more than merely inappropriate; her actions were perverse, and her defense of them indicated an emotional instability that threatened our child.

I began to take stock of my mother's appalling lack of boundaries. It had taken me so long to comprehend the dangerous and abusive nature of what we had been conditioned to label as her "free-spirited" behavior. It was all I had ever known: the flagrant nudity, the inappropriate fondling, and the night visits that she made to me two or three times a week throughout my childhood. I had grown up believing that this was how she expressed her love. I wanted to be loved by my mother, but I had seldom questioned how she chose to demonstrate her affection. As a new mother, something in me finally understood that the person in my life who was supposed to be my greatest protector had actually been my greatest danger.

I was 34 years old. I hadn't fully unraveled all the threads of the story yet, but I knew I needed to protect my child. Hap and I both agreed that we could never leave Zach alone with my mother again. But I realized that if I left him with a babysitter, or anyone except Hap, we could not stop my mother's access to him. She might show up unannounced and exert her "privileges" as a grandmother. I would never be sure of what she might do. We had moved to Hawaii partly because I wanted to live close to my parents. Now we wanted to leave so that we could create a safe environment for our son.

* * *

Once we realized how difficult it would be to keep my mother out of our lives on Oahu, we decided that the best option was to remove ourselves from her life by returning to the Mainland. We had spent eight years in Honolulu and had many friends and professional connections there, but our fear of being unable to protect our child from her bizarre and inappropriate behavior made the decision an easier one.

In 1988, we settled in Ashland, Oregon, a lively town of 18,000 in the Rogue River Valley, and home to the Oregon Shakespeare Festival.

In Oregon, while we were joyfully raising Zach, I began to do a lot of therapy on what had happened to me during my childhood. I realized that what was considered "normal and healthy" within the context of my childhood and our family, was aberrant in the context of healthy parenting behavior. My sense of family loyalty was so strong, and my awareness so deeply buried, that I had never confronted my mother's twisted sexual behavior. I was so inured to how my mother sexualized her love that I had become oblivious to her aberrant behavior. With the help of therapy, I woke up to the sickening truth and understood my mother's nighttime visits for what they were— words that were difficult to speak aloud: Sexual Molestation. Child Abuse. Incest.

At times I felt a strong need to speak the truth to my parents and siblings, but then I would be overcome by doubts and fears. All seven of my siblings had spouses and children and seemed to be leading happy lives. What good could it possibly do to delve into such traumatic memories? And the old Chotzen values—the ones that taught me to prize family loyalty—rose up inside me.

My deepest fear was that if I dared to express myself about the dangers, abuse, and neglect that my mother had perpetrated, the ways that my father had stood by and let her do these things, and the times he had been physically abusive himself, if I tried to burst the bubble of myths, I would be ostracized by my family. Even with an ocean between us, my mother remained a dominant force; I feared both her scary wrath and her powerful influence. And I still wanted my parents' love.

Several of my siblings still lived in Honolulu, and Hap and I had many friends there and had an enduring love for the islands. We returned to visit annually, but we never stayed at my parents' home, and we vowed to never leave Zach unattended with my mother for so much as a moment.

On one Hawaii visit when Zach was three years old, my mom, dad, and I sat at their dining room table, chatting, while Zach played nearby. My parents were telling me about something they had recently learned: that the children in the Miller family—the family that had been our closest friends growing up—had been sexually molested.

"I couldn't believe it," my father announced. 'How could we not have known about it all these years?"

In that moment, I almost couldn't stop myself from speaking up about what had happened in our family—to finally address the truth that had stayed hidden for so many years.

An instant later, as Zach walked by, my mom lovingly reached out and pulled him up to her lap. Giggling, she rubbed her face up and down on the back of his head. She stroked his neck and hair with her fingers, purring, "Oh these beautiful curls, these soft curls." Her voice slipped into a familiar high-pitched tone. Almost as if it were happening in slow motion, I could sense my mother going into a trance-like state, and I was transported back to my own childhood.

Suddenly, she pulled forward the elastic band of his shorts, looked inside, and with an eerily familiar excited voice, squealed, "Oh what do we have here?" Then her hands quickly darted down his pants. She had a delighted expression on her face, and it appeared that she was rubbing his penis.

It only took me a second to react, but it felt as though time had stopped, as if I had frozen, that I was the child being fondled by her. I jumped up from my chair, grabbed Zach off her lap and clasped him tightly in my arms.

Standing close enough that she could feel my rage, I screamed at Mom, "Don't you *ever* touch my child like that!" I felt years of repressed silence pounding against my insides, begging to be let out. I shouted, "When are we going to talk about this in *our* family? When are we going to talk about what happened to *us*?" My parents looked back at me, stunned by my outburst.

The situation degenerated quickly. They both acted as if my reaction had violated them. My father stood up, angry, demanding, "Don't you dare talk to your mother like that! You get out of our house. Leave our home now."

They didn't have to ask me twice. Clutching Zach, I ran outside, where Hap was reading. All I could say was, "We have to get out of here right now!"

As we drove back to the hotel where we were staying, I felt distraught that I had failed to protect our three-year old son from my mother, but I was comforted when I realized that I *had* stopped her and *had* protected him. We booked a flight and returned home to Oregon the next day.

Our second son, Willy, was born at home in 1991. Our relationship with my parents improved with the distance and reached a level of détente. I still loved them, but I knew better than to trust their judgment or to let my mother too close to either of our boys.

They visited us in Ashland after Willy's birth. Hap and I remained vigilant whenever my mother was around our sons. Sometimes I would feel my stomach instinctively tie itself into a knot when she stroked their arms or nuzzled her face into their hair in the same way that she did when we were growing up.

On the morning they were leaving, I couldn't find a blue sweater that I had loaned to her during their visit. After looking everywhere, I asked my mom if she had seen it.

"Oh, that old thing? I didn't think you wanted it. You have so many sweaters."

"Mom, what are you saying? Do you have my sweater?"

"I didn't think you'd care or even notice it missing," she replied.

Calmly, I asked her, "Do you have anything else of mine?"

She turned toward my dad and gave him instructions, "Walter, go down to the car and bring back my suitcase. Claudia wants some of the things I packed."

When she opened her suitcase, I discovered several other pieces of my clothing, and other items from our home, including a beautiful glass candleholder that Hap and the boys had given me for Mother's Day. She was upset that I wanted to keep the items; she had taken them because she liked them. She felt that was her right, her privilege. My father, as always, empathized with her disappointment.

* * *

A few years later, we flew directly to Maui to celebrate my 42nd birthday. My parents came over from Oahu to join us and rented a condo near ours. It had been a great vacation, and it was especially wonderful to see my parents delighting in the energy of seven-year-old Zach and three-year-old Willy.

I was standing next to my mom, knee deep in the warm Pacific Ocean, talking. We were both about to take a swim. Willy and Zach played behind us on the beach with Hap, who was helping them build a moat around their sandcastle. My father lay beside them on the beach, napping peacefully in the sunshine.

"Do you know why Danny won't see me?" Mom demanded.

I did know the answer, but it wasn't my prerogative to explain.

Danny was living in the Midwest with his wife, his five-year old daughter, and his one-year-old son, and he was working on building a healthy life of his own. The first step, he knew, was to heal his anger and discomfort about how Mom had behaved when we were all growing up: her constant nudity and exhibitionism around the house, the way that she would answer the door naked when the mailman delivered the mail, and how she would greet Danny's high school friends wearing a skirt and no underpants, exposing her crotch when she was seated across from them. Danny had chosen to cut off all communication with our mother to protect both himself and his children from her as he learned how to be the parent he wanted to be.

My talks with Danny had been a revelation and a gift: it was the first time I had understood, as an adult, that I was not alone in trying to sort out the pieces of our past, and that I wasn't crazy because the memory of what I experienced behind closed doors in our home was so different than the myths of our perfect family my parents perpetuated.

My mother had complained constantly during that Maui visit about the distance Danny had created between them. She was asking for sympathy and badgering me for hints or answers. Why in the world, she wondered, would a son not want to see his loving mother?

I had enormous respect for Danny's decision, and I was not about to violate his trust to appease my mother. Over and over again I gave her the same response, one that I had discussed and rehearsed with Hap: "I can't speak for Danny, Mom."

Still, she kept asking. "Why won't Danny see me?"

This time, standing in the turquoise ocean, I felt compelled to say something else.

I dug my toes into the wet sand. "I can't speak for Danny," I said, "but I can speak for myself." I could feel myself drawing strength from the ocean, from Hap and our boys playing on the beach behind me, and from my own growing need to tell my mother what, as far as I knew, no one had ever said to her before. I looked right into her eyes as we stood in the water and continued, my voice strong and clear.

"You molested me, over and over, when I was a child. It was *wrong*, Mom. Horrible and very, very wrong."

The color drained from her face. She didn't deny it, but responded, "Well, you have no idea what happened to me. You have no idea what my father did to *me*. You have no idea." She had broken our eye contact and was staring off into the sea. "He used to take me into the bedroom and shut the dark curtains. I remember the dark curtains."

With growing emotion, she described the repeated rapes by her father. It was a horrific revelation, and I was completely derailed by her disclosure. As usual, the conversation had been turned so that it was entirely about her. She needed me to know how terrible her childhood had been, that my pain couldn't compare to hers. I was expected to pity and comfort her, to take care of her. She didn't see the horror in what she had done to me, because, in her eyes, it paled in comparison to the things her father had done to her.

"He did it again and again. I was the one he always picked," she tearfully confided.

"But Mom," I finally interrupted her. "That didn't give you the right to do the same thing to me. That didn't make it okay. It was wrong when it happened to you, and it was wrong when you did it to me."

"You don't know what happened to me," she repeated. "You cannot possibly understand what happened to me."

Frustrated by this impasse, I waded deeper into the water and dove under. I swam for an hour. She had barely heard what I had said to her; nothing had registered. There had been no admission, no apology. What was she telling me? That her repeated violations of me were insignificant and trivial compared to what she had experienced? Or that what she had done to me was somehow justified or fated by the horrors perpetrated upon her? It made my stomach turn.

Late in the afternoon, my parents came over to the condo where we were staying. I was still reeling from my morning conversation with my mom, taken aback both by what she had told me and what she had been unable to acknowledge. While

Hap cooked dinner I sat in the corner of the living room next to my father. We were both reading, though I paid close attention to my mom, who was squatting on the living room floor and playing games with Zach and Willy.

My dad peered around his newspaper at me. "Claudia," he said softly, "Carla told me about your conversation."

I held my breath, hoping that my father was about to acknowledge what my mother seemingly could not. Finally, I thought. Finally, the truth.

"Poor Carla," my father offered. "I had no idea about the details of those horrible things her father did to her. She's been talking about it to me all afternoon. I knew a few things over the years, but I never knew how brutal and how much, the extent of it." His voice was full of concern and sadness and pity. All of it for my mother.

"Dad," I said, "what happened to Mom was terrible. But she did the same kinds of things to me." My father didn't respond. He lifted the newspaper back to his face and pretended to read. I persisted. "Didn't you know what was going on? Didn't you know—or at least wonder—what she was doing all those nights when she left your bed and came to my bed?"

"I left all the parenting decisions to Carla," he muttered. And then he changed the subject and spoke about Clark. "I did know what Clark did to you kids," he admitted. "And we had heard rumors that before we met him, he had been kicked out of the Boy Scouts for being a child molester."

"Then how on earth could you have let him be our babysitter?" I asked, incredulous.

"Like I said, I left all the parenting up to Carla and she liked Clark very much," he repeated.

I sunk into a pit of despair, like I had experienced earlier on the beach with my mother, similar to how I had felt as a child. Why had I expected any more from him? Dad's foremost priority had been, and always would be, Carla. He was so in love with my mother that he was blind to the harm she inflicted on their children. I was stunned to realize that he apparently sacrificed his children's safety, turned his back on her neglect and her molestations, because he was afraid to lose her love. His love for her had both blinded and silenced him. Was he even capable of distinguishing between right and wrong? Had he understood how horrific her behavior had been and chosen not to speak up or interfere, too afraid that he might anger her or, worse yet, lose her? His complicity raised his inaction to the level of being her accomplice.

* * *

I was deeply disappointed by my parents, and I spent years delving into the truth to face what had happened, to understand that the shame I carried wasn't mine. The shame belonged to my mother and to my father.

Our whole world revolved around my mother's needs. It often seemed that the purpose of our existence was to shine attention on her. She expected us to automatically and fully comply with her expectations and her desires, and when we didn't, when she was contradicted or frustrated, we lived in fear of her anger. Somehow, Carla had us all under a spell. Our sense of family loyalty was so strong, and our awareness so deeply buried, that no one could confront her or even acknowledge what she was doing in any way that would stop it.

How does one gain perspective about a mother who was so controlling and all-powerful in our family that everyone was afraid to cross her or stand up to her? I hated that my father was so submissive when my mom openly flaunted her affair with Jerome, yet I was blind to how similarly submissive I had been all the years my mom sexually molested me from the time I was three years old. How long does it take to wake up? What is required to finally set off the alarm that things aren't right? And then what?

For me, awareness first arrived in my early twenties, from being in my own adult relationship, and culminated a dozen years later when I had my own children to love and protect.

Year after year, we still found space in our hearts to spend time with my parents, whether it was a trip back to Hawaii or occasional visits they made to the Mainland. We loved Hawaii and didn't want to feel exiled from a place we enjoyed, where we had many friends, just because my parents lived there. We never stayed with them, and we limited our family visits, often seeing them for just a few days before flying to a neighbor island for our own separate family vacation. We wanted our boys to know and love their grandparents, but under our own cautious conditions.

In 1998, shortly after my father died, we visited my mother in Honolulu. In the middle of a conversation, my mother suddenly remembered that she had bought a blouse she wanted to give to me, and she asked me to follow her into her bedroom while she looked for it.

A narrow hallway led to a large desk against the window in the bedroom. I noticed an oversized journal spread open on the desk with my mother's sprawling handwriting clearly visible. I had never seen this journal before. I caught a glimpse of my name in my mother's large purple cursive writing. "*Claudia says I molested my children. I was just trying to love them. I was just trying to share my love with them.*" That was the only thing written on that page.

I wondered if she had left the journal open to that page deliberately, that this was her way of finally initiating the conversation.

I pointed to the journal and asked. "Mom, do you want to talk about what you've written here?"

She looked right at me and acted as if I hadn't even spoken. "The blouse is somewhere here in the bedroom," she responded. "It might be on a shelf. We'll have to look for it."

That was the closest we ever came to talking about her horrific violations of me for all those years.

It wasn't long after that visit that my mother was diagnosed with Alzheimer's. Soon all of my questions about the past—her schools, her sisters, her parents, her early years with my father—were met with blank stares and helpless shrugs. All the years we had shared, our lives in Seattle, those, too, were lost to her. The ski trips, the camping trips, the protests, the Friday Night Groups, and of course the years of sexual abuse.

She could no longer remember what I could never forget.

AFTERWORD

I must have had an instinct from an early age that at some point I'd attempt to deconstruct my life and my parents' lives because I saved so many letters and journals—mine and ones from my mom, dad, siblings, grandparents, aunts, and uncles. Before Hap and I moved from Hawaii in 1988, I interviewed my parents for two full days on video to record their histories and life stories. I relied on all of this history, as well as family movies from the 1950's and 1960's, to write this memoir.

For years, the most challenging part of telling my story were the two powerful forces continually in conflict inside of me. The first: a deep desire to tell my story. The opposing one: my equally deep desire to not intrude on my sibling's lives, to not re-traumatize them. I am beginning to realize that both powerful needs will continue to live—and surface—in me, side by side.

As refugees from Nazi Germany, my parents created a culture where family was valued above all else. They imprinted on us a message that we were all that each of us had; that having lost so many relatives in the Holocaust, we had a primary duty to love and preserve family.

My mother often reminded us, "No one will love you the way I do. Nobody from the outside can touch the love we have in our family. We're here for each other. We are a unit unto ourselves." These messages became doctrine in our family.

Despite the "we're here for each other" message, my mom

created a competition between us for the little scraps of love each of us could manage to grab. Eight children vied with each other to grasp crumbs of approval—who could be the better skier, the heartier hiker, the best student, the more helpful child? My mother assigned all of us different roles; and we often competed to win her and my father's approval. As a child, I truly believed that my very existence depended on pleasing them in order to be able to survive in our family.

My mother controlled my universe. I had no concept that what she was doing to me at nights was sexual abuse. I didn't have the understanding or the words to question it. She wrapped her molestations with the phrase every child craves, the whispered words, "I love you so much." And my father reinforced that message by telling us that we had the best mother in the world. These two adults created my reality, ruled my world. How could a child know anything different?

During the day, I was focused every minute to win my mom's approval, to be a good girl, *to please her.* I was quiet, obedient, and afraid of her unpredictable angry outbursts. I craved her love, yearned for her motherly affection with every fiber of my being. But her maternal love was completely mixed up with her sexual needs and her sexual appetite—her sexual addiction—which could never be satisfied.

How do you love a mother who does this to you? What choice did I have? This was my daily life. It was constant. During the night, I believed my reason to be alive was to lie on the bed and serve my mother's needs. In the daytime, I was desperate for her and my father's approval. I didn't know it could be different.

Now, as an adult, I know that this is the confusion an abuser creates. My mother was a master manipulator. It took me years to stop wondering if I had done something to make her molest me. There was no part of me that asked for any of this. From the time I was three years old, when she first started to sexually abuse me in the little closet room they built as my bedroom, she removed choice from me. It's taken me decades to understand that the shame I carried all these years really belonged to her, not to me. And to my father who was complicit, who failed to acknowledge what was happening under his own roof and failed to put a stop to it.

As a child in the 1950s and 1960s, if I had ever told anyone about what was happening to me in the dark of night, who would have believed me? My mother had a magnetic control over my father and our family. She was charismatic; she dazzled everyone around her, had them under her spell. She was a well-known professional photographer, a mother of eight children, and a social activist. She was a leader in our Seattle community. My father was adored by friends and respected in the business community. Love in our family existed side by side with my mother's abuse and neglect, the constant unpredictability and danger she exposed all of us to, my father's abdication of his parenting responsibilities, and his physical violence when he flew into rages.

Today, if a child told a doctor, "I'm not in my body," medical professionals would be alert that this might be a sign of abuse. I was experiencing a survival mechanism called dissociation, a common occurrence in an abused child's universe. As a child, I lived with that disconnection all the time, a dual existence. But, back then, no one seemed to notice or know. The Light Ladies were also part of my coping mechanism. I can still see those radiant, ethereal beings and the sun-lit orange groves they took me to. They were my protectors; the safety they provided still brings tears to my eyes.

Experts now realize that people don't usually abuse unless they've been abused themselves. My mom had been molested by her own father when she was a child. She never got the help she needed to stop the cycle of abuse. And so, my mother, the person who should have been my fiercest protector, instead became my greatest danger.

Growing up, the family code implanted in us was: *Our first duty is to one another. Without our family you will have nobody.* We were taught to be so devoted to the belief in family that we couldn't even see or protest the abuse. To name the unspeakable, to call out the secrets that wrapped themselves around our lives like encrusting barnacles, to shine the light of truth on the twisted and the dark, felt inconceivable. Even as an adult, I was terrified that if I spoke the truth I would be ostracized from my family, which felt equivalent to being annihilated.

I now understand on the most personal level that both evil and good can co-exist in a single person. Despite my parents' neglect and abuse, the good values we learned from them have stayed with us. They created wonderful family memories; we hiked, camped, skied, played on beaches, put on puppet shows, and laughed. Growing up, we had invigorating political discussions and fascinating friends. From my parents' examples, we all learned to stand up to injustice. My father founded a family camp when I was three years old; 66 years later it's still going strong—a tradition my parents passed on to their children and grandchildren. My memoir is not just about sexual abuse. It's the complex story of my childhood, in which so many times we were on our own and not safe, in which I was molested, but in which wonderful things also occurred. And it's about my healing.

What has helped me heal the most was having the opportunity to nurture my own healthy marriage and to raise children without repeating the abuse that happened to me. With the love I've nourished with my husband and children, with my determination to face my history and the help of excellent therapists, I've enjoyed an adult life filled with great joy and love.

While I've learned to live with the dark things that happened in my life, for many years they never really went away. The terror and claustrophobia, the ways I felt dirty and bad, the hopelessness I felt that the molestations would never end—those demons that I battled throughout my childhood still lingered and surfaced when I least expected them.

In 1997, we moved back to Seattle for my husband to take a new job. Our sons were six and ten. Despite my love for Hap and our boys, recollections of my mother's sexual molestations as a child under the gray skies of Seattle haunted and overwhelmed me. I sank into deep despair and depression and came very close to suicide. I truly believed my family would be happier without me. But that is also when I first thought about writing this memoir, it became a vehicle to reclaim control of my life.

Even a few years ago, when my mother was 91 years old and living in an Alzheimer's care home hundreds of miles away, there were still times when I would wake abruptly from sleep in the middle of the night in a complete panic. My five or six or seven-year-old self was terrified; I was wide-awake, on red alert to fight off danger. I had to remind myself that I was safe now, that my mother couldn't hurt me anymore; she couldn't travel eight hours by car, come into my home, and climb on top of me while I was asleep in my bed.

Years after my father had died and we visited my mother in Hawaii, our young sons noticed that the moment my mother greeted me and gave me a hug, she would also put her hands under my shirt and reach up to grab my breasts. Reflexively I would take hold of her hands and pull them away from my body. "Why does Carla always try to touch your breasts?" nine-year old Zach once asked.

"It *is* very strange, and it makes me very uncomfortable," I acknowledged. "She's unaware of her behavior."

A few years later, when I visited her in her Alzheimer's care home in Sacramento, she still exhibited this same behavior. Though she no longer knew my name or who we were, she would try to reach under my shirt and fondle my breasts or put her hands down my pants. One of my sisters had the same experience and said, "It is so engrained in her. Just like when we were kids, she starts to reach her hands down your pants."

I have been asked about forgiveness. Do I feel hatred for my mother for violating me and robbing my innocence, and my father for not protecting me from her trespasses? I have certainly felt tremendous rage for what my parents did and worked on that in therapy. To me, forgiveness doesn't mean letting someone off the hook for what they did or for the harm they caused. For me it means that I don't want this to be the main narrative that dominates my life. This is my history, a piece of who I am—but just because terrible things were done **to** me it doesn't define who I am.

Several years ago, my brother Daniel, knowing that I was working on this memoir, asked if he could read it. He acknowledged that he had blocked out most memories of his early life before he was fourteen or fifteen. *"My goal would be to see and understand more and to accept and forgive more so that I can better move forward in my life and allow there to be more love in my heart for Mom as she moves on, too."*

Daniel read an early draft of my memoir carefully, thinking about his own life, and then he gave me a great gift—his memories and corroboration that I had revealed the truth, and a willingness to be my ally. *"As far as carrying it with you, I have no choice now, it is my burden as well. Yet for me it is also a relief to have the truth and a recognition that my years of exile from the family were in response to darker forces than I even knew."*

He wrote to all of our brothers and sisters, encouraging them to read what I had written, saying, *"...because of it, I will never view my life the same again. For me now it's a new day as far as wanting to bring to light forgotten childhood experiences so that they no longer have the power to unconsciously undermine my ability to be the best I can be in the present. It is clear that our parents, while giving us so much that was good, also gave us the legacy of their own wounding. I know I must be willing to see them as the people they truly were lest I continue to pass on the wounds I inherited from them to my own children."*

I have tried to keep this story, as much as possible, about my own experience. The question has come up many times: did your mom molest others in the family? Yes, I witnessed this, as did several of my brothers and sisters. The spouse of one of my siblings confronted my parents about my mother's abuse to a grandchild that was frighteningly similar to what I endured. My mother responded by being outraged to be accused of this; my father was outraged on my mother's behalf. The blind loyalty, the denial in our family, and the covering up for her continued to be the family dynamic.

I wrote this memoir to find my way out of suffering, not to create a constant reminder of it. I wanted to name what happened, to not stay mired in shame. I am no longer serving as my mother's victim, no longer remaining mute, obedient, trapped in despair and self-doubt. By speaking out, I have found a voice that was taken away from me when I was a child. This is a story of hope. My deepest wish is that it inspires clarity, insight, courage, and healing in others.

ACKNOWLEDGMENTS

I could never have started this memoir, and certainly not have finished it, without incredible support from my husband, sons, friends, family, and therapists. Words are inadequate in attempting to thank them for their feedback, enthusiasm, candor, love, and patience, but I'll try.

Elizabeth Wolfson, for helping me to write my first draft when I was too terrified to sit in a room by myself and re-live the trauma. For nine months, I poured out my memories and she transcribed them, giving me stories to work from and encouraging me to keep writing even when I thought my story was too abhorrent to share.

My earliest readers, some of whom read several drafts. They returned my manuscript with coffee-stained pages covered with perceptive reactions, comments, and questions: Jan Lippen-Holtz, Sheila Burns, Sarah Garraty, Monica Jones, Suzi Serbin, Karina Ballantyne, Jackie Finn, Brian Sarvis, Carol Spungen, Bobby Duffy, Ann Sarvis, Rena Smith, Katy Renner, Glen Serbin, Anna Chotzen, Suzanne Edison, Karen Lowe, Molly Holman, Deborah Gibson, Barbara Rosenthal, Daniel Chotzen and Courtney Logue.

Family and friends whose support inspired and helped me to keep going: Steffi Masur, Nancy Fox, Kim Chotzen, Nika Chotzen-Smith, Kira Chotzen, Paula Lilly, Sherry Wetzell, David Ingalls, Diane Berger, Shawn Kibler, Catherine Davis, Clea Stone, Deanna Sundberg, Fran Nunes, Ruthie Painter,

Anna Urrea, Doedy Orchowski, Danuta Bennett, Steve Gorman, Aubrey Pomerance, Dianne Pepper, Lynne Johnson, Tom Rainey and Nina Carter.

Maid Adams and Jean Durning had long discussions with me about my mother's role in the Seattle civil rights movement and the school boycott of 1966, then directed me to a book they co-authored on that subject, *Seattle in Black and White, The Congress of Racial Equality and the Fight for Equal Opportunity*, by Joan Singler, Jean Durning, Bettylou Valentine, and Maid Adams, published in 2011 by the University of Washington Press.

My brothers and sisters for sitting with me for hours of interviews, sharing memories, tears, trauma, and laughter. Growing up together, so often we were on our own and not safe, but we had each other. And we have all not only survived but flourished.

All seven of my siblings have been very supportive, but special gratitude to my brother Daniel who has been steadfast in his encouragement and determination to see my book out in the world where it can be of service to others.

My superb therapists and mentors whose expertise in healing childhood sexual abuse, and whose love, has lit my way: Candace, Ann, Karen, Janice, Gail, Patricia, Devereaux, Jeni, Laurel and Stef.

Susan Ginsburg, of Writers House, for her tenacious and enthusiastic support for my memoir.

My son, Zach, who spent many hours helping to weave my vignettes into a cohesive narrative. His participation brought me hope; his writing brought lightness and humor to my story. And his wife, Rachel, for her perceptive feedback on an early draft and for always being in my corner.

My son, Willy, for his genuine, heartwarming caring and encouragement. From the very beginning, he cheered me on, made me laugh, solved my computer and grammar questions, and gifted me with astute, thoughtful feedback. And his wife, Amy, for her unending heartfelt love and support.

And every day, thank you to my husband, Hap, for being on this journey with me every step of the way. At our wedding in our backyard in Santa Monica in 1979, as part of our wedding vows, he said, *"This relationship has been shaped, molded by the respect, courtesy, love and laughter we have shared. I have loved you since I met you, and probably before then, as I waited patiently for you to appear in my life."* We have been true teammates from the very beginning. Raising children together has been the most creative and fulfilling experience on earth. Sharing the little and big moments of our long love—every day and every year—is the best gift I could ever have. Thank you for spending countless hours editing my memoir, for listening to me in the dark of many nights, and for never wavering in your belief in the value of sharing my story.

To others who told me, "I was abused too, in different ways, and I'm afraid to stand up and speak up because I feel unworthy." This memoir is for you.

Made in the USA
Coppell, TX
26 March 2022